Grief
in Childhood

Grief

in Childhood

**Fundamentals of Treatment
in Clinical Practice**

Michelle Y. Pearlman
Karen D'Angelo Schwalbe
Marylène Cloitre

American Psychological Association • *Washington, DC*

Published by
American Psychological Association
750 First Street, NE
Washington, DC 20002
www.apa.org

To order
APA Order Department
P.O. Box 92984
Washington, DC 20090-2984
Tel: (800) 374-2721; Direct: (202) 336-5510
Fax: (202) 336-5502; TDD/TTY: (202) 336-6123
Online: www.apa.org/books/
E-mail: order@apa.org

In the U.K., Europe, Africa, and the Middle East, copies may be ordered from
American Psychological Association
3 Henrietta Street
Covent Garden, London
WC2E 8LU England

Typeset in Goudy by Circle Graphics, Inc., Columbia, MD

Printer: Edwards Brothers, Inc., Ann Arbor, MI
Cover Designer: Naylor Design, Washington, DC

The opinions and statements published are the responsibility of the authors, and such opinions and statements do not necessarily represent the policies of the American Psychological Association.

Library of Congress Cataloging-in-Publication Data

Pearlman, Michelle Y.
   Grief in childhood : fundamentals of treatment in clinical practice / Michelle Y. Pearlman, Karen D'Angelo Schwalbe, and Marylène Cloitre. — 1st ed.
      p. cm.
   Includes bibliographical references and index.
   ISBN-10: 1-4338-0752-1
   ISBN-13: 978-1-4338-0752-7
   1. Grief in children. 2. Bereavement in children. 3. Grief in children—Treatment.
   I. Schwalbe, Karen D'Angelo. II. Cloitre, Marylène. III. Title.

   BF723.G75P43 2010
   155.9'37083—dc22
                                        2009044714

British Library Cataloguing-in-Publication Data

A CIP record is available from the British Library.

Printed in the United States of America
First Edition

CONTENTS

Acknowledgments .... *vii*

I. Foundations of Treatment 1

Chapter 1.   Introduction to Integrated Grief Therapy
             for Children (IGTC) 3

Chapter 2.   Risk and Protective Factors, Clinical Presentations,
             and Treatment Interventions: A Review of
             the Literature 13

Chapter 3.   Assessing Grieving Children and
             Teaching Basic Coping Skills 37

II. Addressing Problems in Grieving Children 61

Chapter 4.   Treating Depression Symptoms
             in Grieving Children 63

Chapter 5.   Treating Posttraumatic Stress Disorder Symptoms
              in Grieving Children... 83

Chapter 6.   Treating Anxiety Symptoms in Grieving Children..... 105

Chapter 7.   Managing Behavior Problems
              in Grieving Children... 123

III. Addressing Children's Grief and Building Resilience.................. 147

Chapter 8.   Initiating the Grief-Focused Phase of Treatment 149

Chapter 9.   Coping Skills for Grieving Children........................... 165

Chapter 10.   Making Memories and Integrating Past
              and Present 183

Chapter 11.   Fostering Resilience and Concluding
              the Treatment 203

References 219

Index 235

About the Authors.. 243

ACKNOWLEDGMENTS

The work that influenced the writing of this book was supported in large part by the American Red Cross September 11 Recovery Grants and the Silver Shield Foundation. We would like to express our gratitude to these charitable organizations. In addition, we would like to thank Cathy and Stephen Graham for providing generous support to this and many other trauma outreach and intervention endeavors.

Many of our colleagues at the New York University Child Study Center helped us in the development of this book, and we greatly appreciate each of them for their efforts. A special thanks goes to Heather Glubo, for her significant research contribution and endless enthusiasm; Joel McClough, for his unwavering support; and Sandra Juriga, for her creative ideas about how to engage bereaved families in treatment.

We dedicate this book to all of the families we have worked with over the years, who have touched our lives and taught us about the true meaning of resilience, and to our own families, who inspire us every day.

I

FOUNDATIONS OF
TREATMENT

1

INTRODUCTION TO INTEGRATED GRIEF THERAPY FOR CHILDREN (IGTC)

Most young people experience the death of at least one loved one at some point in childhood (Harrison & Harrington, 2001). Approximately 4% of children (through age 18) in Western countries experience the death of a parent (Garmezy & Masten, 1994; Harrison & Harrington, 2001; Social Security Administration, 2000), which is considered one of the most stressful events a child can experience (Yamamoto et al., 1996). Many more experience the death of another loved one, such as a grandparent, other family member, or friend.

Children vary widely in how they respond to the death of a loved one. Much of this variance is influenced by developmental stage, with a 5-year-old's cognitive, emotional, and behavioral responses differing greatly from an 18-year-old's. The variance in how children respond is also influenced by family factors, such as the family's functioning prior to and after the death and the child's relationship to the surviving caregiver. Further variance occurs on the basis of individual child factors, such as temperament, access to and use of social support, and coping style. With such a wide range of responses from child to child, it is impossible to describe any single timetable or series of stages that grieving children necessarily follow.

Nonetheless, certain responses are common among bereaved children. For example, bereaved children are likely to experience confusion, sadness, anger, and worry. For most children, these feelings lessen over time, particularly when they have the support of trusted adults and peers with whom they can talk and share their feelings. Other children seem to have a more difficult time, experiencing psychological distress and social isolation that persist for several months or longer.

Those children who do suffer from significant or prolonged distress following the death of a loved one may be affected in a myriad of ways, including depressed mood, irritability, and significant anxiety about the health and safety of surviving family members (Abdelnoor & Hollins, 2004; Cerel, Fristad, Verducci, Weller, & Weller, 2006; Dowdney, 2000; Genevro, Marshall, Miller, & Center for the Advancement of Health, 2004). They may also exhibit behavioral problems, a decline in school performance, and/or social withdrawal (Luecken, 2008). Finally, emerging evidence suggests that early parental loss may be linked to physical health problems later in life (Luecken, 2008). It is estimated that 20% of bereaved children are likely to have problems significant enough to require clinical intervention (Dowdney, 2000).

Children's difficulties following a significant loss may be related to the inherent stress of grief as well as problems adjusting to corresponding changes in the family system. For example, many parentally bereaved children live with the surviving parent, who may remain single or may eventually remarry. Other bereaved children live with grandparents or extended family members, particularly when both parents have died or when the deceased parent was already a single parent as a result of divorce or other circumstances. Still other children enter foster care or are cared for by other nonrelatives.

Despite the good intentions of the larger family or community, bereaved children often must also deal with the challenge of responding to a social context in which peers as well as adults may not know how to interact with them. Bereaved children often feel isolated and different from their peers, and they may feel that they are treated differently at school or in social settings. Complicating matters further, when the loss is that of a parent or other important adult role model, the child loses a guide to help negotiate various emotional and developmental challenges so that others are needed to step into these roles.

Given the widespread occurrence and potential for trauma and other negative physical and mental health consequences of losing a loved one in childhood, it is important for every clinician who works with children to understand how best to help them cope with these types of loss experiences. To meet this need, this book offers an evidence-based model of treatment—called *integrated grief therapy for children* (IGTC)—that can be applied to various symptoms and circumstances with bereaved children. IGTC goes beyond other child therapy approaches by not only addressing specific presenting symptoms, such as depression and anxiety, but also attending to the child's areas of strength and fostering resilience. Although most of the interventions in IGTC are cognitive–behaviorally based, the theoretical framework also integrates principles from family systems work, interpersonal therapy, and narrative approaches.

This book contains everything needed to successfully implement IGTC, including instructions for specific components of the therapy, sample dialogues to illustrate concepts, and activity handouts that therapists can photocopy and use in sessions. The primary intended audience for this book is the therapists, social workers, psychologists, psychiatrists, and other professionals who provide mental health services to children and families. However, caregivers of bereaved children can also benefit from the book. The remainder of this chapter defines some basic terminology, outlines the components of IGTC, and explains how the book is organized.

TERMINOLOGY

For simplicity and clarity, throughout the book we refer to the current primary caregiver as the *parent*, although we acknowledge that the person may be another relative or adult who is responsible for the bereaved child. Furthermore, we use the term *children* to include those of early childhood age through adolescence, roughly ages 4 through 20, unless otherwise noted. For children younger than the age of 4, the recommendations and interventions geared toward parents and caregivers may be used.

Bereavement refers to the objective experience of losing a loved one by death, whereas *grief* refers to the subjective reactions that people have to bereavement, including the set of emotional, cognitive, behavioral, and physical manifestations and signs of distress that may follow the death of a loved one. *Mourning* is the formalized expression of grief that is practiced by a society or specific cultural group. This includes memorial services, funerals, wakes, and other rituals (Genevro et al., 2004).

IGTC

The IGTC model was developed on the basis of several main beliefs, or treatment principles, and consists of three phases of treatment. This section outlines each of these guiding treatment principles and phases of treatment.

Treatment Principles

IGTC comprises seven treatment principles that serve as a foundation for all clinicians working with grieving children and their families. We discuss each principle in turn.

Principle 1: The Process of Grieving Looks Different From Person to Person—There Is No One Right Way to Grieve

When faced with the death of a loved one, people respond in highly individualized ways. For example, some bereaved children find comfort in openly talking about the deceased, whereas others prefer to maintain their memories in a more private fashion. Contrary to commonly held assumptions, research indicates that people who are grieving do not necessarily follow any particular set of stages and that responses to loss vary greatly from person to person (Weiss, 2008; Wortman & Silver, 2001).

Given the importance of individual differences in the grieving process, clinicians working with the bereaved must tailor their approach to the needs of the individual. It may be argued that this is especially true when working with children, who may face additional challenges depending on their age and cognitive development, such as potential confusion about death itself. For many children, the loss will bring about changes that will alter the course of their lives, and they will experience an array of responses and feelings that may (or may not) accompany such change, including sadness, guilt, ambivalence, fear, and relief, to name a few. The IGTC approach therefore serves as a guide containing a multitude of options from which the clinician can choose aspects that are most relevant for the individual child.

Principle 2: Whenever Possible, Use Evidence-Based Interventions to Guide Treatment

It is our belief that when certain interventions or approaches have been found effective in treating a given problem or disorder, then those are the interventions that should be used. Fortunately, the child therapy literature has expanded significantly over recent decades so that a growing body of research is available regarding what types of treatment approaches may be helpful for specific disorders and symptom areas. This is particularly true for anxiety, for which there is perhaps the most significant amount of treatment outcome data for children (for reviews, see Scott, Mughelli, & Deas, 2005; Silva, Gallagher, & Minami, 2006). There is also evidence regarding which approaches are most effective in helping children with posttraumatic stress disorder (PTSD), depression, and behavior problems (for reviews, see Christophersen & Mortweet, 2001; Target & Fonagy, 2005). Our approach to working with bereaved children who are experiencing problems related to PTSD, anxiety, depression, and behavior problems, as detailed in Part II of this book, is therefore largely based on the existing literature.

Unfortunately, there continues to be a scarcity of evidence regarding the efficacy of treatments designed specifically for grieving children, and those treatments that have been studied have almost exclusively been group-based rather than individual approaches (Currier, Holland, & Neimeyer, 2007). Some of these group approaches have contributed greatly to the child grief therapy literature, such as the Family Bereavement Program (Sandler et al., 1992, 2003), whose outcomes highlight the importance of including the parent in treatment for bereaved children. This has, in turn, informed the IGTC approach, which similarly focuses on parenting skills to promote resilience among grieving children.

Not all bereaved children are in need of treatment, and interventions appear to be most beneficial with children who exhibit adjustment difficulties or other problems after the loss (Currier et al., 2007). Research indicates that when bereaved individuals who are experiencing significant distress receive treatment, outcomes tend to be favorable, with effect sizes comparable with those seen in psychotherapy for other psychological difficulties (Currier, Neimeyer, & Berman, 2008). These findings support our belief that not all bereaved children require a full course of IGTC, which has been specifically designed to allow clinicians to select interventions based on the child's given needs.

We feel strongly that more research is needed in the area of individual therapy for bereaved children, but we also know that clinicians need guidance for how to work with such children based on what we know to be effective so far. Our model therefore attempts to incorporate the given body of literature involving bereaved children (albeit limited) while also drawing from the existing general child treatment literature as well as our own experience with and understanding of this population.

Principle 3: Collaboratively Identify Goals and Determine How to Reach Them

It is important that the therapist present a plan for treatment based on actively discussing goals with the child, and, in some cases (in particular when younger children are involved), the parent. Such discussion not only allows the child some sense of control (which is often disrupted in the face of major loss) over the treatment but also provides a sense of structure and momentum that helps the child and therapist know and agree on what has been accomplished and what work remains. The implication is that a discussion of treatment goals is ongoing, rather than a single occurrence at the start of therapy.

The importance of collaboration in identifying goals is illustrated by the case of Lila, a 17-year-old girl whose father died 1 year before Lila entered therapy. Lila felt overwhelmed by the changes she was facing during her senior year of high school and by the choices she needed to make regarding college applications. Over the course of therapy, there were times during which these decisions were impacted by the loss of her father; for example, she did not wish to attend a college that was farther than a short car ride away so that she could be available to help her mother with her little sister. There were other times, however, that Lila looked to her therapist for guidance about issues that were unrelated to her grief and were more universal to adolescents her age. It was important that Lila's therapist understand what she was looking for in therapy so that they could together move toward those goals.

Principle 4: Build on the Parent–Child Relationship

On the basis of our experience as well as current research (for a review, see Luecken, 2008), the outcomes of the bereaved child are significantly related to the functioning of the surviving parent or caregiver. The inclusion of a surviving parent or caregiver is therefore instrumental in working with bereaved children. The loss of a loved one impacts a whole family and often influences the relationships between family members as a result. Our belief is that bolstering the child–parent relationship is one important component in helping the child to grieve and manage the consequences of a major loss. This may be done in a variety of ways, each of which is described in detail in later chapters, including psychoeducation for the parent around children's reactions to loss, increasing communication between child and parent, and improving parenting skills.

Principle 5: Create and Implement a Treatment Plan Consistent With the Child's Style, Family Culture, and Temperament

As discussed previously, it is important to tailor the approach to the individual. Specificity works in terms of both content (i.e., areas to be addressed through treatment) and process (i.e., how the clinician addresses the child and presents him- or herself and the treatment). In other words, not only is it important to choose which interventions to utilize based on the needs of the child, but it is equally important to choose how to present those interventions based on the child's personality, temperament, age, abilities, likes, and dislikes. For example, whereas a 16-year-old boy may feel comfortable raising his own issues for discussion, a 6-year-old boy might require a more structured environment, including elements of play and art. Similarly, two 10-year-old girls might respond to the same therapist very differently, with one preferring to express herself through art and the other preferring to express herself through talking and storytelling. The important principle here is that there are multiple ways to engage children, and the therapist should take the time to figure out what works best for the individual child.

In the same way, when including the parent in treatment, the parent's style as well as the parent–child relationship must be taken into account. Often, therapists are surprised when a child who was fully engaged during an individual session seems to suddenly clam up when the parent is invited to participate in the session. For this reason, any inclusion of the parent should be fully discussed with the child prior to a joint session. Such discussion should include getting the child's input about what to share with the parent as well as who (i.e., the child or therapist) should share it.

Principle 6: Provide Clear Expectations for Therapy

Bereaved families seeking therapy are struggling with profound life changes and may not be experienced with what therapy typically involves. It is important for the therapist, who is often being looked to for guidance, to offer a safe place in which the child's most private thoughts and feelings may be comfortably revealed. Likewise, it is important for the therapist to disclose to both the child and parent where he or she is coming from, both in terms of the general approach to treatment (e.g., "I know you said you would like to be able to talk to each other about what happened, and I am here to help you do that") and professional responsibilities, including issues of confidentiality and its limits. Issues of confidentiality are particularly important to discuss in a clear way, again with both the child and parent, when the parent will have some role in the treatment process.

Principle 7: Build on Strengths of the Child and Family to Provide Skills That Will Continue to Help Them Over Time

Many of the books currently available regarding clinical practice with children tend to focus on diagnostic issues and how to get relief in key problem areas. Although there is an important place for this type of deficit-based approach, and, in fact, we do include several types of interventions aimed at common problem areas in Part II of this book, we also feel that the strengths of a child are equally important as a focus in therapy for bereaved children. By focusing on and bolstering the strengths of the individual child and his or her family and by using community resources, resilience may be fostered. The fundamental idea is to enhance the child's and family's quality of life by not only reducing problems and symptoms but also by increasing positive interactions and building on what the child and family are already doing to help themselves. In this way, the child will learn how to cope with the loss of a loved one and will be more prepared to adapt to the significant life changes associated with such a loss.

Phases of Treatment

Keeping in mind the basic treatment principles, the clinician administers three phases of IGTC (see Figure 1.1). In the first phase, he or she assesses the grieving child to determine what needs must be met, what symptoms must be addressed, and what resources can be drawn upon to build resilience. This phase is critical for customizing the treatment plan to meet the unique needs of the child. As discussed previously, some children will present with minor difficulties, whereas others will face one or more significant prolonged symptoms. Similarly, children vary in their circumstances and preferences and will therefore require customized interventions to develop coping skills and build resilience. The first phase ends with determining goals for treatment and preparing the child and parent for the work ahead by presenting basic skills that will serve as building blocks for the therapy.

The second phase is to address any presenting symptoms or problems, such as depression, PTSD, anxiety, or behavior problems. Clinicians should address these symptoms prior to focusing on grief and resilience (the third phase) because these symptoms have the most impact on the child's daily life. However, if a child does not present with specific clinical symptoms but nevertheless wishes to benefit from grief-focused treatment, then the second phase may be largely omitted.

The third phase of treatment is to focus more on the loss itself and the grieving process while fostering resilience in the child. One important com-

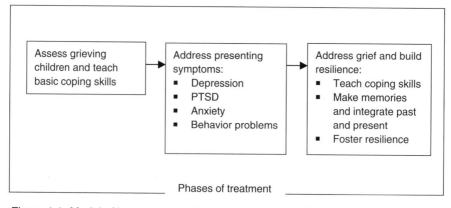

Figure 1.1. Model of integrated grief therapy for children. PTSD = posttraumatic stress disorder.

ponent of this phase is helping the child maintain a connection to the deceased in a way that brings comfort and security while also helping the child to use additional resources, such as the support of other loved ones and their own strengths and coping skills. This continued connection with a lost loved one is thought to be especially important for bereaved children and is in line with other researchers and practitioners who have recognized the importance of maintaining relationships or bonds between bereaved persons and their deceased loved ones (Field, 2008; Klass & Walter, 2001; Malkinson, 2001; Silverman, Nickman, & Worden, 1992; Weiss, 2008).

Within each phase of IGTC, the clinician is encouraged to use those aspects of the treatment that are most relevant and make the most sense for the given child who presents for therapy. For example, a 9-year-old boy who has refused to sleep in his own bed at night and has discontinued many of his after-school activities since the death of his mother may benefit from interventions to address depression and anxiety (second phase of IGTC). Following some symptom improvement, the clinician might then help the boy talk to his father about ways that he would like to preserve his mother's memory (third phase of IGTC).

ORGANIZATION OF THE BOOK

The book is organized into three parts that mirror the three phases of IGTC. Part I introduces the IGTC model, reviews its empirical and theoretical basis, and presents the first phase of treatment. The current chapter lays out the basic tenets of IGTC. Chapter 2 reviews the current literature on bereavement in childhood, including risk and protective factors, clinical outcomes, and findings regarding working with bereaved families in therapy. Chapter 3 further details the first phase of IGTC, provides guidelines for the assessment of bereaved children, and outlines the basic skills of treatment.

Part II focuses on the second phase of IGTC, administering interventions to bereaved children who present with clinically significant problems. This phase of treatment is organized around four major symptom clusters that are most relevant for grieving children: depression (Chapter 4), PTSD (Chapter 5), anxiety (Chapter 6), and behavior problems (Chapter 7).

Part III focuses on helping children to move forward by increasing skills and bolstering strengths. Chapter 8 describes how children understand and cope with loss and learn to thrive despite the loss. The chapter also includes guidelines for presenting these concepts to the child and his or her caregiver, as well as information for parents about how to talk with and help their grieving children. Chapter 9 presents interventions for improving children's coping skills to address thoughts and feelings related to grief. Chapter 10 focuses on facilitating grieving by preserving memories and integrating the loss into the child's current life. Finally, Chapter 11 describes how to foster resilience by strengthening the parent–child relationship and by helping the child to further build on the skills learned throughout the course of treatment. Because therapy termination requires preparation and sensitivity, the chapter also describes how to terminate therapy once treatment goals have been met.

Throughout the book, the text is supplemented with case examples, therapist scripts, dialogues, and activities to illustrate the use of IGTC techniques. Handouts are provided to make many of the strategies ready for use by the clinician. Activity handouts are presented in the chapters in which they are first introduced, each on a separate page so that they may be easily photocopied and provided to the child and/or parent for use in and between sessions. Clinicians should feel free to create their own handouts and activities based on the needs of the individuals they are working with. In fact, we encourage the clinician's creativity throughout the IGTC approach, with an understanding that the treatment is most effective when it is tailored to match the style of the therapist and the unique needs of each bereaved child.

2

RISK AND PROTECTIVE FACTORS, CLINICAL PRESENTATIONS, AND TREATMENT INTERVENTIONS: A REVIEW OF THE LITERATURE

The death of a close family member in childhood is a fundamental loss. In particular, the death of a parent in childhood has long been considered one of the most traumatic events that can occur in a child's life (A. T. Beck, Sethi, & Tuthill, 1963; Lutzke, Ayers, Sandler, & Barr, 1997; Yamamoto et al., 1996). Children, like adults, grieve when someone close to them dies and need opportunities to express that grief in a safe and supportive environment. Although most children tend to experience profound feelings of sadness and despair following a loss, the duration and intensity of grief are unique for each child.

Children may express their grief emotionally and/or as behavioral changes. Research reflects an increased awareness that the nature and expression of children's grief are impacted by a multitude of factors, including family dynamics, social supports, religion, and cultural issues (Genevro, Marshall, Miller, & Center for the Advancement of Health, 2004). Perhaps the most influential variable impacting children's grief is age, or developmental level. Developmental level affects children's capacities to understand the concept of death, how their grief is manifested, and what coping mechanisms are available to them to come to terms with a major loss (Oltjenbruns, 2001;

Worden, 1996). Although commonalities may exist across children at similar developmental levels, it is important to emphasize that children tend to grieve in highly individualistic ways.

Regardless of the manner in which they express their grief, over the course of time, the majority of children come to terms with these feelings and integrate the distressing experience of loss into their lives. Other children may develop emotional and behavioral symptoms that persist over time and have difficulty returning to their baseline functioning. Yet another category of children may seem to be adjusting well at first, even as far as 2 or more years after the loss, but later have problems as they face new developmental tasks or encounter life stressors (Worden & Silverman, 1996).

The latter category of bereaved children is related to the *re-grief* phenomenon discussed by Oltjenbruns (2001), in which children experience a resurgence of grief related to significant early losses as they mature and reach new developmental milestones. Oltjenbruns emphasized that children may need to reprocess the loss from their new, more mature perspective and reaccommodate the past loss in their current life stage. Similar to the re-grief phenomenon, bereaved children are also at risk of demonstrating delayed or distorted grief reactions (e.g., Crenshaw, 2007). In delayed reactions, children may exhibit few or no signs of grieving at the time of the loss but may respond to a subsequent loss of subjectively less magnitude with profound grief and despair. In cases of distorted grief, children may not exhibit intense grief symptoms at the time of the loss but instead at a later point may demonstrate psychosomatic symptoms (e.g., migraines, gastrointestinal symptoms, dizzy spells) and/or interpersonal difficulties that do not appear specific to the loss experience (Crenshaw, 2007). Although these types of delayed or distorted reactions may be normative for children because of their inability to tolerate the pain of ongoing grief (Webb, 2002), it is important to help these children to grieve while remaining cognizant of their limited psychological resources (Crenshaw, 2007). For clinicians, an awareness of the tendency of bereaved children to grieve for short periods at different points and to regrieve as they reach new developmental stages and challenges is essential to optimal treatment.

Regardless of the form it takes, the grieving process may require interventions from a clinician who can provide support for the child and family. When emotional and behavioral symptoms develop and persist beyond a few months after the loss, treatment specifically targeting these presenting issues is recommended. Further guidance about determining treatment needs for this population are provided in Chapter 3. The current chapter reviews the risk and protective factors that predict distress in bereaved children, common presenting problems, and research on treatment interventions. The chapter also indicates how the current research has informed the development of our treatment model, integrated grief therapy for children (IGTC).

RISK AND PROTECTIVE FACTORS

Although the literature on bereavement in childhood has expanded in recent years, the psychological sequelae for children after parental death are still not fully understood. The research findings on the development of psychopathology in bereaved children are inconclusive and often contradictory. Our goal is to discuss how the bereavement process works and to review factors that are believed to play a role in determining how the child adapts to the loss of a parent and the corresponding changes in the family system. These have traditionally been labeled *risk factors* and *protective factors*, and they have important implications for treatment. What has been demonstrated consistently in the outcome research is that children of all ages experience grief, sadness, and despair following the loss of a parent (for reviews, see Dowdney, 2000; Genevro et al., 2004). Several variables have been examined for their potential role in impacting the mental health outcomes of parentally bereaved children, including age and cognitive development, functioning of the surviving parent, parenting skills and family factors, family socioeconomic status (SES), previous functioning of the child and family, gender, relationship to the deceased parent, whether the death was anticipated or unanticipated, and the presence or absence of social support (Cerel, Fristad, Verducci, Weller, & Weller, 2006; Dowdney, 2000; Luecken, 2008). Our understanding of these factors, which is highlighted in the sections that follow, is based on clinical observations and experience with bereaved children and their families, along with emerging research in this area.

Age and Cognitive Development

The following section provides a summary of children's normative reactions to loss across different ages and is based on what we have observed clinically and what has been described elsewhere (e.g., Baker & Sedney, 1996; New York University Child Study Center, 2006; Webb, 2002). Further discussion specific to children's understanding of the concept of death is available (see Speece & Brent, 1996).

Infants: 0–2-Year-Olds

Infants do not have the cognitive capacity to understand death. Still, they may exhibit reactions to the loss, such as searching behaviors, confusion, separation anxiety, and regression to earlier behaviors (e.g., changes in sleep or feeding patterns, increased crying, inability to self-soothe). Infants will not only respond to a change in caregiver, but also to the current caregiver's emotional state. Consistency, routine, and the presence of familiar significant others is essential.

Toddlers and Preschoolers: 2–5-Year-Olds

Children of preschool age are not able to understand the finality of death, and they are likely to react most to the way in which the loss impacts their daily lives. For this reason, young children benefit greatly from the maintenance of routine and structure and need to be reassured of who will be taking care of their daily needs. They will likely be confused about what has happened, and verbal children may repeatedly ask questions about the loved one's location and inquire when the person is coming back. Young children may also exhibit *magical thinking,* meaning they secretly believe that they somehow caused the death or that the death is a result of some wrongdoing on their part.

When experiencing a major life change such as the loss of a loved one, young children may demonstrate behavioral changes, including regression to behaviors that had previously subsided (e.g., bed wetting, excessive crying or crankiness, clinginess, tantrums). They also may exhibit fears and worries that they did not previously have. The regression that occurs in young children may stem from a variety of factors, such as extreme stress in the face of loss, difficulty regulating emotions, and limited self-soothing capacity, and may also be a means of seeking the attention of distracted or distressed caregivers.

Early School-Age Children: 6–9-Year-Olds

By approximately 6 or 7 years of age, children are more likely to have an increased understanding of concepts around death. Although they may continue to express a desire to be reunited with the loved one who has died, school-age children tend to understand that this is not possible. However, they will continue to have questions about what happens to people when they die. They may become very interested or fixated on the details and circumstances surrounding the death. Like younger children, school-age children may regress to an earlier stage of development that makes them appear younger than their actual age. They also may continue to believe that their thoughts or behaviors somehow caused the death and may attempt to be the "perfect child" in an effort to bring the deceased back to life.

Children of this age may become fearful about their own death and/or the death of caregivers, which would leave them alone. It is also common for bereaved children to have mood fluctuations, including times when they are feeling sad and times when they are content and engaging in their usual activities.

Middle School–Age Children: 9–12-Year-Olds

By the time children are approximately 9 years old, they are more capable of abstract thinking and tend to have a mature understanding of death. They are able to comprehend that death is a permanent and necessary part of the life cycle, and they understand that the body completely stops functioning after death. Bereaved children between the ages of 9 and 12 may begin to feel that they are different from their peers because of their loss, and they may withdraw from usual activities as a result. Helping children of this age to maintain and develop relationships with same-age peers is therefore an important component of treatment.

Children at this age may blame themselves for the death of a loved one, or they may feel guilty for things they have said or done that are unrelated to how the person died. They may worry about their surviving family members and, like younger children, may fear their own death and the death of others. Like children of all ages, they will benefit from reassurance that their physical and emotional needs will continue to be met.

Adolescents: 13–18-Year-Olds

Adolescents react to bereavement and loss in a way that is similar to the reactions of adults. They are likely to show emotional distress, often in the form of sadness and depression. They may consider how the experience of loss will contribute to their sense of identity and life purpose and may also begin thinking about personal mortality. Adolescents often imagine the absence of their loved one in future life events and how this absence will influence the course of their lives. Some adolescents may begin to take on increased responsibilities, such as taking care of younger siblings, while others may act out by engaging in risky behavior. Although teens are more able than younger children to express their feelings verbally, they are also more likely to make conscious choices about whether or not to communicate their experiences.

Functioning of the Surviving Parent

One essential determinant of a child's positive outcome after a loss is the availability of a supportive and consistent caregiver. The link between parent mental health and child outcome has been well established in the general child psychopathology literature (e.g., Beardslee, Bemporad, Keller, & Klerman, 1983; Burke, 2003; Carter, Garrity-Rokous, Chazan-Cohen, Little, & Briggs-Gowan, 2001; Downey & Coyne, 1990; Hammen et al., 1987; Orvaschel, Walsh-Allis, & Ye, 1988; Rutter, 1990). This relationship is of particular relevance to bereaved families, where children are often left with a surviving parent who is struggling with his or her own grief and may experience psychological difficulties, such as depression, anxiety, or other mental health problems (Dowdney, 2000; Luecken, 2008). In a recent empirical study, surviving caregivers in bereaved families where there was sudden parent loss (death by suicide, accident, or sudden natural death) were found to have increased rates of depression, anxiety, posttraumatic stress disorder (PTSD), suicidal ideation, and functional impairment when compared with demographically matched nonbereaved control families (Melhem, Walker, Moritz, & Brent, 2008).

In addition to psychological symptoms, caring for a child or children after the loss of a partner has many other implications that can impact a parent's functioning. In both intact and divorced families, the consequences for the living parent are in multiple domains and may include increased financial stressors, change in residence, increased responsibility in parenting, and loss of social supports. A parent's capacity to manage these pressures is essential to the child's ability to cope effectively with the loss.

There is considerable evidence demonstrating an inverse relationship between mental health of the surviving parent and child distress. In a recent large-scale investigation of psychopathology in parentally bereaved children ages 6 to 17, Cerel et al. (2006) found lower levels of depressive symptoms in the surviving parent to be associated with better outcomes for the child, based on interviews at regular intervals during the first 2 years after a parental death. Another study involving parentally bereaved children and their surviving parents found parent adjustment to be the best predictor of the child's emotional adjustment (Kalter et al., 2002). An earlier prospective study of acute bereavement in preschoolers who had lost a parent within the previous 6 months found depression in surviving parents to be the most significant predictor of childhood behavioral disturbance (Kranzler, Shaffer, Wasserman, & Davies, 1990). Melhem et al. (2008) also found higher caregiver functioning to be a protective factor against depression in bereaved offspring. Finally, higher scores on a global measure of psychopathology administered to bereaved children (ages 2 to 17) were associated with having a mentally ill, usually depressed, surviving mother (Van Eerdewegh, Clayton, & Van Eerdewegh, 1985).

These studies demonstrate the importance of parents' psychological health with regards to bereaved children's outcomes. The IGTC treatment principles therefore emphasize the need to include the surviving parent in any treatment approach for bereaved children. In some cases, parental psychoeducation and guidance as a component of the child's treatment is sufficient. Some examples include encouraging parents to follow their children's lead when discussing the death, to support their children's experiences, and to facilitate children's expression of feelings. In other cases, such as when the parent is experiencing his or her own depression or other problems in need of clinical attention, a separate course of individual therapy for the surviving parent may be warranted.

Parenting Skills and Family Factors

It has long been believed that factors such as how the loss of a parent is experienced, coped with, and resolved by the child are often determined by the family context (Reese, 1982). As previously mentioned, research has consistently demonstrated that the psychological well-being of the surviving parent is a strong predictor of mental health outcomes for a bereaved child. Over the past few years, researchers have tried to better understand specific family and parenting factors that mediate this relationship. The ability to engage in *positive parenting* has been identified as a variable that may account for how parental psychological distress impacts bereaved children's coping (Kwok et al., 2005). Positive parenting is the creation of a supportive, stable, and structured environment, characterized by a warm relationship between parent and child and consistent discipline by the parent (Kwok et al., 2005). In their implementation of the Family Bereavement Program, an intervention that targets parenting and other family variables, Sandler and colleagues found that improvements in parenting are associated with a decrease in mental health problems for children in bereaved families (Sandler et al., 1992; Tein, Sandler, Ayers, & Wolchik, 2006). Conversely, negative parenting practices and the stress associated with bereavement in the surviving parent has been suggested as placing the bereaved child at risk (Luecken, 2008).

Other researchers have also examined the ability of the surviving parent to provide stability and consistency in the child's family environment and daily life as an essential factor in decreasing the child's risk of developing behavior problems. In a longitudinal study of families with children aged 6 to 16 coping with the loss of a parent, Saldinger, Porterfield, and Cain (2004) also found that child-centered parenting was associated with less symptomatology and more positive perceptions of the surviving parent by the child. A nonintervention study of families in which a parent died of cancer found that positive family coping, characterized as the ability to communicate effectively, resolve conflicts, and express feelings, was associated with better outcomes (less depression and better social adjustment) for both the child and the surviving spouse (Kissane, Bloch, & McKenzie, 1997).

These findings are consistent with what we and others have observed clinically with bereaved children and their parents, which is that outcomes for the bereaved child are inextricably linked to the functioning and responses of the surviving parent. The IGTC approach emphasizes the importance of involving the parent in treatment in the following ways. First, we teach or review parenting skills and coping skills that may have been compromised as a result of the loss and related adversities. Second, the parent is recruited to reinforce the principles and coping strategies that the child learns throughout the course of treatment. Third, we facilitate positive communication between the parent and child, including the expression of feelings and communication about the loss. Finally, we help the family to make decisions regarding funerals or other mourning rituals and encourage them to find continuing ways of memorializing the deceased. Rituals may include aspects of the funeral service as well as ongoing activities that allow children to remember their loved one in a structured and meaningful way, such as writing letters, engaging in the deceased parent's favorite activities, or setting aside family time to remember the lost parent.

Family SES and Secondary Stressors

The death of a parent may result in financial strain for the bereaved family, particularly if the deceased parent was the primary source of income. However, results from research examining the role of family SES in determining outcomes for bereaved children are mixed. Some research has indicated that family SES is an important variable in determining degree of child psychopathology after bereavement (e.g., Cerel et al., 2006). Additional studies found lower social class of bereaved families to significantly predict mental health problems in adulthood (Harris, Brown, & Bifulco, 1987; Parker & Manicavasagar, 1986). Other researchers have found different results. A study of predominantly minority children who lost a parent through either natural death or homicide did not find any significant impact of SES on child outcome (Thompson, Kaslow, Price, Williams, & Kingree, 1998). Similarly, Lin, Sandler, Ayers, Wolchik, and Luecken (2004) did not find a relationship between level of income postloss and mental health problems in bereaved children. However, these authors speculated that their measurement of SES may account for the negative findings, as a decline in income is likely to be a more accurate predictor of mental health problems than current level of income.

The mixed results from this research may be explained by further exploring the pathway from SES to child outcomes in bereaved families. Financial problems after the death of a parent increase the likelihood of secondary stressors for the surviving family members. These may include a need to move and/or change schools, which impacts the child's sense of stability and may result in loss of friendships and social supports for the family. In addition, financial problems can also interfere with a family's ability to cope practically with the loss, such as being able to afford child care (Cerel et al., 2006).

Evidence of an association between reports of significant life events and child psychiatric symptoms has been demonstrated in bereaved families, indicating that it may not be SES per se but rather the experience of life changes that are often related to economic problems that impacts a child's outcome (Pfeffer et al., 1997). It seems clear that in some situations, economic problems may not play a role in outcome or may simply have an additive effect when combined with other stressors. In other cases, economic problems might contribute to the development of or exacerbate other risk factors. IGTC suggests a thorough review of financial concerns as well as related sources of distress in bereaved families, for their practical implications and for their potential impact on adherence to treatment. Helping the parent and child to develop more effective coping skills is helpful in reducing the impact of these types of stressors.

Previous Functioning of the Child and Family

In general, there is limited research exploring children's previous functioning as a predictor of psychological distress following parental death (Lin et al., 2004). Furthermore, methodological issues complicate our ability to interpret the findings. A child is typically assessed after the death occurs, at which point it is difficult to discern whether the symptoms were present previously or, alternatively, whether they developed following the loss. In addition, there tends to be a reliance on parental report to assess the child's baseline functioning, despite the demonstration that more psychological symptoms in children are endorsed by self-report than by parent report after a loss (e.g., Weller, Weller, Fristad, & Bowes, 1991). Whether this is also true for child symptoms prior to loss has not been established empirically.

Children who were vulnerable psychologically before the loss of their parent may have a more difficult time when confronted with parental death and are likely to demonstrate an increase in previously displayed symptoms and possibly new symptoms. Evidence for the impact of a prior individual or family history of psychological or psychiatric disturbance on outcome in bereaved children has been found. Specifically, bereaved children with pre-existing untreated psychiatric disorders, as well as bereaved children with a family history of depression, have significantly more depressive symptoms than other bereaved children (Weller et al., 1991). Children who have suffered previous losses, even if seemingly minor, may also be at increased risk of developing symptoms (Elizur & Kaffman, 1983; Webb, 2002).

It is important to assess the previous functioning of bereaved children because it is likely to influence the course and severity of postdeath symptoms, as well as the way in which the child copes with and adapts to the loss. Again, this information is typically gathered by conducting a thorough interview with the parent and child, as well as obtaining relevant school and health records.

Gender

Conclusions from research on whether the gender of the child impacts their level of distress following the death of a parent are mixed. Bereaved girls have been found to be more susceptible than bereaved boys to the development of mental health problems in several studies (Reinherz, Giaconia,

Carmola Hauf, Wasserman, & Silverman, 1999; Rotheram-Borus, Stein, & Lin, 2001; Schmiege, Khoo, Sandler, Ayers, & Wolchik, 2006; Worden, 1996). Researchers have speculated that girls may be more at risk because of the nature of their role in the family and their sensitivity to stress within the family. Girls may be more likely to take on greater responsibility after a parental death and tend to demonstrate more concern about the well-being of the surviving parent (Tein et al., 2006). Consistent with other literature on gender-related vulnerabilities, some studies have shown that bereaved girls develop more internalizing symptoms (e.g., Raveis, Siegel, & Karus, 1999), whereas bereaved boys have higher global levels of psychopathology with more aggression and acting-out behaviors (Dowdney et al., 1999; Kranzler et al., 1990). However, others have found that gender does not play a role in predicting mental health problems in these children (e.g., Lin et al., 2004).

When treating bereaved children, it is important that behaviors that may not appear grief related (e.g., acting-out behavior in boys) are attended to and understood as possibly connected to the loss experience. It is also helpful for the clinician to recognize how gender roles may impact a child's response to the loss of a parent and to communicate the importance of balancing new responsibilities among family members. Although a child realistically may need to take on increased responsibilities after the loss of a parent, it is important that the responsibilities are age appropriate and do not lead to parentification of the child.

Relationship to the Deceased Parent

Basic attachment theory (e.g., Bowlby, 1969, 1973, 1980) states that the loss of a parent through death or abandonment is a significantly upsetting event because it represents a loss of the major attachment figure on whom the child was emotionally dependent. This theory is supported by research indicating that the duration and intensity of the child's grief reaction may depend on the extent to which the child perceived the lost parent as essential to their protection and security (Shaver & Tancredy, 2001). Children also appear to be more profoundly impacted by the death of a parent when they had a closer relationship to that parent and perhaps relatively less of an emotional connection to the surviving parent (Kranzler et al., 1990). Melhem et al. (2008) found that one factor influencing outcome for children bereaved by sudden parent loss was the nature of their last conversation with the deceased; specifically, bereaved children who recalled a more confiding conversation were at increased risk of depression after the loss, supporting the idea that a closer relationship conveys a greater risk. These findings are important clinically, as often a key part of the work in treatment is helping the child to cope with his or her overwhelming feelings of grief and loss as well as to develop a stronger emotional attachment to the surviving parent or caregiver. The surviving caregiver may require guidance from the therapist about how to reassure the child of his or her psychological and physical safety.

Anticipated Versus Unanticipated Death

Clinicians have often presumed that when a death is expected, the ability for loved ones to begin mourning in anticipation of the death may facilitate better outcomes. Conversely, when a death is sudden and shocking, it is perceived as a more disturbing loss. There is in fact a potential link between type of loss and outcome, as parents who die suddenly are more likely to have had higher rates of psychiatric disorder, including mood, substance abuse, and personality disorders, and these illnesses are associated with an increased risk of mortality not only from suicide but also from accidents and cardiovascular diseases (see Melhem et al., 2008). These factors may place their children at additional risk of psychological problems.

However, studies that have directly examined the relationship between type of death and general outcomes for the child have found little evidence that either expected or unexpected death is linked with greater child disturbance (Cerel et al., 2006; Dowdney, 2000; Saldinger, Cain, Kalter, & Lohnes, 1999). This issue has been addressed in the child literature, primarily with children whose parents had a terminal illness, and research suggests that the impact is more on the grief process itself than on the psychological sequelae for the child. Evidence suggests that children may exhibit the most intense grief when a parent is in the terminal stages of illness and that symptoms may subside after the death itself (Siegel, Karus, & Raveis, 1996). Although there is intense distress associated with a sudden death, the experience of living with a terminally ill parent is also a burden for the child and family (Cerel et al., 2006).

Although anticipated versus unanticipated death does not seem to significantly impact general outcomes, children who experience the death of a parent through murder or suicide may be at greater risk of developing PTSD (Yule, 1994). The loss of a parent by homicide or suicide may carry a particular risk because of the trauma and shame associated with these types of deaths. Children bereaved by the suicide of a parent have reported higher levels of depressive symptomatology than children who have lost a parent to cancer, for example (Pfeffer, Karus, Siegel, & Jiang, 2000). Feelings of anxiety, anger, and shame were also more likely to be reported by children bereaved by parental suicide than other children who lost a parent (Cerel, Fristad, Weller, & Weller, 1999). Children who lost a parent to homicide have been found to be more likely than controls to present with behavior problems, whereas children who lost a parent to natural death were not more likely than controls to develop these types of symptoms (Thompson et al., 1998). It is interesting to note that A. C. Brown, Sandler, Tein, Liu, and Haine (2007) found contrasting findings when examining outcomes following parental death from suicide or other violent causes as compared with death from illness. These authors found that the cause of death had little impact on children's mental health problems, grief, or risk and protective factors, and they concluded that cause of death from violence or suicide is generally not useful in determining bereaved children's need for treatment. Finally, in a study that looked specifically at the psychological sequelae of sudden parental death, including death from suicide, accident, or sudden natural causes, Melhem et al. (2008) found no evidence of increased risk for those who lost a parent to suicide compared with those who lost a parent suddenly from other causes.

In summary, type of death does not, in and of itself, determine the outcome for the child. However, IGTC highlights that eliciting the circumstances surrounding the death is essential to the therapist's understanding of the nature of the child's response. This is a sensitive discussion, and the therapist should use his or her clinical judgment to determine when the family is ready to disclose these details. When the circumstances of the death are traumatic, it is important for the clinician to assess for symptoms of PTSD. In addition, the therapist should assess on an ongoing basis how the child and parent are making sense of the loss experience and guide them in integrating the experience of loss into both their self- and worldviews (see Chapter 10).

Social Support

Clinicians often assume that social support is a key factor in determining outcome after bereavement (W. Stroebe, Zech, Stroebe, & Abakoumkin, 2005). Research in this area has focused on bereaved adults, rather than children, whose social network is determined largely by their parents. However, findings from the adult research are applicable to child treatment for that reason; the degree of social support received by the surviving caregiver is likely to influence his or her ability to cope, which, in turn, influences the child. However, it is important to emphasize that it is the social support of the surviving parent rather than of the child that has been primarily examined.

In their exploration of resiliency factors that enable successful adaptation in families after the loss of a parent, Greeff and Human (2004) found that the most important coping resource identified by bereaved families was social support obtained from extended family and friends. Sherkat and Reed (1992) also found that the quantity and quality of social support contributed to well-being in adults who were suddenly bereaved by the suicides or accidental deaths of family members.

In contrast, in a review of studies on the role of social support as a moderator of the impact of loss on the psychological health of conjugally bereaved adults, W. Stroebe et al. (2005) found limited evidence that social support accelerates time of recovery or buffers against depressive symptoms following a loss. Individuals who had high levels of social support had lower depression levels; however, this finding was true for both the bereaved individuals and married controls, indicating that this effect was not specific to bereavement.

Although the research does not uniformly demonstrate that social support significantly influences outcome, it does not appear to have any negative effects that would deter clinicians from encouraging bereaved individuals to seek support. Based on clinical observations, parents of bereaved children who have stronger social networks appear to function more effectively than those parents who feel isolated and perceive a lack of support from their community. Social support is especially important for parents of young children in managing everyday caretaking responsibilities. Additional research is needed to further determine the importance of different types of support (e.g., emotional, financial, practical), which may lead to a better understanding of the needs of bereaved individuals.

An area of concern that often surfaces when working with bereaved children is their tendency to isolate themselves socially for many different reasons that can include shame, feeling different from their peers, preoccupation with their own grief, and fear that closeness can lead to future loss. Although to our knowledge no studies to date have specifically looked at the impact of the child's social circumstances on outcome, basic attachment theory would suggest that close, secure relationships with others would play a protective role. Therefore, IGTC suggests that a child's social functioning should be assessed and included as a treatment goal when warranted.

Summary of Risk and Protective Factors

Common variables that increase the likelihood of adverse outcomes for bereaved children were reviewed, including age and cognitive development, functioning of the surviving parent, parenting skills and family factors, family SES and degree of additional family stressors, previous functioning of the child and family, gender, relationship to the deceased parent, anticipated versus unanticipated death, and social support. To work therapeutically with these children and promote resilience, clinicians must understand and address these factors in treatment. The importance of addressing parent–child communication and parenting skills in treatment was also highlighted. This can be accomplished through skills training that focuses on effective parenting along with psychoeducation for parents about how to support their child's grieving (see Chapters 7 and 8).

CLINICAL PRESENTATIONS IN BEREAVED CHILDREN

Bereaved children are affected by the death of a loved one in various ways, with the effects of the loss being manifested as diverse clinical presentations (Luecken, 2008). Following the death of a parent, bereaved children may exhibit signs of depression, anxiety, PTSD, behavioral disorders, and general adjustment difficulties. These different presentations are further elaborated on in the sections that follow.

Depression

The most consistent finding in the literature with regard to outcomes following child bereavement is the relationship between the loss of a parent and depression in the bereaved child (Lutzke et al., 1997). Several studies have demonstrated that recently parentally bereaved children (up to 18 months postdeath), of ages ranging from preschool to adolescence, have significantly higher levels of depression than do nonbereaved, demographically matched comparison groups (Cerel et al., 2006; Gersten, Beals, & Kallgren, 1991; Kranzler et al., 1990; Melhem et al., 2008; Van Eerdewegh et al., 1985). In these studies, depressive symptoms, including dysphoria, declining school performance, sleeping and eating disturbances, and withdrawal, were all found to be increased in bereaved children. We have observed clinically that bereaved children sometimes report thoughts that resemble suicidal ideation; for example, a child might state that he or she "would like to be in heaven with [his or her] father." However, we have found that these thoughts are typically based on a desire to be reunited with the lost parent and are not something upon which children will act. This phenomenon has also been noted in the literature (Weller et al., 1991).

Although these studies show evidence of depressive symptoms in bereaved children, it appears that only a minority will meet full criteria for a depressive disorder. Compared with nonbereaved children diagnosed with major depression in inpatient and outpatient settings, bereaved children have been shown to have less depressive symptoms (e.g., Cerel et al., 2006; Weller et al., 1991). This is not to suggest that grief never leads to major depression; some bereaved children may develop major depressive episodes at some point after the loss or at a later point in adolescence or adulthood. There has been evidence that early parent loss is one factor that can lead to later major depressive episodes and even suicidal behavior (see Brent & Melhem, 2008). Moreover, the observation of depressive symptoms by a parent, teacher, or other caregiver is often one of the factors that brings bereaved children to seek clinical intervention. For further guidance on the treatment of depression in bereaved children, refer to Chapter 4.

PTSD

It can be argued that whenever a child loses a parent, it is a traumatizing experience. However, bereavement and trauma do not always overlap diagnostically. The sudden death of a parent may be considered particularly traumatic, and if followed by symptoms including reenactment of the traumatic event, avoidance of stimuli associated with the event, or general withdrawal and hyperarousal, a diagnosis of PTSD may be warranted. Children who lose a parent because of suicide, murder, accidental death, or unexpected medical complications have been found to be at risk of PTSD (Melhem et al., 2008; Yule, 1994). After the terrorist attacks of 9/11/01, which left thousands of children bereaved, it was found that children who lost a parent in this specific tragedy were more likely than nonbereaved children to have at least one current anxiety disorder, the most common being PTSD (Pfeffer, Altemus, Heo, & Jiang, 2007). PTSD may also follow deaths that appear to be expected, such as following a long illness (Breslau, Andreski, & Chilcoat, 1998).

In recent years, researchers have proposed a distinct diagnosis of traumatic grief, separate from PTSD, depression, or normal grief. *Childhood traumatic grief* may be defined as a condition in which a child loses a loved one under subjectively traumatic circumstances, and trauma symptoms interfere with the tasks of grieving (Cohen & Mannarino, 2004). The proposed symptom profile includes trauma symptoms such as intrusive reminders or preoccupation with the death; avoidance of places, people, or situations that are reminders of the loss; and increased arousal symptoms such as irritability, sleep disturbance, increased startle reaction, and feeling generally unsafe (Cohen, Mannarino, & Knudsen, 2004). Another proposed diagnosis, *prolonged grief disorder*, formerly called *complicated grief*, has been used to describe a form of grieving in bereaved adults that includes symptoms of elevated and chronic separation distress along with cognitive, emotional, and behavioral symptoms such as difficulty moving on with life after the loss, avoidance of loss reminders, feeling that life is empty and meaningless, numbness, and inability to trust others (Lichtenthal, Cruess, & Prigerson, 2004; Prigerson, Vanderwerker, & Maciejewski, 2008). The cluster of symptoms that constitutes prolonged grief disorder is considered distinct from the set associated with PTSD, major depressive disorder, and adjustment disorder (Lichtenthal et al., 2004; Prigerson et al., 2008). However, the best criteria for defining a complicated grief reaction in adults and the relationship of traumatic grief to other syndromes and conditions are subjects of continued debate in the field (e.g., Demi & Miles, 1987; Rando, 1985; M. Stroebe, Hansson, Schut, & Stroebe, 2008; M. Stroebe et al., 2000).

While establishing accurate diagnostic criteria for both children and adults has important implications, IGTC is designed to treat all bereaved children, first targeting their primary symptoms and areas of distress even when criteria for particular diagnoses are not met. Chapter 5 presents the IGTC approach for helping children who exhibit any significant trauma symptoms following the loss of a loved one.

Anxiety

Bereaved children often experience increased anxiety, which typically emerges in the form of worry about separation from their remaining parent and/or the safety or well-being of their family members (Dowdney, 2000). Specific anxieties related to attachment, separation, and death are common reactions to the loss of a parent, even in nonclinical groups of children (Sanchez, Fristad, Weller, Weller, & Moye, 1994). These anxieties may generalize to worries about daily life, social fears, and specific phobias. In one study, the authors found that the anxiety items demonstrating the most difference between bereaved and nonbereaved groups were secret fears, worries, and difficulty sleeping (Abdelnoor & Hollins, 2004). Other studies have looked at generalized anxiety symptoms and found parentally bereaved children to be significantly more anxious than controls. They tend to experience higher levels of withdrawal, nervousness, anxiety, and social problems (Abdelnoor & Hollins, 2004; Kranzler et al., 1990; Luecken, 2008; Saucier & Ambert, 1986). Bereaved children have also been found to be more socially withdrawn than their peers 2 years following parental loss, with the most pronounced effects for preadolescent girls and adolescent boys (Worden & Silverman, 1996).

Bereaved children have also been known to report somatic complaints, such as headaches and gastrointestinal problems (e.g., Sood, Weller, Weller, Fristad, & Bowes, 1992; Van Eerdewegh, Bieri, Parrilla, & Clayton, 1982), which are common manifestations of anxiety. Anxiety may also develop in response to bereavement-related changes that disturb children's familiar patterns of living and challenge their assumptive worlds (Siegel et al., 1996).

IGTC emphasizes that the treating clinician should assess for the presence of anxiety by eliciting specific worries from the child as well as noting behavioral changes. It is essential that the child's fears and worries be addressed and that the parent is enlisted to help reassure the child of his or her safety and security. Other strategies that help with the reduction of anxiety in children are elaborated on in Chapter 6.

Behavior Problems

Although disruptive behaviors and conduct problems may not be commonly thought of as grief reactions, children's responses to loss are widely variable. These reactions may not be recognized as part of normal grief and therefore may be pathologized, overlooked, or result in blame directed at the child. However, anger and rage are natural reactions to bereavement, as the parent who has died was essential to the stability of the child's world. From an attachment perspective, children who present with high levels of externalizing problems in the context of a chaotic home environment may be attempting to connect with or get attention from preoccupied and distressed caregivers (Allen & Land, 1999).

As noted earlier, Kranzler et al. (1990), on the basis of teacher and parent report, found bereaved boys to have significantly more conduct problems. Dowdney et al. (1999) found boys to show higher levels of psychological disturbance in general, particularly acting-out and aggressive behaviors. Higher levels of aggressive behavior have also been observed in preadolescent girls 2 years after parental loss (Worden & Silverman, 1996). Other authors have not found a significant relationship between parental death and behavior problems (e.g., Gersten et al., 1991; Van Eerdewegh et al., 1982).

From our observations as well as research involving parentally bereaved children (Kwok et al., 2005; Luecken, 2008), it appears that surviving parents often have problems parenting effectively and maintaining consistent discipline after the loss of their spouse. This is often due to the parent's feelings of guilt about what the child has been through and/or is related to the impact of parent psychological distress on energy level, ability to keep up routines, and global functioning. IGTC emphasizes that issues regarding routine and discipline be addressed in treatment, as problematic parenting practices have been found to be an important risk factor for the development of conduct problems in children (see Webster-Stratton, Reid, & Hammond, 2004). Chapter 7 provides guidance on how to address these issues in the treatment of bereaved families.

Summary of Clinical Presentations in Bereaved Children

The review of the literature indicates that children grieve in different ways. Bereaved children may present with an array of different symptoms, such as depression, anxiety, posttraumatic stress, and behavior problems. Clinical presentations can also vary by gender, temperament, developmental level, and coping style. The treating therapist should be aware of these multiple presentations, as bereaved children do not always look the same. Understanding these varying presentations is key to successful treatment, as there is not one uniform way to treat these children. The IGTC approach uses the presenting symptoms to guide the treatment process while understanding them in the context of bereavement. The second phase of IGTC, as detailed in Part II of this book, provides step-by-step guidelines for addressing these clinical problems.

It is also important to underscore that the child and/or parent seeking help may not always have a diagnosable disorder. Some bereaved individuals may report symptoms of the disorders described previously. For example, some bereaved children might be anxious when faced with reminders of the death but may not meet criteria for an anxiety disorder. The IGTC treatment is most helpful for those children who have symptoms that are interfering with their daily functioning. Others may express difficulty adjusting to the loss, along with anxiety or discomfort about how to talk about death within their family. These families are often seeking direction and may need psycho-education and/or a short course of treatment.

INTERVENTIONS FOR FAMILIES
COPING WITH PARENTAL LOSS

A recent meta-analytic review of the existing controlled outcome literature on the effectiveness of bereavement interventions for children suggests that although not all bereaved children benefitted from treatment, those presenting with significant problems or distress showed favorable outcomes following bereavement intervention, particularly when the treatment was closer to the time of the loss (Currier, Holland, & Neimeyer, 2007). In another comprehensive quantitative review of intervention studies for bereaved adults and children, Currier, Neimeyer, and Berman (2008) found that the interventions did not benefit all bereaved individuals but rather were most beneficial when targeted toward individuals who were having significant difficulty adapting to the loss. In those cases, the effectiveness of the bereavement interventions was comparable with psychotherapy for other difficulties.

In the literature specific to bereaved adults, there has been some indication that grief counseling may not be helpful and may even be contraindicated for adults experiencing normal grief (e.g., Jordan & Neimeyer, 2003; Schut, Stroebe, van den Bout, & Terheggen, 2001). However, counseling has been shown to be helpful for adults experiencing complicated grief (e.g., Shear, Frank, Houck, & Reynolds, 2005).

The research findings for both bereaved children and adults are consistent with our belief that not all bereaved children necessarily require therapy. It is only when symptoms persist and interfere with daily functioning that a course of IGTC treatment is recommended. Given the opportunity, treatment should begin as close to the loss as possible to maximize effectiveness and to potentially prevent delayed or distorted grief reactions. Treatment objectives should be based on the presenting problems specific to the child, including grief-focused interventions when necessary. Different types of therapeutic interventions for bereaved children are discussed in the following sections.

Bereavement Support Groups

Support groups are the most common and well-studied intervention for both bereaved children and adults. Group-based strategies for bereaved families often consist of parallel parent and child groups and provide both educational and therapeutic support (e.g., Zambelli, Clark, Barile, & de Jong, 1988). Parent groups typically offer psychoeducation about loss, teach coping skills, and provide the opportunity to express emotions in a supportive atmosphere. Children's groups are usually designed to help children understand the meaning of death in a developmentally appropriate manner, and they often use techniques such as artwork, bibliotherapy, and game play to help children communicate their feelings (Zambelli & DeRosa, 1992). Examples of possible effective group treatments for bereaved children are elaborated on next.

Tonkins and Lambert (1996) found that children who participated in an 8-week bereavement psychotherapy group had a significant decrease in both emotional and behavioral symptoms compared with a waiting-list control group. The authors developed a treatment model that was designed to provide a sense of safety for children to explore thoughts and feelings about the deceased. Different methods of expression, including discussion, art, and bibliotherapy, were used to help the children express sadness and fear, as well as feelings of anger and guilt. Psychoeducation about the grief process was provided. Although the study did not measure causal factors that accounted for patient improvement, the authors stated their belief that expression of feelings through symbolic communication, feelings of sameness to peers, facilitation of memories and thoughts of the deceased, and education about the grief process were all curative factors. Another evaluation of a 6-week peer support group for parentally bereaved children found no improvements in self-esteem, depression, or problem behavior for the group members compared with controls (Huss & Ritchie, 1999). However, group participants reported that their loss experiences were normalized by participating in the group.

Grieving children who participated in music-therapy–based bereavement groups demonstrated a significant decrease in grief symptoms on the basis of home evaluations, although teacher reports and self-reports were less clear (Hilliard, 2001). Hilliard (2001) described the group as a cognitive–behavioral intervention that used music and movement along with discussion to facilitate behavior modification, recognition and expression of emotions, and cognitive restructuring. Education about death and the nature of grief was also provided, and the use of adaptive coping mechanisms was promoted. Another more recent study by Hilliard (2007) also demonstrated the benefits of a music therapy group in reducing grief symptoms and behavioral problems for bereaved children, as compared with a social work group, which reduced behavioral problems but not grief symptoms. Although both studies had a relatively small number of participants, they suggest that music therapy is potentially a powerful and effective intervention for bereaved children.

Pfeffer, Jiang, Kakuma, Hwang, and Metsch (2002) evaluated the effectiveness of a manual-based bereavement group intervention for children bereaved by the suicide of a parent or sibling. Their intervention focused on children's understanding and reactions to death in the family, unique problems for suicide-bereaved children, and loss of resources in their environment. The treatment consisted of psychoeducation about the nature of death and suicide, how to recognize feelings of grief, prevention of suicidal urges, and improving problem-solving skills. Supportive aspects helped children to express their grief and to identify positively with the deceased while avoiding suicidal thoughts. Children were also helped to manage traumatic thoughts and concerns related to the stigma of suicide and to feel more optimistic and develop new relationships. Concurrently, parents received a separate group intervention in which they were able to express their own feelings of grief and received psychoeducation about childhood bereavement and how to best help their children. The authors found that the group improved coping skills and decreased levels of anxiety and depressive symptoms for this population significantly more than a nonintervention control group. However, posttraumatic stress symptoms persisted, and there was no change in social maladjustment. It was also noted that parents did not show significant changes in depressive symptoms compared with controls. The authors speculated that this was because the parent intervention focused on educating parents to help their bereaved children rather than on the needs of the parents themselves.

Sandler and colleagues (1992, 2003) have conducted rigorous evaluations of a theory-based intervention they developed for bereaved families called the Family Bereavement Program. As described earlier, they looked at the family environment as a mediator of the effects of parent loss on child outcome. Their preventive intervention program specifically targets coping skills for the surviving parent, improving family cohesion, and developing warmth in the parent–child relationship. They have found the program to be effective in reducing risk and improving protective factors immediately following the program, as well as reducing both internalizing and externalizing problems for girls (but not boys) 11 months after completion of the program (Sandler et al., 2003). In a follow-up study looking only at girls, potential mediation effects of several child variables on the Family Bereavement Program were examined (Tein et al., 2006). Two important findings were that negative life events mediated program effects on behavior problems and that active inhibition of emotional expression mediated program effects on mental health problems. These authors also found, consistent with an earlier study (Sandler et al., 1992), that improvements in parenting resulting from program participation led to reduced mental health problems for children in bereaved families.

Additional group treatments have been studied for their effectiveness in treating trauma-exposed children. Goenjian et al. (1997) found brief trauma–grief-focused psychotherapy to be effective in reducing PTSD symptoms and preventing the worsening of depressive symptoms in adolescents exposed to an earthquake in Armenia. Layne et al. (2001) developed a therapeutic school-based group intervention that was found to significantly reduce posttraumatic stress, depression, and complicated grief symptoms in war-exposed Bosnian adolescents.

Although groups can be an effective form of treatment for bereaved populations, some children and parents may benefit from or prefer individualized interventions. Furthermore, clinicians are bound to encounter individuals who present for treatment following a loss, so it is important to have a sound model for use in these cases. Clinical insight can be gained from the group therapy research—specifically, the importance of providing psychoeducation about death and loss and normalizing children's feelings of grief, along with reducing children's feelings of isolation; the need to use creative approaches when working with children; the focus on improving coping and problem-solving skills; and the value of including the parent in treatment and developing parent–child communication skills. All of these components are included in IGTC.

Individual and Family Therapy Approaches

Although numerous essays, case studies, book chapters, and articles have been published regarding psychotherapy for bereaved children, these writings tend to be descriptive in nature and not empirically based. To date, there has been little research that examines the efficacy of therapeutic interventions for a bereaved population. Empirical research studies that have been conducted have typically examined the effectiveness of group treatments (see the previous section). Other treatment modalities, such as individual and family therapy, are often implemented by clinicians working with bereaved children but have not been empirically tested.

One commonly used form of therapy with children is play therapy, an approach aimed to help the child to express him- or herself symbolically through play. To date, no empirical research has examined outcomes for bereaved children who received play therapy treatment, although many authors have provided guidelines for this type of treatment (e.g., Glazer & Clark, 1999; Webb, 2002).

Another common form of treatment is family therapy. Family therapists typically work within the family unit to impact change in the interactions between its members. In bereaved families, therapists typically provide guidance for the family through the grieving process and help them to work though issues surrounding their loss (Glazer & Clark, 1999). Again, there has been no empirical research to date that explores the effectiveness of this type of treatment with bereaved families.

Cognitive–behavioral therapy (CBT) is another form of treatment that addresses multiple symptoms understood as cognitive, physiological, and behavioral responses to various emotions, including sadness and fear. One specific CBT approach is trauma-focused CBT, originally developed for sexually abused children and since used to successfully treat children exposed to other types of traumatic events (Cohen, Mannarino, Murray, & Igelman, 2006). An adaptation of this treatment, called CBT for childhood traumatic grief, was developed to treat childhood traumatic grief and includes both trauma- and grief-focused components (Cohen, Mannarino, Murray, & Igelman, 2006). Some aspects of the grief work include psychoeducation about responses to loss, helping children to verbalize what is missed about the deceased as well as ambivalent feelings, and discussion of positive memories of the deceased. Joint parent–child sessions are a key component of treatment. Results from a pilot study of this treatment demonstrated its effectiveness in improving childhood traumatic grief, PTSD, internalizing and externalizing symptoms, and behavior problems in children who lost loved ones from violent or sudden deaths, along with a reduction in PTSD and depressive symptoms for participating parents (Cohen, Mannarino, & Knudsen, 2004).

It is important to note that although CBT for childhood traumatic grief and other treatments for children exposed to trauma may be helpful in working with children with traumatic grief and posttraumatic stress reactions, these approaches were not designed as therapeutic interventions for bereaved children with symptoms other than those related to trauma. The IGTC model attempts to fill the gap in the literature about how to effectively treat all bereaved children.

Given the lack of evidence on effective individual therapies for these types of children, we looked to the research on therapies for bereaved adults for guidance. Sireling, Cohen, and Marks (1988) examined the difference in effectiveness of two grief treatments in a sample ranging in age from 16 to 70. They found that guided mourning, in which patients were exposed to avoided stimuli related to bereavement, improved avoidance of and distress related to bereavement cues significantly more than antiexposure, in which patients were encouraged to stop thinking about the loss and move on. Time-limited dynamic psychotherapy has also been found to reduce symptoms and improve social and occupational functioning in adults who experienced the death of a parent or husband (Horowitz, Marmar, Weiss, De Witt, & Rosenbaum, 1984).

A randomized controlled trial was conducted with adults who met criteria for complicated grief to compare the efficacy of a treatment designed specifically to treat complicated grief with a standard psychotherapy treatment, interpersonal psychotherapy (Shear et al., 2005). The complicated grief treatment was based on interpersonal psychotherapy but adapted to include cognitive–behavioral techniques for reducing trauma symptoms, such as retelling the story of the death and modified exposure work to help the patient confront loss-related situations that were being avoided. Although both treatments were effective in improving complicated grief symptoms, complicated grief therapy showed both higher and faster response rates, demonstrating the importance of specifically addressing trauma and grief symptoms when treating complicated grief.

Summary of Interventions and Implications for Treatment

Although limited data are available on evidence-based treatments for bereaved children, significant insights can be gained from the studies discussed in this chapter. Most treatments to date include interventions that elicit the expression of emotions about the deceased, including positive, negative, and conflicted feelings. This appears to be a key component of effective treatment for bereaved individuals demonstrating grief symptoms that interfere with their daily functioning and require therapeutic support. Another valuable intervention is psychoeducation, for both parents and children, about the nature of death as well as common reactions to such a significant loss. This helps the parent to assist the child with his or her grief, and it helps the child to understand the finality of death and to normalize his or her feelings about the loss. Current evidence also suggests that effective interventions may help the parent and child to memorialize the deceased and to integrate the memories of their loved one into their lives in a positive way. Helping to foster healthy coping skills for both child and parent also appears to be extremely beneficial, as bereaved families are typically faced with multiple stressors secondary to the loss itself. Finally, recent interventions (e.g., Sandler et al., 2003) have also highlighted the importance of parenting skills as an integral part of treatment, and this component may be the missing piece in studies with mixed results. Direct involvement of the parent in treatment, including specific strategies to help the parent maintain consistency and stability in the home environment, appears to be essential to positive outcomes.

The IGTC approach described in this book includes many of the aforementioned strategies that have been shown to be effective in the research. Our method is largely based on the principles of CBT, which we have found to be a powerful intervention for addressing not only grief but also the specific symptoms commonly seen in this population. CBT approaches have been successful as a treatment for children and adolescents with anxiety and depressive disorders (for reviews, see Compton et al., 2004; Kazdin & Weisz, 2003) and have also been supported for use with children with PTSD (Cohen, Berliner, & March, 2000). Considering that the presenting problems reported by bereaved children are often consistent with these disorders, these techniques are useful in the treatment of this population. The chapters that follow describe how to effectively treat bereaved children with varied clinical presentations.

3

ASSESSING GRIEVING CHILDREN
AND TEACHING BASIC COPING SKILLS

When seeking clinical services, bereaved families present with various needs, including guidance regarding what to expect and how to cope as well as help in dealing with specific symptoms or problems that follow the death of a loved one. A thorough assessment should always be conducted to determine treatment needs. This chapter presents the clinician with guidelines for assessing and educating bereaved children as well an introduction to the basic skill components of integrated grief therapy for children (IGTC).

ASSESSING THE NEEDS OF GRIEVING CHILDREN

When parents seek psychotherapy or other clinical services for a grieving child, there is often an underlying worry that the loss has irrevocably changed the child in such a way as to have made him or her different or vulnerable to behavioral or emotional problems. Though most children are resilient, it is important to conduct a thorough assessment of each new client to determine the needs of the individual child and the proper course of treatment. The assessment must screen for the presence of clinically significant symptoms, determine how the child and family are currently functioning, and gather relevant information about the death of the loved one and the consequent grieving process.

A comprehensive evaluation, including structured or semistructured clinical and diagnostic interviews, should be conducted. Standardized clinician rating scales along with self-, parent, and teacher report instruments may also be included to help create a clear picture of the child's functioning in various settings (i.e., home and school). For example, results from the child's self-report can be compared with information obtained via parent interview and teacher ratings. Some examples of general screening measures commonly used to assess global psychological functioning of children and adolescents include the Behavior Assessment System for Children, Second Edition (Reynolds & Kamphaus, 2004), the Child Behavior Checklist (Achenbach & Rescorla, 2001), and the Schedule for Affective Disorders and Schizophrenia for School-Age Children—Present and Lifetime Version (Kaufman, Birmaher, Brent, Rau, & Ryan, 1996). Developmental variations in the presentation of symptoms should also be taken into account.

In general, the psychological evaluation of children and adolescents must include assessing for thoughts of hurting oneself or others. Assessing for risk of suicide may be particularly relevant for bereaved children, who may express a wish to be reunited with their deceased loved one (Webb, 2002). Such an expressed desire may or may not indicate true suicidality involving an intent or plan to harm or kill oneself. It is therefore important for the clinician to clarify through direct and careful questioning whether there is an intent or plan to carry out suicidal thoughts or ideas when they are present. Pfeffer (1986) provided information and specific questions for the clinician to use when assessing children for suicidal risk.

The evaluation of a child presenting for clinical services should also include an assessment of the child's protective factors and risk factors. A child's emotional and behavioral strengths (such as coping skills, prosocial behaviors, and the like) may serve to protect a child facing negative life events such as the death of a significant loved one. A more detailed discussion of the role of protective factors in promoting resilience follows in Chapter 11, but the important point regarding assessment is that such emotional and behavioral elements should be asked about and taken into account when formulating a complete picture of any child. Clinicians should also screen for potential risk factors, such as previous functioning of the child, family psychiatric history, school or learning problems, and parental psychopathology.

The strong correlation between parent functioning and child functioning is well known and evident to any practicing child therapist. Given the established impact of parent psychological health on child well-being, it is advisable to routinely include a general screening or assessment of the parent's mental health and general functioning as part of a comprehensive assessment of all factors that directly influence the child. The evaluation of the parent or caregiver is particularly relevant in the case of working with bereaved children, whose outcomes have been shown to be strongly influenced by the psychological health of their surviving parent or parents (Cerel, Fristad, Verducci, Weller, & Weller, 2006; Kalter et al., 2002; Kranzler, Shaffer, Wasserman, & Davies, 1990; Van Eerdewegh, Clayton, & Van Eerdewegh, 1985). It is also important to assess for and address parental psychological difficulties, as they may interfere with the parent's ability to participate in the child's treatment, which we consider to be essential to positive outcomes.

In addition to an assessment of general child and parent functioning, including the evaluation of potential psychopathology as well as risk factors and protective factors, it is important to assess domains that are specifically relevant to grieving children. These domains are described in the sections that follow, and related questions are presented in Table 3.1.

Nature of the Death

When beginning to work with grieving children and families, it is helpful to understand the key circumstances around the death. For example, was the death sudden or expected? Was there a prolonged period of illness? Did the child witness the death (or was he or she present during the moments immediately before or after the death)? The answers to these types of questions provide a context for better understanding the child's experience. For example, when the death of a parent follows a long and difficult illness, the child may have been involved in activities such as caretaking for the sick parent, visiting the hospital, witnessing invasive medical procedures, and the like. Children of terminally ill parents are also more likely to have prepared, to some extent, for the death or at least for the possibility of death. Some children may feel relieved that the stress of the illness has come to an end, whereas others may feel that they lost their parent well before the actual death occurred. Taken together, these types of experiences may impact how a child experiences and copes with the loss of a parent following an illness.

In contrast to the experience of the death of a loved one following a terminal illness, a sudden death, such as one that occurs following an accident or disaster, is likely to be associated with its own unique set of circumstances and related feelings. For example, some report days, weeks, or even months of shock during which the family operated in a haze of denial or chaos, such that the grief and mourning processes seem to occur some time after the death itself. A sudden death also means that family members did not have a chance to say goodbye or resolve interpersonal issues between themselves and the deceased.

TABLE 3.1
Assessment Questions for Grieving Children and Families

Area of assessment	Questions
Nature of the death	What does [your child] know about the circumstances of the death and the details about how it happened?
	If unclear based on the answer to the question above, proceed with more detailed questions about the nature of the death. For example, was the death sudden or expected? Was there a prolonged period of illness?
	Did [your child] witness the death (or the moments immediately before or after the death)?
	Are there certain aspects of what happened that have not been discussed?
	What does [your child] know or understand about what happens to people when they die? For example, have you discussed religious beliefs about death? Does [your child] ask questions about [the deceased] or about what happened? If so, what kinds of questions do you hear most?
Rituals and beliefs	What types of beliefs does your family have about death?
	What does [your child] understand about what happens when people die? For example, have you talked about heaven or an afterlife?
	Describe the wake, funeral, or memorial service that took place. What was [your child's] role during these ceremonies?
	What types of mourning rituals have occurred or might occur in the future? What kinds of things do you do (either together as a family or individually) to remember the person who died?
	What role does religion play in the family's grieving, and has the family's involvement in church or other religious activities changed since the loss?
Ongoing stressors	How has [your child's] routine changed since the loss?
	Who was the primary caregiver before the loss, and has that changed? How has [your child's] relationship with [the current primary caregiver] changed since the loss?
	How has [the current primary caregiver] responded to the loss?
	What reminders of the deceased seem to be most upsetting for [your child]?
Coping strategies	What are the types of things that have helped your family following the loss?
	What supportive resources are available to your family? To what extent are friends and extended family members involved in day to day support?
	How does [your child] respond or soothe him- or herself when feeling upset or sad?
	Do family members tend to talk to one another about their feelings, or are they more likely to keep these types of things to themselves?
	Have the children been continuing to go to school during the period of mourning?
	What are some of the things that you would like help with?

Yet another issue that may be more likely following a sudden death is the involvement of the larger community or even the media and the tendency to portray the deceased in a certain way. Depending on the cause of death, some children come to perceive their deceased loved one as a hero (such as might occur in the case of a parent who was a police officer killed in the line of duty) or a villain (such as might occur in the case of a parent who died following a drug overdose). These perceptions may be further complicated by the fact that they do not always correspond to the way the child viewed his or her loved one while he or she was alive.

In addition to finding out how the loved one died, it is equally important for the clinician to be aware of the extent to which the child has been informed of these details. In some situations, children may not have been exposed to the whole story regarding what happened to their loved one. For example, a child may know that his father was very sick before he died but not that the illness was related to his father having AIDS. It is important for the therapist to be aware of what the child has been told regarding the death of a loved one to facilitate communication among family members as therapy progresses. For most children, the therapist will discuss these issues with the parent well before discussing the actual death with the child. (For teenagers, it is more likely that they understand what it means to die and the circumstances surrounding the death of their loved one.) Information about the child's understanding regarding what has occurred will better help the clinician to understand the child and his or her grief experience.

Rituals and Beliefs

Rituals tend to play a large role in how people grieve and mourn their loved ones. Rituals may include aspects of the funeral service (including how long after the death the funeral may occur and what happens during the funeral service) as well as how the deceased is remembered. These rituals are influenced by various factors, including religion, family traditions and beliefs, and societal and cultural influences. Likewise, beliefs about death (e.g., existence of heaven or afterlife) are influenced by similar factors, all of which contribute to what children are told following the loss of a loved one. It is important for the clinician to be aware of the family's rituals and beliefs to better understand the context surrounding the child's understanding of the death.

Ongoing Stressors

The death of a loved one is often followed by several related life changes, including changes in family roles (e.g., who is the primary caretaker, who is responsible for helping with homework), finances (e.g., loss of income), and relocation, to name a few. By asking about changes for the child and family that have occurred since the loss, the clinician is able to gain an understanding of the child's day-to-day life and all of the changes and potential stressors that are having an impact. In addition, such questions demonstrate an understanding that loss and its consequences are ongoing and complicated, as opposed to discrete and time-limited, events.

Coping Strategies

In addition to finding out the problems that the grieving family is seeking help with, it is also helpful for the clinician to inquire about the types of things that have aided the family members thus far through the grieving process. For example, are friends and other family members involved in day to day support? Do family members tend to talk to one another about their feelings, or are they more likely to keep these types of things to themselves? What types of things have helped the child in the grieving process thus far? Asking questions about coping skills is another way in which the clinician may focus on the child and family's strengths in addition to identifying potential problem areas.

On the basis of the initial assessment, the therapist will make a decision about the proper course of treatment. A major factor in this decision is whether the child presents with any clinically significant problems or symptoms. If the child is in fact functioning well, then the therapist may determine that a few sessions providing guidance and education (rather than a full course of therapy) are sufficient. In these cases, the goals would be to reassure the family and normalize their experience of the grieving process, to guide the parent in helping the child now and in the future, and to discuss warning signs that would indicate that additional services are necessary. The following section reviews the content areas we have found most helpful and relevant to review in these types of sessions. This content also represents some of the basic ideas and skills of IGTC.

TEACHING BASIC SKILLS: BUILDING BLOCKS OF IGTC

Several themes or building blocks of the therapy approach will be revisited throughout the course of treatment. These building blocks include elements of our basic understanding about loss and grief as well as strategies to cope with the effects of grief in children. The remainder of this chapter discusses these two themes.

Guidance and Education for Grieving Children and Their Parents

Often, requests from parents of grieving children are for general advice or education about normative grief reactions. The parent may be worried about the long-term impact of the loss on the child. Parents may also have questions about how to talk to their children about how a loved one died, or they might want to better understand what their children do and do not comprehend about death. In these cases, the role of the clinician is to provide parents with psychoeducation about children's responses to loss and to address their immediate questions and concerns. This helps to provide support and reassurance and occasionally sets up a therapeutic relationship, should the need for additional services arise.

Specific information about children's understanding of death at different ages was outlined in Chapter 2, and additional information about children's normative reactions to grief is presented in Chapter 8. The reader should review the relevant sections of these chapters to prepare for the types of content areas that are most often asked about in sessions where psychoeducation is the primary goal. In addition, the handout *Helping Children Cope With Death* (Activity 3.1) presents some general guidelines for parents of grieving children that are likely to be helpful. After reviewing the information in session, this handout may be photocopied and provided to the parent.

Whereas certain families presenting for clinical services are simply seeking reassurance and psychoeducation as previously described, in other cases, additional services are necessary. Studies show that a sizable proportion (estimated to be approximately 20%) of bereaved children will demonstrate significant emotional and behavioral problems after the loss (Dowdney, 2000; Worden, 1996; Worden & Silverman, 1996). In cases where the clinical assessment reveals that the child is experiencing symptoms of distress that are interfering with his or her ability to function at home or at school, therapy will be indicated. The following section provides an introduction to the basic coping skills for grieving children that are used throughout the IGTC approach.

Basic Coping Skills for Grieving Children

As mentioned previously, one of the fundamental elements of IGTC is the premise that bereaved children must receive help with clinical symptoms before they move on to face the grief itself. Because bereaved children presenting with persistent problems tend to have symptoms that can be categorized as depression, anxiety, posttraumatic stress, and behavioral problems (Cerel et al., 2006; Dowdney, 2000; Worden & Silverman, 1996), our treatment draws from evidence-based treatment in these domains.

Based on the current literature regarding evidence-based practice, behavioral therapy and cognitive–behavioral therapy (CBT) approaches compose the primary treatments of choice for children and adolescents with various problems, particularly anxiety and depressive disorders (for reviews, see Compton et al., 2004; Kazdin & Weisz, 2003). Evidence has also supported the use of CBT

Activity 3.1 Helping Children Cope With Death

- Provide your child with honest and direct information about what has occurred. To the extent that your child wishes to discuss what happened, engage in open conversations about the cause of the death and encourage questions. When adults avoid discussion of death, this can convey that the topic is "taboo," which may ultimately result in increasing children's fears and worry.

- Allow your child to retain as much of his or her daily routines as possible during stressful times. By maintaining familiar schedules, children will gradually reestablish feelings of normalcy, and their anxieties about the loss will be significantly reduced. Encourage your child to express and communicate his or her feelings. Memorial ceremonies and other rituals are important for some children, whereas others may feel more comfortable expressing their emotions through art or through connecting with peers. Help your child to identify constructive methods to express feelings such as anger and sadness.

- Do not judge your child's reactions to loss according to another's reactions. Some children find solace by spending time with friends and relatives; others prefer to process the event in solitude. Reassure your child that it is normal to experience many different reactions to loss, including anger, guilt, and sadness—and that a person may feel sadness without necessarily crying.

- Be available to discuss the death on more than one occasion, as children's interest in and questions about what happened will change over time. Every child will process loss at his or her own pace.

- Be aware of and patient with possible fluctuations in your child's emotional world. Mood changes are to be expected in children following a significant loss or upsetting events.

- Consider how much detail to provide about the death based on your child's cognitive understanding, temperament, and desire for information. Children's ability to process loss is influenced by their age and other factors.

- Understand that it is normal for feelings of grief to come and go over time and for certain life events to intensify the feelings of loss even years later.

- Seek the help of a professional if your child indicates a sense of hopelessness or seems to have trouble functioning at home, in school, or in relationships with family and friends.

approaches for children with posttraumatic stress disorder (Cohen, Berliner, & March, 2000), and behavioral approaches in particular have been supported for helping children with behavior problems and their parents (Kazdin, 2003; Webster-Stratton & Reid, 2003). Given the preponderance of support for the use of CBT in the kinds of problems commonly seen among bereaved children, IGTC includes several CBT strategies in its approach, particularly in its approach to addressing symptoms (as presented in Part II of this book). Techniques aimed specifically at working with children suffering from depressed mood, difficulties related to trauma, anxiety, and behavioral problems are reviewed in Chapters 4 through 7, whereas more general strategies are presented in the paragraphs that follow. This section reviews basic CBT principles and coping skills that may be used throughout the course of treatment to improve overall functioning and reduce symptoms that may impact grieving children.

IGTC may be considered a coping skill therapy in that it focuses on the use of strategies to decrease the impact of negative events (Mahoney & Arnkoff, 1978). The patient is taught a variety of skills designed to help him or her cope with a range of stressful situations. Some of these techniques will be used with the children themselves, whereas others are geared toward providing skills for the parents or caregivers to better help their children. The strategies presented are referred to throughout the course of treatment.

Cognitive–behavioral techniques can help patients cope with a wide range of symptoms, including potentially disturbing thoughts and feelings that may accompany grief. The introduction of coping strategies primarily involves teaching new skills, and the process will vary depending on the child's age, cognitive understanding, and abilities. Some of these skills are more cognitive (e.g., identifying and changing thoughts), whereas others are more behavioral (e.g., facing fears) in nature.

For cognitive work, developmental considerations are important, as children prior to the age of 6 may not have the capability to understand metacognition or to reflect on their thinking process (Harter, 1982). For these young children, the therapist may skip the cognitive coping strategies and instead focus on more concrete behavioral strategies, such as relaxation and behavior management. The age of 6 is an approximate guideline, and skills presented in this chapter should be chosen by the therapist on the basis of the child's age and observed developmental capacities. With children of all ages, it is important for a therapist to engage children in a playful manner, using developmentally appropriate materials (e.g., artwork, workbooks, blackboards) to aid the teaching process (Braswell & Kendall, 2001).

The Triangle of 3

A fundamental component of CBT is the *cognitive triangle*, which is a representation of the connections among thoughts, feelings (including emotions as well as physiological reactions), and behaviors. Throughout the remainder of this book, the cognitive triangle is referred to as the *Triangle of 3* to facilitate the child's ability to remember and use this concept. The handout *Triangle of 3* (Activity 3.2) provides an illustration to be used while introducing this concept in session. The therapist can introduce the handout as follows:

> *Therapist:* A lot of the work we will be doing together is based on the idea that our thoughts, feelings, and behaviors are connected. The Triangle of 3 shows how this connection works, with each of the three points relating to one another. Let's use an example from your own life. Tell me about a time that you recently felt stressed or overwhelmed.

The therapist should encourage the child to provide an example in which there was some degree of mild negative emotion, but not one in which there was excessive difficulty, such as often occurs in the presence of reminders of the deceased. Using the child's example, the therapist will lead a discussion to illustrate how a change in one element (i.e., thoughts, feelings, or behaviors) promotes change in each of the other elements. The following case example demonstrates how to present these concepts in session. The therapist is talking with an 8-year-old girl named Jessica a few weeks into their working together.

> *Jessica:* The teacher asked us if we wanted to read our book reports to the class yesterday. I thought she was going to make all of us do it, but then she asked for volunteers. I think I'll still have to go next week, though.
>
> *Therapist:* OK, so let's fill out the Triangle of 3 to see what your thoughts, feelings, and behaviors were in that situation. Think back to yesterday, when the teacher said that reports were going to be read out loud. How did you feel?
>
> *Jessica:* I felt scared.
>
> *Therapist:* You felt scared, that makes sense. How did you know you were scared? Where did you feel it in your body?
>
> *Jessica:* I don't know. I just didn't want to go in front of the class.
>
> *Therapist:* Lots of times, when we have strong feelings, our body reacts in specific ways. For example, when I'm anxious, my face gets red.
>
> *Jessica:* Oh, yeah, me too. My face was really red yesterday.
>
> *Therapist:* Your face got red. Did your face feel warm and flushed, too?
>
> *Jessica:* Yup.
>
> *Therapist:* OK, so let's write that down on the triangle, under feelings. Did any other part of your body react to feeling scared? Like your head or belly?

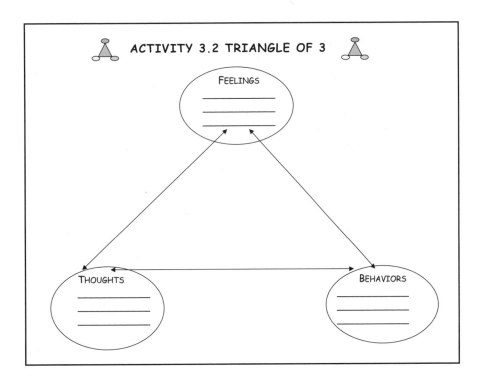

ACTIVITY 3.2 TRIANGLE OF 3

FEELINGS

THOUGHTS

BEHAVIORS

Jessica:	I think my stomach hurt, too.
Therapist:	OK, so we'll write that, too. Now, you've done a great job of telling me all about your feelings, and we've written those down. Let's move on to your thoughts. What were you thinking when you were about to read your report in front of the class?
Jessica:	I'm not sure. I guess I was trying to remember what to say.
Therapist:	OK, what were you thinking about yourself at that time? Do you remember saying anything to yourself, like about what you would do if the teacher called on you?
Jessica:	Oh, yeah, I was telling myself not to mess up. And I was thinking that I'm really not good at talking in front of the class. And that if I got called, everyone would see how embarrassed I was.
Therapist:	Oh, I see. I'm going to write those thoughts down, too. So your stomach was hurting, you were feeling uncomfortable and flushed, and you were telling yourself that you are not very good at speaking. Sounds rough. What did you do next?
Jessica:	Nothing. The girl sitting next to me raised her hand, so she went first. I'm pretty sure we all have to do it, though.
Therapist:	Oh, so you sat and waited, hoping you wouldn't have to go, right? So we can fill in another thought, which is "I hope I don't have to go," and a behavior, which is waiting. A behavior can either be something you do, like talking to a friend, or it can be something you *don't* do, like not volunteering or avoiding speaking in front of the class.

After personalizing the cognitive triangle with an example from the child's own life, the therapist may begin to point out how a change in the thoughts, feelings, or behaviors leads to a change in each of the other elements. It is usually best to focus on one element at a time (e.g., feelings) and to keep the examples as concrete as possible, as in the following example, which is continued from above.

Therapist:	Now what if, instead of your stomach hurting and feeling flushed, you instead felt calm and relaxed. What would you think then?
Jessica:	Maybe I wouldn't have been so afraid to be called on. I wouldn't have to worry what other people thought as much, because my face wouldn't be red.
Therapist:	Right, so if your body felt different, your thoughts would be different, too! Does that make sense?

Jessica:	Yeah.
Therapist:	Now what if your thoughts changed first? For example, what if, instead of thinking "I'm not good at speaking in class," you instead thought, "I can do this"?
Jessica:	Then I really wouldn't feel so bad.
Therapist:	So the arrow goes both ways. Your feelings influence your thoughts, and your thoughts influence your feelings. Actually, the whole triangle works that way, with all three things being related. The feelings in your body affect your thoughts, your thoughts affect your feelings, and both your thoughts and feelings affect how you behave or act in any situation.

The cognitive triangle and the ways in which one is able to change one's feelings, thoughts, and behaviors should be presented to the parent in much the same way that these topics are presented to the child. After introducing the concepts to the child, the therapist may invite the parent to join the child in session so that the child and therapist can teach the parent about the Triangle of 3 together. The fundamental point to convey is the interrelationship among thoughts, feelings, and behaviors, so that a change in one of these three elements usually causes a change in the other two.

When working with very young children (usually children less than 6 years old) who will not be able to work on abstract concepts like the Triangle of 3, the therapist may decide to meet with the parent individually to help improve his or her coping skills, which, in turn, will benefit the child (e.g., by decreasing stress in the home environment, improving the child–parent relationship, and ultimately providing skills for the parent that will be mirrored by the child). The therapist may ask the parent to talk about a recent situation in which he or she felt stressed or overwhelmed. Common examples may include arguments between family members or worries about the future. Time should be spent talking about the parent's feelings and physiological responses, thoughts, and behaviors that are common in these situations.

The next step in introducing basic skills is to teach the child and parent how to change feelings (particularly the body's responses to emotions), thoughts, and behaviors. It is often easiest to begin by introducing coping strategies that involve changing the patient's physiological response to stress, but the therapist may decide which element to start with on the basis of the individual's needs.

Physiological Exercises

At this point, the child already understands that the way his or her body reacts to stress influences the way he or she thinks and behaves. Common physiological reactions include increased muscle tension, headaches, fatigue, stomach upset, increased body temperature and blood pressure, and joint pain. The therapist may help the child understand his or her body's responses in situations that elicit negative thoughts and feelings:

> *Therapist:* Our bodies tend to react to stress in specific ways. For example, you may notice that when you feel stressed or anxious, your heart starts to beat faster inside your chest. What are some other ways that your body responds to stress? Where in your body do you feel changes when you are feeling worried or overwhelmed? How often do you feel this way?

The therapist should engage the child in a conversation about times in which he or she feels sad, anxious, angry, or otherwise overwhelmed with emotion. The child may need a bit of extra encouragement to talk about these feelings, particularly if he or she has become accustomed to avoiding situations that prompt his or her own negative emotions or those of family members. The latter seems to be a common trend among children who have lost a parent, and this avoidance may itself eventually become a target of treatment. If this is the case, then extra time should be spent helping the child to identify negative or otherwise difficult emotions early on in treatment and to then share these feelings with the surviving parent.

Depending on the child's age, interest, and learning style, the therapist may want to provide a brief explanation of why the body reacts this way. When faced with a stressor, our bodies are designed to react in a way known as the "fight or flight" response, which involves an increase in blood pressure, heart rate, breathing rate, and muscle tension, along with a decrease in blood flow to the extremities and digestive system. This is helpful during times that our body needs to react quickly, but may not be helpful during times that we would rather remain calm (Davis, McKay, & Eshelman, 2000).

After talking about the child's individual reactions to stress and other potentially negative emotions, the therapist may begin to teach the child how to alter these physiological responses through relaxation. The primary means of relaxation are diaphragmatic breathing (or breathing retraining) and muscle relaxation. It is often helpful to let children and their parents know that although people often think of relaxation as a simple task that they either already do or know how to do, it is actually a coping skill to be learned through proper instruction and repeated practice.

Diaphragmatic Breathing. Children of any age should be able to complete simple breathing retraining exercises in which they are encouraged to breathe through the diaphragm or abdomen as opposed to the upper chest. The therapist will ask the child to sit comfortably with both feet on the floor, to inhale slowly through the nose, and then to slowly exhale. It is often beneficial for the child to place his or her hand over his or her belly to feel it rise while inhaling and fall while exhaling. This is in contrast with what happens with shallow breathing, which occurs higher up in the chest.

If the child is unable to "belly breathe" while sitting, then the therapist may encourage him or her to try again while lying on the floor. Legs should be straight and slightly apart, and arms should be at the sides of the body with palms facing up. In this position, a small book or other object may be placed over the belly, which will noticeably rise and fall. Children generally tend to understand that deep breathing feels relaxing, particularly when viewed in contrast with the shallow breathing that occurs when they are crying or when they are running fast.

Relaxation Exercises. Progressive muscle relaxation (PMR; Jacobson, 1938) has proven beneficial in reducing symptoms of stress, pain, and anxiety in adults. PMR is based on the fact that one cannot feel relaxed and well at the same time that one feels anxious and stressed, and vice versa. The strategy involves going through each body part, one at a time, alternating between tensing and relaxing the muscles. The end result is an overall feeling of relaxation throughout the body. It is thought that the practice of PMR allows one to combat feelings of distress in various circumstances.

In children, muscle relaxation techniques have been found to induce a short-term and immediate feeling of calmness (Lohaus & Klein-Hebling, 2000). For this reason, relaxation of the major muscle groups of the body may be considered another possible tool for helping children manage their physiological reactions to stressful situations. The handout *Relaxation for Children* (Activity 3.3) presents PMR in a way that may be fun and easy for use with children and adolescents. This handout should be used to introduce the relaxation technique in session and then provided to the patient for use at home. When adapted for use in session, it is helpful to audiotape the exercise so that the patient may bring the tape home to practice the relaxation exercise, preferably daily.

For younger children who are unable to sustain focused attention on each muscle group, a more general muscle relaxation strategy may be used. A common technique is to have the child make his or her body stiff, like a noodle before it is cooked, and then to make him- or herself soft, like a piece of cooked spaghetti. This technique was used with a 5-year-old boy whose father died the year before his mother brought him in for therapy. After learning the strategy in session, he eventually began to use it at home during times that he became overwhelmed or upset. A short-hand developed between the boy and his therapist, such that one or the other could say "spaghetti!" when emotions ran too high, and the boy would automatically stand up straight, and then allow himself to totally relax and drop onto the floor like a wet noodle. The therapist may teach relaxation in the following way:

> *Therapist:* We're going to practice an exercise that will help you to go from feeling tense to feeling relaxed. To do that, we're going to pretend

Activity 3.3 Relaxation for Children

These exercises will help you feel calm and relaxed whenever you use them. They should be practiced every day at the same time of day, such as bedtime, until you feel that you have really mastered the art of relaxation. Then, you will be able to use the strategies to help yourself whenever you feel nervous or upset!

I'd like for you to get comfortable by sitting upright, with your feet flat on the floor and your arms to your sides or in your lap. You might want to close your eyes to shut out everything else but the sound of my voice and the way your body feels. We can start by taking a few deep breaths. Next, you will slowly tense and relax each muscle group in your body, from the bottoms of your feet to the top of your head. After going through each muscle group, you will find yourself totally relaxed.

1. Feet and toes
Let's start with your toes. I'd like you to scrunch your toes all the way in to your feet, as if you were at the beach, digging your toes into the sand. Keep your toes like that for 5 seconds, 4, 3, 2, 1. Ok, now relax your toes, and notice the difference in the way you feel.

2. Legs
Now, picture yourself back at the beach. Use your leg muscles to push your feet all the way down into the sand. Feel the tension up and down the front and back of your legs. Hold that tension for 5 seconds, 4, 3, 2, 1, and then relax. You are now feeling relaxed all the way from the tops of your legs to the bottom.

3. Stomach

We're moving on to your stomach, now. Suck in your stomach, so that you are pulling your belly button as far into your body as it will go. Imagine that you want to squeeze through a narrow door and need to make yourself as skinny as possible to get through. Hold in your stomach (5, 4, 3, 2, 1)...and then relax. Slowly, take one or two extra deep breaths so that you can really focus on that feeling of relaxation. Again, notice the difference between the feeling of tension and relaxation.

4. Arms and shoulders

Next, you are going to stretch your arms up and back, way up over your head. Pretend that you are a cat that is very sleepy and just about ready for a nap. Pull your arms all the way back and hold them (5, 4, 3, 2, 1) and then relax. Allow your arms to once again fall comfortably to your sides. Notice the difference in feeling between tension and relaxation.

5. Hands and fingers

Now that your arms and shoulders are relaxed, we can move along to your hands and fingers. Make a fist and squeeze as tightly as you can. Bring your fingers all the way in to the palms of your hands. Hold your fists (5, 4, 3, 2, 1) and then relax.

6. Face

To relax your face, open your mouth as wide as you can. Your top lip is almost as high as your nose, and your bottom lip is stretched down to your chin. Hold your mouth open (5, 4, 3, 2, 1) and then relax and bring your lips comfortably back together again.

7. Head

We're going to finish with your forehead by bringing your eyebrows all the way up to the top of your head, as if you just heard some really surprising news. Feel the wrinkles that are now on your forehead, and notice how tight they feel. Hold that tension (5, 4, 3, 2, 1) and then relax.

8. Finish

You have relaxed your whole body, from your feet to your head. Notice how your feet, legs, stomach, arms, hands, face, and head all feel relaxed, and how your whole body feels calm. Take a few slow, deep breaths at your own pace. When you are ready, open your eyes.

like we're spaghetti. I know that sounds silly, but wait until you see how it works! Have you ever seen what a piece of spaghetti looks like before it's cooked? It is hard and straight, like this. (*Stand up and show the child how you can make yourself stand up straight, with arms down at your sides.*) But when it's cooked, it is loose, like this. (*Again, show by example.*) Now you try. How does that feel? Notice the difference between feeling tense and relaxed. Now you can practice getting loose and relaxed whenever you are feeling tense or worried.

Cognitive Coping Strategies

Once children are able to successfully use deep breathing and relaxation techniques to change their physiological response to negative affect, they are ready to move on to changing their cognitive responses. As with the physiological exercises, it is important to consider the child's abilities before choosing how to proceed. As a reminder, this section may not be appropriate for children prior to the age of 6.

The cognitive therapy model is based on the ideas that thoughts influence emotions and behaviors and that modifying dysfunctional thoughts consequently leads to an improvement in mood, behavior, and general functioning (J. S. Beck, 1995). Cognitive restructuring techniques are used to modify dysfunctional thoughts and establish more adaptive patterns of thinking. With children, the first step is to elicit negative thoughts that may be the target of cognitive intervention.

When introducing any new strategy, particularly ones that target abstract ideas like cognitive processes, it is often helpful to use concrete examples from daily life to illustrate the principles being discussed. In introducing cognitive therapy, the therapist may try to remember a concrete time in which the child previously talked about feelings. This may be the same example referred to by the child when reviewing the cognitive triangle, or it may be an example provided by the child during a previous therapy session. The use of an example from the child's life that was previously shared will show that the therapist is listening and attentive, even when the child is simply talking about his or her day.

For the given situation, the therapist will ask about the thoughts that were running through the child's mind. The therapist should guide the child to talk about his or her thoughts concerning both the situation and him- or herself, explaining that these types of thoughts are known as *self-talk* because they are the things we tell ourselves in a given situation. Self-talk often involves answers to questions such as, "What do you think will happen?" and "How do you think you will handle it?" Children and adults may be relieved to hear that we all engage in this type of self-talk and that we can monitor our thinking to look for negative patterns. Examples of negative self-talk might include thoughts about expectations (e.g., "Something bad will happen") or thoughts about one's abilities to cope (e.g., "I can't handle this" or "I will be embarrassed and everyone will know"). In general, we can identify negative thoughts as ones that continue to promote negative feelings and/or behaviors, thus creating a cycle of feeling bad.

The following is an example dialogue between a therapist and a 14-year-old boy named Aiden.

> Therapist: We're going to begin talking about strategies for changing negative thinking, which, as you know from our work with the cognitive triangle, increases negative feelings. I remember last week you were telling me about not wanting to go to your friend's upcoming party, and I thought we would use that as an example. Is that okay?
>
> Aiden: Yeah, I still don't think I want to go.
>
> Therapist: OK, can you tell me more about that?
>
> Aiden: Well, I feel like I probably wouldn't have any fun anyway, so I might as well stay home. I haven't really been out since my dad died, and I don't think my friends want me to go to the party anyway.
>
> Therapist: So, you've been thinking that if you went to the party, you wouldn't have any fun. And that your friends don't want you there anyway. Well, then, of course you don't want to go!
>
> Aiden: (Laughs) Yeah.
>
> Therapist: OK, well, that makes sense, but I want to talk about these thoughts a little more. First of all, these kinds of thoughts that you are having about what you expect to happen at the party are called *self-talk* because they are the things you say or think to yourself but don't usually say out loud.

When the concept of self-talk seems to be understood, the therapist may then begin to work with the child to examine the evidence that supports or challenges his or her specific negative ideas. In CBT, the therapist helps patients not only to identify and evaluate their thoughts and beliefs but also to change those thoughts determined to be dysfunctional in that they perpetuate a negative cycle (J. S. Beck, 1995). This is done by asking questions that will challenge negative thoughts and promote the creation of new, less negative ideas. A simple question such as, "What evidence do you have for this belief?" may be a good place to start.

Generating alternative thoughts may be encouraged by asking questions such as, "Is there another way of looking at or explaining this observation?" or, more simply, "What else do you think might be happening here?" Similar questions such as "What do you expect might happen next?" and "How would you respond if you had a different expectation?" might also be applicable. Finally, the therapist may ask the child to think about what would be so bad if the negative thought were actually true. This is known as a "What if . . . ?" question, in that the therapist asks the child to consider that even if the dreaded thought were proven correct, the situation would not be catastrophic. By identifying negative self-talk and using cognitive restructuring techniques to change those perceptions, children ultimately learn how self-talk can help them to alter their emotional responses (Braswell & Kendall, 2001).

The following dialogue, continued from the example between 14-year-old Aiden and his therapist, illustrates how the concept of cognitive restructuring may be presented in session.

> *Therapist:* Let's talk more about the thought that your friends don't want you to go to the party. Do you know this for a fact?
>
> *Aiden:* No, I just think it's true.
>
> *Therapist:* So you see there is a difference between facts and thoughts or beliefs. Now, I want us to pick at this thought that you're friends don't want you at the party, kind of like we are detectives trying to solve a mystery and determine the facts of the case. What is the evidence that your friends don't want you at the party?
>
> *Aiden:* Well, they told me about it last week and a bunch of them asked me to go, but they haven't brought it up again since.
>
> *Therapist:* So you think that because they haven't asked again, they don't want you there?
>
> *Aiden:* Yeah, I mean, they know it's been hard for me and they should ask again.
>
> *Therapist:* Hmm, are there any other reasons that they might not have asked you about the party again, aside from not wanting you there?
>
> *Aiden:* Well, I did tell them that I didn't think I could go.
>
> *Therapist:* So we know that they asked you to go to the party, and that you told them that you didn't think you could go. But you believe that they don't want you there since they haven't asked again.
>
> *Aiden:* Well, I don't know, maybe they didn't ask again because they thought I wouldn't go anyway. Lately, since everything happened, it seems like they don't want to bother me.
>
> *Therapist:* So another thought is that they didn't ask again because they didn't want to bother you. How would you feel about

the situation if you believed that your friends haven't been talking about the party because they don't want to bother you, and not because they didn't want you there?

Aiden: I'd feel better about it. I'd feel like they care about me, and that maybe I should go to the party to spend time with them.

Therapist: It sounds like thinking that your friends care about you makes you want to spend more time with them, and that makes sense. It turns out that changing one thought has a large effect on your feelings and your choices about what to do in a given situation.

The process of cognitive restructuring is similar for children and adults, but of course adults are better able to reflect on the consequences of their thinking as well as the influences on their thinking. The cognitive restructuring technique is largely based on A. T. Beck, Rush, Shaw, and Emery's (1979) cognitive therapy for depression, which is a useful reference for further reading on this topic. When speaking with parents, it is important that the clinician be attentive to their beliefs about themselves and their children, as expectancies regarding child behavior and child rearing have a direct impact on parenting behavior (Braswell & Kendall, 2001).

Changing Behaviors: Choosing Approach Over Avoidance

One of the basic principles that the reader sees running through this and most cognitive–behaviorally based therapies is to approach anxiety-provoking situations, rather than avoid them. The premise is that avoidance serves to reinforce the belief that the feared situation is in fact dangerous or that the patient cannot actually cope. This is an important concept to review with the parent as well as the child.

Encouraging parents to help their children face rather than avoid stressful situations may be met with resistance. Although most parents are inclined to take steps to prevent having their children experience negative emotions, this inclination may be even more salient among parents of grieving children, who have already experienced loss and all that goes with it (e.g., sadness, rapid changes in daily life) early in life. Consequently, parents may aim to shield their children from experiencing more pain, and they may try to avoid situations that increase feelings of grief. For example, some grieving families cope by not talking about the deceased or by quickly changing the topic when someone from outside the family mentions the deceased person's name. Although the therapist should of course convey empathy in cases like these, it is important to point out that such avoidance tends to have unwanted consequences, like teaching children that the deceased loved one may not be talked about or that the family is unable to remember the person in a healthy way.

Others may avoid situations that seem unrelated to their grief but prove to be connected upon further reflection. For example, many families who have experienced the loss of a parent or caregiver change the sleeping arrangements in the home so that one or more child is sleeping in the same bed with the surviving parent. Bedtime is typically a time for reflection about the day, and it is also a time during which spouses tend to spend quiet time together. Those who have lost a spouse may therefore have their children sleep in their bed with them to avoid the loneliness and sadness they feel there. It is not our view that cosleeping is necessarily problematic, but rather that having the child sleep in the parent's bed so that the parent does not have to be alone is not in the best interest of the child. At this point in the therapy, the goal is to simply present the idea that avoidance of negative emotions often backfires, either because it exacerbates the feelings that were trying to be avoided or because it decreases self-efficacy in relation to general coping.

Behavior Management Skills

As part of the introduction to basic CBT principles, the therapist may want to review with the parent strategies for managing children's behaviors. This is especially true when working with young children through school age. Although many behavioral concepts may be familiar to parents, we have found that a review is often helpful, given that discipline may have been compromised as a result of the stress and life changes associated with the loss of the loved one.

A simple review of the power of parental attention may be quite informative. Parents may benefit from being taught how they can increase positive behaviors through positive attention (e.g., praise, incentives) and decrease negative behaviors either by removing attention or by imposing consequences. More specifically, the therapist may instruct the parent to "catch the child being good" and to reinforce desirable behaviors appropriately to increase their likelihood.

Appropriate reinforcement may vary by a child's age, personality, and temperament. For example, younger children from preschool through early school age are likely to respond well to verbal praise (e.g., "I like the way you cleaned up all of your toys after playing") and to simple tangible rewards, such as stickers. Children who are older may respond better to rewards that are more symbolic, such as earning privileges or spending special time engaging in a fun activity with a parent.

In addition to providing attention to increase wanted behaviors and withdrawing attention to decrease unwanted behaviors, many parents may benefit from learning about setting clear expectations and providing consequences. This is especially true for parents who are finding that their children are not following instructions or are breaking rules at home or at school. Parenting strategies and ways in which the therapist may incorporate behavioral management into the child's treatment, particularly when behavioral problems are present, are more fully described in Chapter 7.

SUMMARY

This chapter presented guidelines for assessing the bereaved child that will enable the clinician to make decisions about viable treatment options for grieving children. Some children may require a full course of treatment, whereas for others a few sessions involving guidance and education about children and grief may suffice. This chapter also introduced basic principles about helping bereaved children and about the grief process itself, as well as basic cognitive–behavioral skills used in IGTC. These concepts are revisited as needed and more specifically applied to working with bereaved children in a clinical setting in the remainder of this book. By presenting the ideas introduced in this chapter, the therapist will inform both the child and parent about the basic principles and components of the IGTC approach.

II

ADDRESSING PROBLEMS
IN GRIEVING CHILDREN

4

TREATING DEPRESSION SYMPTOMS IN GRIEVING CHILDREN

The most common outcome associated with the loss of a parent in child-hood is depressive symptoms in the bereaved child (Lutzke, Ayers, Sandler, & Barr, 1997). Several studies have demonstrated that bereaved children have significantly higher levels of depression than nonbereaved comparison groups (Cerel, Fristad, Verducci, Weller, & Weller, 2006; Gersten, Beals, & Kallgren, 1991; Kranzler, Shaffer, Wasserman, & Davies, 1990; Van Eerdewegh, Clayton, & Van Eerdewegh, 1985). Some of the depressive symptoms reported by bereaved children include dysphoria, declining school performance, sleeping and eating disturbances, and withdrawal. It is important to note that children who are bereaved may not necessarily meet the full criteria for a major depressive episode but may present with subthreshold depressive symptoms, which places them at risk of more serious depression at a later point (Clarke et al., 1995; Lewinsohn, Clarke, Seeley, & Rohde, 1994). In addition, there is evidence that early parent loss may be one factor contributing to later major depression and suicidal behavior in adolescence and adulthood (see Brent & Melhem, 2008). Therefore, children and adolescents who have elevated but subsyndromal symptoms of depression for an extended period of time are likely to benefit from treatment.

This chapter introduces specific strategies from the integrated grief therapy for children (IGTC) model for treating symptoms of depressed mood in bereaved children. It also provides directions for addressing areas that may be impacted by child and adolescent depression, such as school performance and relationships with peers and family members. Interventions to address the child's negative thoughts, improve self-esteem, and increase pleasurable events and activities are also included.

In line with our general approach of integrating evidence-based treatments for a specific problem, the IGTC model for treating depressive symptoms combines components of approaches for treating children and adolescents with depression, including interpersonal therapy for adolescents (IPT-A) and cognitive–behavioral therapy (CBT; American Psychological Association [APA] Working Group of Psychoactive Medications for Children and Adolescents, 2006), as well as family systems approaches (Carr, 2009). IPT-A, originally developed for use in the treatment of adult depression, was adapted for adolescents by Mufson and her colleagues and has been found effective in the treatment of adolescents with severe depression symptoms (Mufson & Dorta, 2003). There has also been support for CBT in the treatment of both child and adolescent depression, although the superiority of CBT over other forms of psychosocial and psychopharmacological treatment has not been established (APA Working Group of Psychoactive Medications for Children and Adolescents, 2006). Family-based interventions that focus on decreasing family stress and increasing support within the family through enhanced parent–child communication, effective problem solving, decreasing critical interactions, and promoting secure attachment have been found to be as effective in treating depressed children as individual CBT approaches and psychodynamic therapies (Carr, 2009; Trowell et al., 2007).

In addition to psychotherapeutic interventions, a thorough assessment should be conducted by the therapist to determine whether a referral for psychiatric medication is also needed. Although the need for medication should be determined on a case-by-case basis, research suggests that a combination of CBT and medication may be an effective form of treatment for depression (Treatment for Adolescents With Depression Study Team, 2004).

THOUGHTS, FEELINGS, AND BEHAVIORS THAT ACCOMPANY DEPRESSION IN BEREAVED CHILDREN

Many bereaved children describe feelings of sadness, commonly expressed as tearfulness and crying (Worden, 1996). However, sadness or depression in children presents differently across developmental stages. For example, younger children who have difficulty expressing their feelings with words may act out their irritability through tantrums or defiance. Adolescents tend to have more appetite and sleep problems than younger children who are depressed and may also be at risk of sexual promiscuity and drug or alcohol use. The following is a list of symptoms, based on the *Diagnostic and Statistical Manual of Mental Disorders* (4th ed.; American Psychiatric Association, 1994) and clinical observations, that a therapist may notice in a bereaved child or adolescent who is depressed:

- tearfulness;
- trouble falling or staying asleep;
- low energy or restlessness;
- changes in appetite;
- somatic complaints, such as stomachaches or headaches;
- difficulty concentrating or paying attention (e.g., poor school-work);
- stopping of activities they used to enjoy, particularly those enjoyed with the deceased parent;
- feelings of guilt and rumination about the deceased;
- feeling different from peers and feeling misunderstood;
- feeling like death of parent and other things are their fault;
- spending more time alone and avoiding friends and family; and
- thoughts about their own death and/or reuniting with their lost parent.

As noted, some bereaved children may feel that the death of the parent was somehow their fault and/or struggle with thoughts or beliefs that they could have done something to prevent the death from occurring. Young children may exhibit magical thinking, or a belief that their thoughts made their parent die. For example, 6-year-old Claudia believed that if she had been nicer to her sister, her dad would not have been angry as much and would not have gotten sick with cancer. After her father died, she worked hard to be "perfect" all the time so that her mother would not also get sick.

Also common are guilty feelings or ruminations about what children believe they could or should have said to the deceased. These can be positive things the child wished he or she had said, such as "I love you" or "You're a great mom." Other unsaid thoughts may be more conflictual or involve the expression of angry or negative feelings. For example, 17-year-old Mary had noticed in the months before her dad died in a car accident that he was always on the Internet late at night. She was aware that it upset her mother, but still she had been reluctant to ask him about it. After he died, she questioned why she had been unable to confront him and felt guilty for her feelings of anger toward him about it.

Other children may describe symptoms of withdrawal, such as feeling alone and isolated, not wanting to socialize with friends or family, and feeling different from their peers. Common statements by bereaved children include things like "No one understands me" or "No one gets what I'm going through." Michael, a 13-year-old boy who lost his mother, described how his friends called him the first week after his mother died but "now they never do." He complained about being home a lot of the time and how his family "annoyed him." He further elaborated that although he had not felt like spending time with friends in the weeks after his mom died, he now felt that he was no longer part of his social group. This is a common concern, as some children may avoid friends in the immediate aftermath of the death and then later feel they do not have friends to return to.

Another common source of sadness in bereaved children and adolescents is imagining future events for which the deceased parent will not be present, ranging from events in everyday life to special occasions. These children may ruminate about missed activities with their parent. A teenage girl who came for treatment described how she would often think of the absence of her father at her future wedding. This thought made her feel very sad, and she often coped by isolating herself in her room and going to bed early.

INTRODUCTION TO HELPING CHILDREN WITH DEPRESSION

Parents of bereaved children who are having symptoms of depression often describe their children as moody, moping, or difficult to cheer up. They may express concerns such as, "Will my child ever be like he used to be?" It is important to instill hope and inform the parent that one important goal of treatment will be to help the child cope with feelings of sadness and to communicate more effectively. It may be helpful to reassure the parent and child that although the experience of loss may have changed him or her in some ways, many things about him or her remain the same.

The IGTC model emphasizes the importance of providing psychoeducation to bereaved families. Education should be provided about what depression is, particularly in the context of bereavement, and how it can impact daily functioning. This discussion may include a review of the child's symptoms, general education about depression, and ways in which therapy might be helpful. Psychoeducation in the early stages of treatment can help to normalize what the child is experiencing for both the child and the parent and has typically been included in evidence-based treatments for depression (e.g., Mufson & Dorta, 2003).

Therapist: I understand that you have been feeling sad (and/or empty, irritable, or a loss of interest in things that used to be enjoyable). You may find that it has been more difficult to think, make decisions, or concentrate. You may also feel like many things are your fault and you may even have thoughts about death. These things can influence the way your body works—you may feel tired, lose or gain weight, feel slowed down or agitated, and have trouble sleeping.

Sometimes kids feel this way after they lose a parent. When someone we love dies, it makes sense to be sad and to wish things could be different. One of the things we can work on in therapy is to help you to cope when you are feeling this way.

The therapist can then ask several questions about the child's depressive symptoms:

- Can you tell me some of the things that make you feel sad?
- What do you do when you are feeling sad?
- Is there anything that you do that helps you feel better?
- Are there any situations that seem to make things worse?

Therapist: OK, it seems like things have been pretty rough for you lately. Another word that describes what you're going through is depression. Depression can be hard to beat, but we're going to work really hard together to fight depression, and we're going to get your (caregiver) and the rest of your family to help too!

CHANGING BEHAVIORS

CBT emphasizes a collaborative relationship between therapist and patient (A. T. Beck, Rush, Shaw, & Emery, 1979) and assumes that psychopathology is greatly influenced by a system of faulty beliefs and behavior. Therefore, the reconstruction of these thoughts or behaviors is essential to successful treatment. Behavioral techniques used with children often consist of strategies to help patients to increase their involvement in pleasant activities or to improve problem-solving and social skills. The IGTC model adapts CBT techniques for work with bereaved children.

A hallmark of depression is a decrease in positive, healthy activities or behaviors. Activity scheduling is one important intervention to promote the increase of these types of behaviors and may be of particular use with a bereaved child who is depressed and isolative. This intervention essentially means having the child prioritize fun and pleasurable activities. As a first step, the therapist can provide the child and parent with the handout *My Daily Schedule* (Activity 4.1) to monitor the activities they are currently participating in throughout the day for a period of 1 week. They should be encouraged to try to rate their mood during each activity using a "feeling thermometer."

Activity 4.1 My Daily Schedule

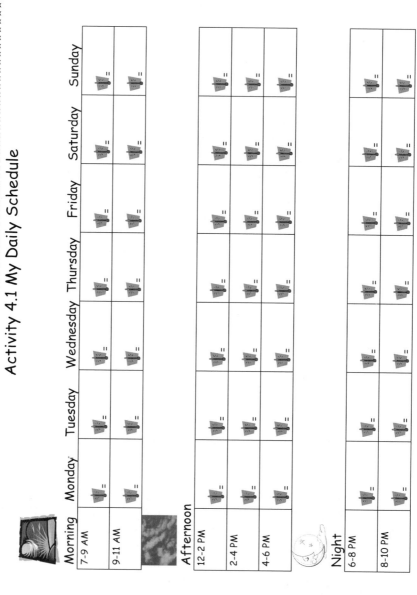

	Monday	Tuesday	Wednesday	Thursday	Friday	Saturday	Sunday
Morning 7-9 AM							
9-11 AM							
Afternoon 12-2 PM							
2-4 PM							
4-6 PM							
Night 6-8 PM							
8-10 PM							

The concept of a feeling thermometer, or an index of emotional intensity, can be explained to the child in the following way.

> *Therapist:* The feeling thermometer helps us to understand how we're feeling and how strong those feelings are. The feeling thermometer goes from 0° to 10°. Ten degrees means feeling the most sad and down you could possibly feel. Zero degrees is when you feel totally calm, happy, and peaceful.

To get the child used to the feeling thermometer, the therapist asks the following questions:

- On a scale of 1–10, how are you feeling today?
- Can you give an example of a time when you felt like a 10?
- Can you give an example of a time when you felt like a 0?

After the child spends a week monitoring his or her activities with the handout *My Daily Schedule*, the child and therapist can then review together how the child is spending his or her time and how much pleasure he or she is taking in his or her current activities. The next step is to generate a list of activities the child has stopped participating in since the death of the loved one, or at least since the depressive symptoms began. It is important to note that bereaved children may have stopped activities that they used to participate in with the deceased parent. The therapist can help the child to verbalize their concerns by specifically asking questions like the following:

- Are there things you used to do when (mom) was alive that you no longer do?
- Can you name them?
- What makes it hard to do those activities now?

The therapist should help the child to express feelings around this topic, as they will likely be themes that will surface repeatedly over the course of treatment (e.g., feelings of guilt, loss, concerns about "replacing" the deceased parent). The therapist should be supportive of the child's feelings and provide empathy about the range of feelings they are likely to express (e.g., guilt, sadness, loneliness, anger about the unfairness of the loss experience).

For the purposes of activity scheduling, it is important to problem solve with the child to identify substitute partners or activities that the child can do without the deceased parent. Problem solving, described in Chapter 8, involves thinking of all the possible solutions to a problem and helping the child to choose the best or most feasible one.

A point system, as illustrated in the handout *My Goals* (Activity 4.2), is helpful in fostering the child's commitment to engaging in fun activities. The number of points associated with an activity should be based on how challenging an activity is for an individual child. The therapist can help the

Activity 4.2 My Goals

Basket (2 points)	# of Points
eat dinner with dad and sis	2
_watch favorite TV show____	2
_go out for ice cream_____	2

Grand Slam (4 points)

_ride bike to the park_____	4
play with next-door neighbor	4
_go to movies with dad_____	4

Touchdown (8 points)

_join swim team_____	8
_invite friend for sleepover_____	8

Activity 4.2 My Goals

Basket (2 points)   # of Points

_____   _____

_____   _____

_____   _____

Grand Slam (4 points)

_____   _____

_____   _____

_____   _____

Touchdown (8 points)

_____   _____

_____   _____

_____   _____

child to identify easy, medium, and more difficult activities. The first part of the handout illustrates a sample list of goals for a school-aged bereaved child, and the second part is blank and is for clinical use.

For some children, the point system itself will be reinforcing, whereas for other children, it may be helpful to set up a reward system with the parent to reinforce achievement of goals. When working with adolescents, a list of goals can be written on a blank sheet of paper. This type of collaboration is extremely important with teenagers to give them a sense of autonomy and agency in taking care of their own psychological health.

The following dialogue focuses on increasing positive activities with Ruby, an 11-year-old girl whose mom died 6 months ago.

Therapist: Remember how last time we talked about how you've been having a hard time doing fun things when you're feeling sad and depressed, and we made a list together of fun things that you want to start doing again?

Ruby: Yeah, but it's hard to have fun when you're feeling so bad.

Therapist: I know it's hard to imagine doing those things again—so we'll start really slow. What do you think the easiest one on the list is?

Ruby: I guess air hockey with my sister.

Therapist: That sounds like a good one to start with. Maybe you can try and play one game this week and see how it goes. Does that sound OK?

Ruby: Yeah, I think so.

Therapist: Are there other fun things on the list that you want to try?

Ruby: Well, I guess going to the movies. That was a special thing I used to do just with my mom. (*Becomes tearful*)

Therapist: I know thinking about that makes you feel really sad.

Ruby: Yeah, it's not fair that I don't get to do that anymore.

Therapist: It's true that you won't be able to go to the movies with your mom anymore, and of course that makes you sad. I'm wondering if there is someone else that you might like to go to the movies with?

Ruby: Yeah, my dad asks me sometimes if I want to go.

Therapist: What do you think that would be like for you?

Ruby: Actually, it would be nice to do something fun with my dad outside of the house. We watch TV together and stuff, but it's not the same. I do want to see a movie that's playing now.

Depending on the level of depression, some children may have more difficulty than others. For children with more significant depressed mood who are finding it hard to engage in new activities, the therapist should acknowledge and empathize with their lack of interest but encourage them to try a given activity despite their reluctance. This is important because once the child has the experience of participating in a pleasurable activity, the positive feelings elicited from this experience are likely to be self-reinforcing.

The next step is to create a new activity schedule to help the child schedule pleasurable activities for the coming week. The number of activities should increase incrementally each week according to the individual child's progress. Increased activity often results in an improvement in mood, enabling the child to begin working at a more cognitive level (Stallard, 2005).

CHANGING THOUGHTS

A cognitive technique that is beneficial for children with depressive symptoms involves first helping them to identify distorted cognitions or thoughts and then develop more realistic countercognitions (Curry, 2001). Cognitions that occur in response to everyday situations are known as automatic thoughts, which are essentially assessments or interpretations of events. In a depressed child or adolescent, automatic thoughts are likely to be distorted in some way. Cognitions of depressed individuals tend to be overly self-critical and biased toward the negative, with positive outcomes attributed to external rather than internal factors, and with perceived failure in one domain generalized to one's whole life. Children and adolescents who are experiencing symptoms of depression are therefore likely to interpret situations in a way that results in an overly negative view of the self, experience, and future (Belsher & Wilkes, 1994).

Eliciting Negative Thoughts

The first step to begin changing negative cognitions is to help the child or adolescent identify a specific situation in which he or she felt sad or depressed. One way of eliciting a child's automatic thoughts is to simply ask what he or she was thinking in that situation. To help the child describe his or her thoughts in further detail, the therapist may find the following prompts helpful:

- What thoughts went running through your head?
- What did you say to yourself at the time?
- What ideas popped into your mind?

Some negative thoughts that are common in depressed children may connect to how they view themselves as compared with others, along with beliefs that others think negatively of them (e.g., "I'm just not as smart as the other kids," or "They really think I'm a dummy–nerd–loser"). Bereaved children in particular might identify thoughts like, "Kids are looking at me funny," or "Everybody feels sorry for me." The therapist should explore the feelings and beliefs behind these types of thoughts and help the child to replace them with corrective or more realistic thoughts, as discussed in the next section.

Challenging Negative Thoughts

When a child or adolescent presents with sadness and accompanying negative thoughts about the self and the world, it is important for the therapist to determine whether the thoughts are in need of challenging. It is understandable for children who have lost a parent to experience negative thoughts at times about what has happened to them and the world around them. For example, a bereaved child may become sad when thinking about the absence of his deceased mother during his upcoming birthday. The therapist should of course empathize with the feelings of sadness and loss. However, if the child indicates negative thought patterns that serve to maintain his feelings of sadness (e.g., "I'll always feel this bad"), then the therapist may work with the child to challenge the accuracy of those cognitions.

When negative thoughts are identified that are in need of modification, the therapist can work with the child to examine the evidence that supports or challenges the thoughts. As elaborated on in Chapters 3 and 9, questions such as, "What's the evidence to support this view?" and "How would you respond if you had a different expectation?" may be used to guide this exploration. The handout Be Your Own Detective: Questions to Ask Yourself When Having Negative Thoughts (Activity 4.3) lists typical questions that may be used during this process and is an important tool for the therapist to help the child to challenge maladaptive thoughts.

As negative thoughts are elicited and challenged, it is also helpful to teach awareness of basic irrational or negative thought patterns. These include mind reading, should statements, and all-or-nothing thinking. Examples of these negative thought patterns, or cognitive distortions, in bereaved children are provided in the paragraphs that follow. Mind reading is when people make predictions about what other people are thinking without sufficient evidence to draw conclusions. Should statements, or "should-y" or "must-y" thinking, are another type of cognitive distortion (Belsher & Wilkes, 1994). Individuals with this type of thinking tend to be hard on themselves or others about things that they unrealistically feel should and must be done. All-or-nothing thinking is another type of negative thinking and is the

Activity 4.3 Be Your Own Detective:

Questions to Ask Yourself When Having Negative Thoughts

O What evidence do you have to support this thought?

O What evidence do you have that goes against this thought?

O Is there another way of seeing what is happening?

O What else do you think may be happening?

O How would you feel if you thought differently about what was happening?

O How would you feel if you had a different expectation about what is going to happen?

O What would your best friend (or parent, teacher, or sibling) say if he or she knew you felt this way?

O What would you say to your best friend if he or she was in this situation, thinking the same thing?

O What if your thought was found to be true?

      - What would happen next?
      - How bad would that be?

tendency to place all experiences in two extreme and opposite categories (A. T. Beck et al., 1979).

Recognizing these patterns is particularly useful when working with adolescents, who are typically able to understand cognitive errors. With practice, adolescents can also learn to challenge their negative thoughts. The therapist should help the teenager to identify the patterns or themes in his or her thoughts and illustrate how to challenge these thoughts and generate more corrective or helpful statements. The following example with 13-year-old Kate demonstrates how to help adolescents label and challenge negative thinking.

> *Therapist:* So, can you tell me what positive activities you did this past week?
>
> *Kate:* Well, I went to my friend Amanda's sleepover.
>
> *Therapist:* Wow, that's great! I know being able to go to sleepovers again was one of your goals. How did it go?
>
> *Kate:* Well, it was good at first but then all the girls started complaining about things their moms won't let them do. I just stayed quiet and then Amanda changed the subject to how much she hates her gym uniform.
>
> *Therapist:* What thoughts ran through your head?
>
> *Kate:* Well, things like "They all wish I wasn't here so they could talk about their moms," and "They think I'm pathetic."
>
> *Therapist:* Did anyone say either of those things?
>
> *Kate:* No.
>
> *Therapist:* Wow, you never told me you could read minds!
>
> *Kate:* (*Laughs*)
>
> *Therapist:* Yes, it's a funny way of thinking about it, but when people are depressed they sometimes tend to read minds. They think that they can tell what other people are thinking and they usually think it's something negative. But a lot of times, there's no real evidence for it. Like the party—what evidence did you have that they didn't want you there and thought you were pathetic?
>
> *Kate:* Well, when Amanda changed the subject, it was like they couldn't even talk about what they wanted to, just because I was there.
>
> *Therapist:* So when Amanda changed the subject, you immediately thought that your friends didn't want you around. Are there

other reasons that they might have stopped talking about their own moms?

Kate: I don't know—I think she changed the subject because it was weird to talk about in front of me. It really seems like they don't know what to say around me.

Therapist: Hmm, so another possibility, besides them not wanting you around, is that your friends don't know what to say around you.

Kate: Yeah, exactly.

Therapist: Actually, that happens a lot—even adults don't always know what to say when someone they care about is having a rough time.

Kate: I didn't think about it like that. Maybe they thought that I wouldn't want to hear about their moms, so they were just trying not to hurt my feelings.

Therapist: OK, so we can spend some talking about what you can say and do in those situations. Also, the more we work together, the easier it will be for you to notice when you are having these types of negative thoughts, or being a mind reader, and try to challenge them like we just did together.

As noted, "should-y" or "must-y" thinking is another cognitive distortion that may be present in bereaved children and adolescents who are depressed. For example, a bereaved teenage boy who lost his father might have thoughts like, "I should be in charge of the house now that my dad is gone," or "I can't leave my mom alone." Bereaved children and adolescents may attempt to grow up quickly and may take on adult behavior in an effort to replace the parent who has died. They may experience guilt about resuming their normal lives and worry about abandoning their surviving parent. A common theme that emerges in family therapy for childhood depression is the tendency of the child to serve as a confidant or support system for a parent, usually the mother (Campbell et al., 2003). This dynamic is likely to be exacerbated in bereaved families. These types of issues that involve the child's role in the family are best addressed with the parent and child together in joint sessions. Specifically, the therapist should communicate to the parents the tendency to expect bereaved children to mature quickly and take on new roles, just as their own worlds are changing in so many ways. Statements such as, "You are the man (or woman) of the house now," or "You'll have to take care of your mother now that your dad is gone," may be well intentioned but are rarely helpful. Although it is realistic that some changes will occur in the home, it is important for the therapist to facilitate communication about these new roles and increase understanding of the age appropriateness of different responsibilities.

All-or-nothing thinking is another type of negative thinking common in individuals with symptoms of depression. Considering their loss experience, bereaved children in particular may display an exaggerated response to minor negative cues and may have a tendency to expect the worst outcome. Some common all-or-nothing thinking errors that we have observed in bereaved children faced with stressful situations are thoughts like, "I can't handle this," or "Things always go bad for me." Other common distortions related to feelings of sadness after losing a parent are thoughts like, "I'll always feel this way," or "I'll never be happy again."

The cognitive strategies described previously are most applicable to preteens and adolescents. At times, teaching cognitive errors may also be a useful strategy when working with younger children, provided that they are at least school age (or 6 years old). However, when teaching this age group about cognitive processes, therapists should simplify them and make them concrete using games and metaphors. The handout *What Are My Negative Thoughts?* (Activity 4.4) can help children identify the types of cognitive distortions that often happen when people are depressed. This handout describes the different types of negative thinking that are common in children who have symptoms of depression and encourages the child to come up with examples from his or her own life.

With younger children, it is also helpful to use creative methods to assist the child in identifying negative thoughts and figuring out what a new thought might be. It is important to first make sure the child is able to grasp the concept of self-talk and how thoughts influence feelings and behaviors (Review Chapter 3 for more on information about self-talk). Once the child understands the concept of self-talk, the following exercise is designed to help the child identify and challenge his or her own negative thoughts.

Draw, or have the child draw, a simple picture of a person in a situation previously discussed, which may have involved a negative or sad thought expressed by the child. For example, if the child said that he sometimes doesn't want to go to school because he would miss his mother, then the child would draw a sad face and the therapist would write out "I miss my mother." Talk about what the child in the picture is feeling and doing. Next, ask the child what else he thinks about in the given situation, prompting for more positive thoughts. Continuing the example, the therapist would ask the child what he likes about school, which might lead to more positive statements such as "I play with friends at school." Then have the child draw a picture showing how he would feel with the new, more positive thought. This process highlights how less negative thoughts lead to decreased feelings of sadness, and is similar to the use of "thought bubbles" which are elaborated on in Chapter 6.

Activity 4.4 What Are My Negative Thoughts?

Dark glasses—I can only see negative things that happen!

Mind-reader—I can tell what everyone else is thinking—bad thoughts about me!

Fortune-teller—I think bad things will happen before they happen!

No-good—Good things that happen don't count!

Exploder—Little negative things get really, really big!

Examples from my own life:
A time I wore dark glasses was _____
_____

I read somebody's mind _____
_____

My bad fortune was _____
_____

I decided a good thing was no-good _____
_____

I exploded over a little thing _____
_____

Increasing Self-Esteem

It is important to help children generate positive thoughts about themselves not only to replace negative ones but also to improve self-esteem. A sample activity designed to bolster self-esteem and increase positive thoughts is the creation of a book highlighting the child's special traits. Specifically, the therapist might encourage the bereaved child to consider what personal qualities his or her deceased or surviving parent might indicate they value(d) about the child. This provides an opportunity for the child to build self-esteem by identifying positive traits about his- or herself that are perceived by others and by feeling a connection to the deceased and his or her current caregiver. This activity also allows room for creativity in the therapeutic process. It is important to allow the child to generate ideas to include in the book and pick arts and crafts supplies. If the child is stuck, then the therapist may provide suggestions, such as making a drawing of the self with family or friends, writing about favorite aspects of self, favorite games–foods–activities, and/or adding clippings from magazines and photographs.

With adolescents, age-appropriate activities can also be conducted to engage the teen in positive self-exploration and expression. This may include journaling, poetry, story writing, or creating a collage. The therapist may ask directed questions to inspire the teen in this activity. These may include asking the teenager to list, draw, or make a collage of his or her favorite things; asking about what authors–artists–individuals he or she admires; and asking other questions that help the teenager formulate how he or she would like to view him- or herself. As with younger children, the therapist can also use this as an opportunity to help bereaved adolescents to reflect on qualities about them that were perceived by the deceased or other friends and family members. During this activity, the therapist can highlight positive self-statements that the adolescent may later use as coping statements in times that are more difficult.

IMPROVING RELATIONSHIPS

Children who lose a parent may subtly alienate themselves from others to reduce the risk of future losses (Wolfelt, 1983). It is important to look for signs of this in a bereaved child who becomes isolative and avoids close relationships. In general, children and adolescents who are depressed may have difficulty keeping their friends and/or making new friends. We have observed that some bereaved children, particularly adolescents, respond to feeling different from their peers by forming new friendships with other children who have faced similar life stressors. A change in social circles may result, which may be a positive source of identification but may also represent another experience of loss and major transition.

Psychoeducation should be provided about the impact of depressive symptoms on family relationships and peer relationships. The therapist may emphasize that it is common for bereaved children to feel stigmatized and acknowledge that some bereaved children feel that they are labeled as different. Feelings of isolation and stigmatization may contribute to or be exacerbated by feelings of depression.

The therapist can facilitate a discussion about changes in social relationships by asking questions such as the following:

- Who can you go to for support when you're feeling sad?
- How have your friendships changed since the loss?
- What does it feel like to be around other kids who haven't lost a parent?

During this discussion, if it appears that the child is withdrawn and his or her social activities are limited, then it is important to work with the parent to ensure that the child has access to social activities at scheduled times throughout the week. These should be included in the daily activity schedule. If the child presents with symptoms of interpersonal conflict, then the therapist can role play current problem areas with the child, asking him or her to take turns playing himself–herself and the other child. The therapist should aid the child in finding solutions to difficult problems.

As noted earlier, anger and irritability are common in depression. This can be hard for the entire family, who may feel that no matter what they do, they are unable to soothe or cheer up their angry child or teen. Jenna, a 14-year-old girl who was away at summer camp when her father died, was described by her mother as being "angry most of the time." Jenna was in agreement that she did indeed feel angry that she was not at home when the death happened. With the help of the therapist and her mother, she was able to express other feelings surrounding both being away from home and the death itself, including guilt and sadness.

PARENT AS HELPER

Evidence-based treatment protocols for depression in children and adolescents typically recommend at least partial involvement of the parent (e.g., IPT-A; Mufson & Dorta, 2003). IGTC emphasizes that including the parent in treatment is instrumental to achieving and maintaining a positive outcome with bereaved children and adolescents who have symptoms of depression. During this part of the treatment, the parent and child typically attend some sessions together, allowing for the opportunity to address conflicts and communication problems in the parent–child relationship and creating an improved family environment that is beneficial for the child well after the treatment ends.

Families of children with depression are often characterized by stress and conflict (e.g., Kaslow, Deering, & Racusin, 1994; Marmorstein & Iacono, 2004), and family conflict may in fact precipitate or exacerbate depressive symptoms, particularly among adolescents (Mufson & Dorta, 2003). Also, one of the markers of childhood depression is irritability (*Diagnostic and Statistical Manual of Mental Disorders*, 4th ed.; American Psychiatric Association, 1994), which is a feature that may also be associated with interpersonal conflict. In some cases, the depressed child may exhibit more acting-out behavior, whereas in other cases, the child may be withdrawn from family activities. The parent might be acting differently as well, particularly if he or she is having his or her own symptoms of depression or grief. This has implications for the dynamic between child and parent; for example, the parent might misinterpret the child's misbehavior as willful or antagonistic, when the child is really trying to express his or her feelings of sadness or reactivate a depressed or withdrawn parent. The first step is to reframe these types of parent–child problems as a familial response to their experience of loss and related feelings of grief and depression.

The second step is for the therapist to encourage the parent to identify and reinforce positive attributes of the child and help the parent to see the child's efforts to please him or her. As the parent begins to see his or her child more clearly and positively, the therapist should guide the parent as to how to convey increased parental interest and warmth. Specific strategies for improving parent–child interactions can be found in Chapter 7. The family should also be encouraged to schedule enjoyable family activities, and special time should be allocated for the parent and child to spend alone together. Finally, it is important to help the child and parent to communicate about changes in role expectations following the death of a parent that may be contributing to depressed mood.

SUMMARY

This chapter outlined IGTC interventions to be used when working with bereaved children and adolescents who are presenting with problems related to depression. Specific characteristics of depressed children who experienced a loss were identified and discussed, along with common symptoms and clinical presentations. The approach described in this chapter highlighted the use of cognitive–behavioral, interpersonal, and family-based strategies to modify depressive thoughts and behaviors in bereaved children and also included techniques to improve and strengthen family and peer relationships.

5

TREATING POSTTRAUMATIC STRESS DISORDER SYMPTOMS IN GRIEVING CHILDREN

The death of a loved one is a potentially traumatic event that creates risk for the development of posttraumatic stress disorder (PTSD). According to the *Diagnostic and Statistical Manual of Mental Disorders* (4th ed.; American Psychiatric Association, 1994), traumatic events are sudden, unexpected, and uncontrollable events that result in actual or threatened death or threat to bodily integrity of oneself or others and that produce feelings of intense terror, horror, or helplessness. Studies in the past 2 decades have determined that events such as the unexpected death or suicide of a family member, motor vehicle accidents, witnessing or being the victim of domestic or community violence, and exposure to war or terrorism are associated with PTSD in children (Pine & Cohen, 2002). It has been suggested that PTSD can also result from deaths that appear to be expected, such as the death of a grandparent or parent after a long illness (see Breslau, Andreski, & Chilcoat, 1998). These observations suggest that children may perceive a death as shocking and unexpected, regardless of its objective nature as expected or predictable. Thus, evaluation of the impact of a death should be understood through the child's view of the event and its impact on his or her life.

The presence of PTSD related to the loss of a loved one among children and youth may be more frequent than has been recognized in the mental health community. Indeed, a large community sample study of PTSD in young adults found that the death of a family member or friend was the most common cause of PTSD, accounting for 31% of all cases (Breslau et al., 1998). These findings suggest the importance of assessing children for PTSD after the death of a loved one and the value of being familiar with interventions that facilitate the resolution of PTSD symptoms.

This chapter presents the integrated grief therapy for children (IGTC) approach for treating symptoms of PTSD following loss. The way in which PTSD manifests in bereaved children, as well as risk factors for the development of this disorder, is described, and appropriate interventions are introduced. Primary interventions include coping strategies to improve functioning and the creation of a trauma narrative to reduce PTSD symptoms.

SYMPTOMS OF PTSD IN BEREAVED CHILDREN

PTSD comprises three distinct symptom sets that may present in the following ways when stemming from the death of a loved one: (a) reexperiencing symptoms, such as unbidden images of the death, nightmares, and preoccupying thoughts about the trauma or person who died; (b) avoidance of traumatic reminders of the death, including specific places, people, or activities; and (c) hyperarousal symptoms, such as irritability, anger, poor sleep, poor concentration, and heightened startle response. The expression of these symptoms varies depending on the age of the child.

The unique or signature symptoms of PTSD are the reexperiencing symptoms, and these have been observed in children as young as 3 years of age (Scheeringa, Zeanah, Myers, & Putnam, 2003). In younger children and toddlers, these symptoms can be seen through repetitive play or reenactment of the event or repeated drawing of salient aspects of the trauma or traumatic death (Terr, 1981, 1983). For example, following the terrorist attacks of September 11, 2001, we observed bereaved children repetitively building blocks and knocking them down or drawing sheet after sheet of the twin towers. Middle school and older children's reexperiencing symptoms are more likely to come in the form of images or nightmares about the death or about the person who died.

Avoidance symptoms and emotional numbing appear less often in children of preschool age or younger. In middle school and older children, such symptoms may be expressed in social withdrawal from family and friends and lack of interest or enthusiasm for activities that the child used to enjoy. Among teens, reduced interest in the future or in planning a future for themselves may be observed.

Symptoms of hyperarousal vary by age. Following a death, young children may begin to show increased aggressiveness and destructiveness; toddlers may regress to behaviors such as loss of toilet training. These symptoms are viewed as resulting from children's difficulties in managing increased arousal relative to their stage of development (Dyregov & Yule, 2006; Eth, Silverstein, & Pynoos, 1985; Scheeringa et al., 2003). Among adolescents, and to some extent among middle school children (Hoven, 2003), use or increased use of alcohol and drugs has been reported, presumably as a maladaptive coping strategy for hyperarousal symptoms (see Kilpatrick et al., 2003).

RISK FACTORS AND INTERVENTIONS

Several factors increase risk of PTSD among children. Many of them are similar to those observed in adults and include gender, with girls more likely to develop PTSD than boys; history of previous trauma; and history of previous psychopathology or psychological difficulties (see Pine & Cohen, 2002). Still, the past 3 decades of research on trauma in children indicate that the most powerful influences in mental health status of children following a trauma are parental reactions and overall family functioning.

The literature concerning traumatic exposure among children indicates that parental PTSD symptoms are the most powerful and most consistent predictors of the development of PTSD and other psychological difficulties in children (e.g., Earls, Smith, Reich, & Jung, 1988; Green et al., 1991; Kilic, Ozguven, & Sayil, 2003; Landolt, Boehler, Schwager, Schallberger, & Nuessli, 1998; McFarlane, 1987a, 1987b). Of this group, three studies focused on parental death, and the results were consistent in finding that the response of the remaining parent is a critical factor in the mental health status of the child. These studies suggest the importance of the parent–child relationship in recovery from loss and in maintaining the child's well-being. The nature of the parental death in each study differed, with one related to the World Trade Center attack (Pfeffer, Altemus, Heo, & Jiang, 2007), the second as a result of a suicide (Pfeffer et al., 1997), and the third following parental death from a variety of causes (Stoppelbein & Greening, 2000). The authors of the last study reported no differences in PTSD or other psychopathology among children related to the nature of parental death (e.g., suicide, accident, disease) or to anticipation of death.

The IGTC model suggests that it is most beneficial to organize treatment of children with PTSD related to the death of a loved one into two relatively distinct components or tasks. The first component focuses on ensuring that the child has sufficient and appropriate resources to cope with the loss and that the child stays or gets back on track developmentally in regard to social and emotional competencies. This includes the introduction of coping strategies for managing distress and symptoms and can extend to more general life skills, such as emotion regulation and effective communication, which can be undermined by the impact of a traumatic loss.

The second component focuses on developing a narrative of the death for the purpose of resolving PTSD symptoms such as nightmares or repetitive play. For children who are having traumatic symptoms related to the death or loss, it is essential that the elements of the narrative that are aimed at reducing PTSD symptoms be completed before moving on to Chapter 10. In Chapter 10, the child is helped with the larger task of making memories about the loved one's life and death to commemorate and preserve memories of the deceased. When the child is not experiencing PTSD symptoms and/or did not experience the loss as traumatic, the creation of a trauma narrative is not a necessary precursor to memory making.

COMPONENT 1: BUILDING SKILLS AND MAXIMIZING ADAPTIVE FUNCTIONING

The first component of IGTC treatment for PTSD revolves around managing symptoms and improving day to day life. The particular tasks include (a) coping strategies that specifically target the management of PTSD; (b) exploration of beliefs about the death and their impact on the child's sense of self and the world around them; (c) guidance around the development of roles, routines, and responsibilities in a family changed by the loss of one of its members; and (d) skills training concerning emotion regulation, communication, and emotional expression.

Coping Strategies for PTSD and Related Trauma Symptoms

PTSD symptoms such as intrusive thoughts, nightmares, and increased startle response are often experienced as occurring in an uncontrollable and unpredictable fashion, sometimes exacerbating a sense of loss of mastery and control that often happens following a traumatic event. In addition, PTSD by definition results in substantial emotion dysregulation in which a child can swing from feeling emotionally numb and shut down to suddenly being overwhelmed by feelings of fear, anger, or sadness. Sometimes the feelings are so intense or of a nature that the child does not recognize what they are feeling, leading to confusion, increased fear, and greater uncertainty. The handout *Feelings Monitoring* (Activity 5.1) can help the child give names to his or her feelings, track when and why they happen, and implement a coping strategy or more adaptive response. Note that two versions of this handout are included,

Activity 5.1 Feelings Monitoring

Feeling	Intensity (0–10)	Trigger	Thought	Response	Next time I'll...
Scared	10	Sound of bus	Someone is going to get hurt	Froze on spot Refused to get on bus	Use deep breathing to calm down
Angry	8	Heard people screaming outside	Why do people shout? Don't they know they should save it for when something serious is happening?	Screamed out window and told them to shut up	Put on my favorite song and try to forget about it
Sad	6	My first birthday without my mom	Birthdays are no fun anymore	Cried all morning on my birthday	Talk to my sister about my feelings—she had a hard time on her birthday this year, too

Activity 5.1 Feelings Monitoring (*Continued*)

Feeling	Intensity (0–10)	Trigger	Thought	Response	Next time I'll. . .

one completed and one blank. The blank handout is included for the therapist to give to the child to complete between sessions. The completed handout provides specific examples of situations that trigger negative feelings for a child based on the following case example, illustrating how to help the child track these feelings and situations and practice more adaptive coping skills learned in session.

Ten-year-old Sally and her mother had both been struck by a bus turning a corner as they were crossing a street. Sally survived the accident, but her mother did not. Sally and her 14-year-old sister had been living with her grandmother for 6 months since her mother died when they began therapy. Her grandmother worked two jobs and was dealing with the loss by keeping things as "normal" as possible. This included not talking about the loss and having the girls "be grown up" and take on more responsibilities at home. Sally was not doing well at school and was having temper tantrums and crying jags. She felt confused and scared.

Sally: I just don't feel normal.

Therapist: Well, you're not alone in this experience. You've gone through something really difficult. Most people who lose someone they love experience a lot of intense feelings, whether it shows or not.

Sally: But mine come out of the blue, I don't know why.

Therapist: I know it may be hard at first, but it might be worthwhile to track what you're feeling when you're feeling it. This strategy will help you to understand what types of situations trigger your feelings, it will show you that they are not as unpredictable as they seem. This technique is called *feelings monitoring*. You can start by writing down a word to describe what you're feeling, and then describing the situation. This will help you see connections between your feelings and the situation you are in.

Sally: I don't think I can do that. It sounds hard. I don't think I can figure out why I feel what I do.

Therapist: Here's a handout that can help make it easier. We can practice one together. You are likely to find that you actually do have a good reason for why you feel the way you do. Something has happened, or some one said something that reminds you of your loss and all the scary things that have happened.

Sally: Well, that scares me too! I don't want to remember, and then those feelings pop out from nowhere.

> *Therapist:* It's scary, I know. But once you figure out where your feelings are "popping out" from, they'll be less scary and they'll make more sense. Then you can figure out ways of managing them better.

Over the next couple of weeks, Sally monitored her feelings using the handout provided. The therapist helped her to become more aware of exactly what bothered her, which was most often reminders of the accident. Together, Sally and her therapist worked on figuring out which types of situations triggered her symptoms—from general situations, such as "where there are loud noises and sounds," to very specific situations, such as "sounds from buses and sounds of people screaming." Once the association between these types of sounds and the bus accident was identified, Sally felt less confused and "not so crazy." The therapist reinforced the message that although painful, Sally's feelings were normal and natural. Her therapist also helped her to begin identifying ways that she could manage her feelings and not be as overwhelmed by preparing for the types of situations that triggered her difficulties (see Activity 5.1, *Feelings Monitoring,* completed handout). Although the feelings remained and continued to be painful, Sally no longer felt out of control. Furthermore, as she came to understand and accept her feelings better, she was able to manage them better too. She felt proud of herself.

The therapist and child can use any number of coping strategies that are relevant to the feeling or situation. These include relaxation techniques, such as focused abdominal breathing, progressive muscle relaxation, and positive imagery or positive self-statements. The selection of the exercise is based on the child's individual preferences, ideally building on skills that are already present, followed by the development and practice of new strategies that are a match to the children's interest, developmental age, and home life or routines. IGTC suggests that a collaborative pick-and-choose method is most helpful, in that it engages the child's interest and creates a greater likelihood of being practiced out side of the session. Building on strategies that are already in use can lead to relatively rapid success in implementing the strategy and build confidence in the child. The reader is referred back to Chapter 3 for more detailed instruction around how to work with children on these types of cognitive and behavioral strategies.

Exploring Beliefs About the Death

Traumatic deaths, like any other trauma, can change children's beliefs about themselves and about the world. Children, like adults, will search for reasons why something terrible has happened. If no immediate rational or plausible explanation is found, then children and even teenagers may believe or fear that that they are to blame for the death. For example, a child may think a bad behavior led to a parent's illness or that a recent argument led to a sibling's accident. These types of thoughts are due, in part, to the nature of cognitive development in younger children, where the interpretation of events is filtered through a reference to self. It may also, particularly in older children or teens, reflect self-blame or guilt related to a troubled or ambivalent relationship. In either case, however, such beliefs are not necessarily a sign of any particular pathology.

Deaths that are the result of human intent, such as terrorist attacks or murder, are known to create greater risk of PTSD compared with those that are believed to occur randomly or by nature (Charuvastra & Cloitre, 2008). Such events also can disturb beliefs in the benevolence of the world, leading to negative reformulations (Janoff-Bulman, 1992) and/or reinforcing negative beliefs that are already present (e.g., "The world is not safe," "People are bad"). Negative beliefs can lead to behavioral choices that create self-fulfilling prophesies and risk for a range of negative outcomes. For example, the belief that "people are bad and not to be trusted" may lead to hostile behavior toward others, which increases the likelihood of others responding with hostility or withdrawal (Safran & Segal, 1990).

The exploration of misconceptions of self-blame or highly generalized negative beliefs about others is critical in posttraumatic work, as such cognitive symptoms contribute to the maintenance of PTSD and related trauma symptoms (Resick & Schnicke, 1996). Misperceptions or highly negative beliefs will differ in their nature and include misperceptions about causality (e.g., "If I were good, this would not have happened"), black-and-white thinking (e.g., "Bad things happen to bad people"), and overgeneralization (e.g., "You can't trust anybody" or "Everyone breaks their promises"). Revision of these beliefs to more adaptive perceptions of self or the world occurs through the generation of alternative points of view supported by counterexamples. Counterexamples need to be realistic, developed collaboratively with the parent, and have an experiential base, including development of exercises or "evidence collection" as homework.

Table 5.1 provides examples of distressing beliefs related to the self and proposed adaptive alternatives that may be explored and supported with the help of a therapist. The following is a case example of using the IGTC model to work through negative thinking in a preadolescent boy.

Twelve-year-old Bobby came to therapy following the recent death of his father from colon cancer. Bobby told his therapist that he had not been doing well in school even before his father got sick and proceeded to cry. Upon further discussion, during which the therapist provided support as well as asked challenging questions, Bobby admitted that he believed his bad grades may have been the cause of his father's illness. He also stated that he wished he could now bring back his dad by raising his grades.

TABLE 5.1
Alternatives to Negative Thoughts

Negative belief	Alternative
Beliefs about myself	
My father died because I stressed him out all the time with my bad behavior. He even said so.	Dad said he loved me. (My mom reminded me) there were plenty of times I made him happy.
My sister was in a car crash with her friends. If I had been nicer to her she wouldn't have gone out and she might still be alive.	Even if I would've been nice to my sister, she'd have gone out. It was Saturday night and she always went out on Saturday, no matter what. I miss her.
I feel guilty because maybe if I had said more to my mom about watching her health, about not smoking, it would have made a difference. I did not try hard enough.	I told her lots of times to quit smoking. My Dad did, too. Everyone did. But she would just laugh . . . that was her way. It's not my fault.
Beliefs about the world	
The world is full of evil people who can hurt you in a minute.	Not everyone is evil. All my life my grandmother has been really good to me. There are three people I can count on to take care of me: my sister, my grandmother, and my best friend.
I will only be safe if I never ride in a car again.	Before the accident, there were lots of times we drove around and nothing bad happened. It's probably safe most of the time.
People from a different religion are scary.	Jimmy is from a different religion and a different country. He looks OK and has always been nice.

> *Bobby:* I know my bad grades stressed my father out. He would get so upset and angry with me. And I read that stress can make people sick or make sick people get worse. So, either his being sick was my fault or his worry about me pushed him over the edge.
>
> *Therapist:* Whoa! Hold on there for a second. As I recall, your dad was sick before you moved from elementary to middle school. And that's when your grades went down, is that right?
>
> *Bobby:* Oh, yeah, I forgot about that. But my bad grades made him feel worse, I'm sure.
>
> *Therapist:* Did he say so?
>
> *Bobby:* Yeah, he would complain that my grades made him feel sicker and then we would get into stupid fights.
>
> *Therapist:* Well, he was pretty sick then, and sick people are often cranky. Also you were under the stress of a new school and

	a lot of change at home. So both of you were stressed and had a lot to deal with.
Bobby:	Hmm, yeah, it was a really bad time.
Therapist:	Right—a bad time for both of you. Do you remember good times with your dad before he got sick or even when he was sick? Times when you felt close?
Bobby:	Oh, sure, we were close. Even when he was sick, he said he loved me.
Therapist:	So, maybe that's something to remember. He loved you. That's important.
Bobby:	Yeah.
Therapist:	He loved you and enjoyed your company. I'd like for you to keep that in mind, especially when your thoughts focus on how bad things got between you. How are your grades now?
Bobby:	Getting better.
Therapist:	Good, your dad would be happy to know that after such a tough time, things are getting better.
Bobby:	I think he would definitely like that.

In this case, the therapist shifts the blame away from Bobby for making his father sick, suggesting that the sickness made his father grumpy, and even points out that the sickness adversely affected Bobby and his relationship with his dad. Of most importance, the therapist speaks with compassion for both Bobby and his father: The illness had been difficult on both of them. The therapist points out the positive bond between father and son as the enduring quality of their relationship. The therapist is also suggesting that Bobby have more compassion for himself and for his Dad when reflecting on the difficult time they went through together.

Review of Routines, Roles, and Responsibilities

The death of a family member, particularly a parent, often leads to significant changes in family routines and some changes in roles and responsibilities. Such profound changes in the daily rhythm of life can be disorienting to children, particularly for those children who are feeling less safe and secure, as often occurs in the face of trauma and PTSD. Other family members often take on the roles and responsibilities of the deceased, and the family system as a whole tends to experience a shift to accommodate these changes. The surviving caregiver(s) are left to fill in tasks for which they may not be well suited, whether it be homework review or attending a sports event. Adjustment among siblings or younger family members about responsibilities as simple as who sets the table or walks the dog can be flash points for conflict and confusion, reminders of loss, and an increased sense of unwanted responsibility.

Providing information about the impact of changes in routines on emotional well-being can be helpful to parents and children and can normalize the presence of emotional distress. The therapist can identify what routines the child misses or which changes have been most upsetting and develop strategies to address or compensate for them. Parents should be encouraged to provide essential routines related to regular sleep and eating habits. PTSD and its symptoms undermine circadian rhythm, and, with it, healthy patterns of sleeping and eating. The stressors of a new environment, workload, and financial concerns can distract a parent from maintaining these important routines for both the children and themselves. Directing parent's attention to these activities and providing guidance and support in developing logistically feasible routines can be crucial for some families. See Chapter 8 for additional information about helping families cope with the myriad of changes they may face following the death of a loved one.

Along with changing roles, some grieving parents may experience difficulty in limit setting or in implementing consistent discipline. An inability to maintain consistency in discipline can stem from a parent's feeling sorry for their children because of the pain they have experienced and the desire not to inflict any more suffering or the belief that being more lax can assuage some of the children's pain. Some parents set up rules, but because of depression, exhaustion, or distraction, change the rules or fail to implement them. Other parents are inconsistent because their children are exhibiting problem behavior or acting differently and they are uncertain how to proceed. PTSD is characterized by alternating patterns of irritability–aggression and emotional numbing–social withdrawal, and so strategies for maintaining routines that once were effective may be variably productive or entirely counterproductive.

Clinically, we have noted that in bereaved families, there is often a strong positive correlation between parental report of inconsistent discipline and children's report of increased anxiety, reduced peer competence, and reduced academic performance. These observations reinforce the idea that inconsistent discipline may increase anxiety and undermine a sense of security among bereaved children, particularly among those with symptoms of PTSD, which is itself characterized by heightened arousal and reduced sense of security. The following case example illustrates how a therapist may go about discussing consistent discipline with a grieving parent.

Twelve-year-old Paul had been in therapy related to the death of his father for a few weeks when his mother, Betty, asked the therapist for help navigating her changing relationship with her son. The therapist offered to meet with the mother for a separate individual session to discuss these issues.

Parent: When Paul complains about being forced to study for tests and that no other kid in his class studies as much, I feel bad and often back down. I can't tolerate seeing him so upset and angry. Underneath, I know he's feeling different from the other kids. Also, he's suffered so much, I just can't bear to add to it.

Therapist: I can see that it is difficult. One thing you can do is first find out how much homework there is and how much study time the teacher expects.

Parent: That's a good idea. I've just been so exhausted and busy, though, that taking time for one more phone call and one more appointment just seems too much.

Therapist: Well, I've noticed this is an issue that keeps coming up. You and Paul have been having conflicts about homework for quite some time. You probably have spent more time in arguments with him—and making then unmaking rules—than the time it would take to find out for certain what the expectations are for him in school. Once you know, you might have more information and more confidence in rule-making at home.

Parent: Put that way, it makes sense. Still, he'll probably be upset that I'm investigating this and going on and on about it.

Therapist: Well, I understand what you are saying about not wanting to increase his distress. You might find, though, that if you set specific and reasonable rules and routines regarding after-school and homework time, things will actually improve. Having rules and routines can actually be very comforting to kids who have experienced loss and trauma. Their lives become more predictable and safe feeling, which contrasts with the insecure feelings and worry about the unpredictable. There is some measure of security in that.

Parent: Yeah, that makes sense.

The IGTC model emphasizes the importance of setting limits with bereaved children, whose daily lives have often become less structured and are likely to have changed dramatically from that which occurred before the loss. This occurs for a variety of reasons, including the strain on the parents (who are themselves bereaved) as well as the parent's feelings of guilt and remorse regarding the child's suffering (as in the case example). Time should be taken to identify and clarify appropriate limits and rules for the child, to plan with the parent for ensuring its implementation, and to role play between parent and therapist to establish appropriate language and behavior for the implementation of the rules at home. Basic skills that can be reviewed, supported, and refined include the use of praise, effective time-out procedures, and contingency reinforcement schedules. The reader is referred to Chapter 7 for specific instructions regarding these and other parenting skills.

Emotional Expression and Modulation

PTSD is, by definition, a disorder in which feelings of hyperarousal and intense distress alternate with avoidance of feelings, thoughts, and situations related to the traumatic event (American Psychiatric Association, 1994). Avoidance of feelings related to the trauma or loss can lead to distancing or avoidance among family members. Children may avoid their siblings or other family members, and parents may avoid their children, particularly when the child begins talking about the death (Scheeringa & Zeanah, 2001). Ironically and sadly, family members can become "traumatic reminders" to each other, and thus the death of a family member can drive survivors apart rather than closer together.

Alternatively, children and parents may avoid talking about the death in an effort to protect one another from becoming upset. Parents may not want to pry into children's thoughts or may avoid discussing their children's thoughts and feelings for fear of exacerbating any problems. At times, children may feel inhibited in talking to their parents about thoughts that frighten or confuse them, as they fear upsetting their parents, particularly if they have already observed their parents having difficulty themselves. Clinically, we have observed instances of mutual protection in which both parent and child avoid conversations related to the death, which often leads to reduced communication, understanding, and sense of connection between the child and parent. These circumstances may be problematic, as absence of discussion about traumatic events between parent and child have been related to negative outcomes in children, including exacerbation of PTSD symptoms (e.g., Laor, Wolmer, Mayes, & Gershon, 1997).

Reduction in the inhibition of emotional expression among bereaved children has been found to be a strong predictor of improved mental health functioning (Sandler et al., 2003). More generally, parental openness about both parents' and children's feelings have been found to foster the development of emotional competence over time (Lutz, Hock, & Kang, 2007) and the ability to cope constructively with challenging situations (Bronstein, Fitzgerald, Briones, Pieniadz, & D'Ari, 1993; Valiente et al., 2004).

In line with these findings, IGTC suggests that a critical task in the treatment of bereaved children, with and without symptoms of PTSD, is to facilitate the development of affective expression and modulation skills. Ideally, if both children and parents gain greater ability to express and modulate the expression of their feelings, they may have less need to use avoidant strategies. Such skills development may also support the child in staying on track in developmental tasks related to effective emotional expression and associated social competencies.

Parallel sessions for children and their parents can be implemented in which each has the opportunity talk about their feelings. Initial conversation between child and therapist can begin with a discussion of everyday feelings. This will allow the therapist to gauge the child's capacity to accurately identify and express a range of feelings. Moreover, the therapist can model the expression of a variety of feelings for the child, including likes and dislikes and positive and negative feelings. This discussion will help set an environment where the child feels comfortable talking about a range of feelings and exploring the names for feelings not yet well understood. The therapist can enlist the use of games such as the "Mad, Sad, Glad Game" (1990) or, for older children and adolescents, the use of the "Feelings Wheel" (e.g., Cloitre, Cohen, & Koenen, 2006). The handout *Feelings Wheel* (Activity 5.2) may be used to help individuals identify and label a variety of emotions, from general emotions, such as sadness, to more specific and complex emotions, such as humiliation and despair. The clinician may use the feelings wheel by asking the child or adolescent to identify which feelings he or she experiences in different circumstances, particularly when discussing the loss. For the child or adolescent with a limited emotional vocabulary, the handout may be kept out during therapy sessions to refer to if he or she is struggling with verbalizing feelings or for the therapist to assist in these types of situations.

Parents can be instructed in a similar fashion (e.g., using feelings wheels), which serves the dual purpose of helping them discover their own feelings and identifying and encouraging the expression of emotions in their children. Some bereaved or PTSD-distressed parents may not be able to respond to their children's feelings about the death itself. However, a simple but extremely useful skill that most parents can easily master is reflecting back the emotions that the child is describing. The therapist can note to the parent that such simple listening and reflecting can be very comforting and validating to the child. This, in turn, can provide the adult with some sense of mastery in a difficult and painful situation and enhance confidence in his or her ability to parent his or her child. Further and more specific instruction in active listening and acknowledgement of feelings can be provided for skills practice at home (see Chapter 7 for further information about reflective listening).

IGTC proposes a variety of strategies to help the child in modulation of feelings, particularly feelings that the child fears being overwhelmed by. One approach is simply to suggest that the child pay attention to the feeling and think about it. The child can do this in the presence of the therapist and

ACTIVITY 5.2 FEELINGS WHEEL

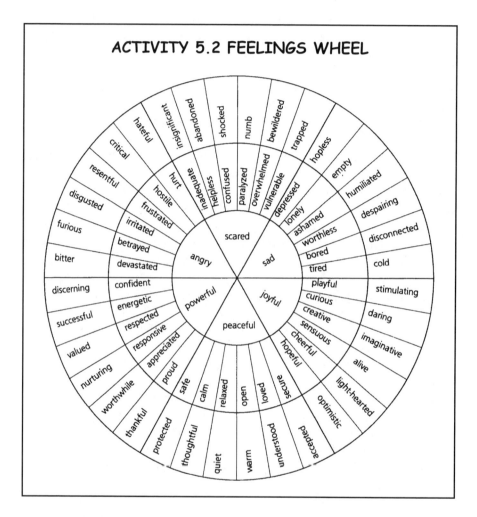

From *Treating Survivors of Childhood Abuse: Psychotherapy for the Interrupted Life* (p. 148), by M. Cloitre, L. R. Cohen, and K. C. Koenen, 2006, New York: Guilford. Copyright 2006 by Guilford. Reprinted with permission. Permission to photocopy this handout is granted to purchasers of this book for personal use only (see copyright page for details).

practice with the parent at home. In addition, the child can describe the feeling to the therapist, parent, or even to him- or herself in words, as in a diary or poem. The transformation of feelings into words can resolve the sense of being overwhelmed by them. The use of this strategy early on in the treatment about day-to-day feelings and conflicts ideally provides the child with success experiences and a personal understanding of the value of putting words to feelings.

When staying with the feeling or thought may not be maximally adaptive to the immediate situation (e.g., during a test, a social interaction, or sports), alternative strategies, such as cognitive or behavioral distraction, may be used. For example, a child on his way to school who finds himself feeling sad about his father's death or frightened by the idea that his mother could die in the same sudden way may return and reinvest attention to interacting with friends on the bus or to thinking about the basketball game he is going to play that afternoon. Chapters 3 and 9 describe useful strategies for stress reduction and distraction in more detail.

Enhancing Social Skills and Social Support Behavior

There is substantial evidence that PTSD is associated with increased conflict among family members (Johnson, Feldman, & Lubin, 1995; McFarlane, 1987b), reduced family cohesion (McFarlane, 1987b), and deterioration of social relationships in general (Riggs, Byrne, Weathers, & Litz, 1998; Shalev, Tuval-Mashiach, & Hadar, 2004). Assessment of such problems in either the child or parent is important for several reasons. First, the deterioration of the parent–child relationship leads to slowed recovery for the child and increased strain on the parent in the management of the home. Moreover, PTSD may contribute to deterioration in the child's social relationships among his or her peers. The off-putting symptoms of PTSD, such as irritability, emotional numbing, and social withdrawal, may indeed lead to some distancing by peers, which, in turn, may lead to or exacerbate feelings of being alone, alienated, and misunderstood, which so commonly accompany PTSD. Although members of the extended family and the community reach out to individuals who have experienced a loss, they may do so with some trepidation about the appropriateness of their efforts. Families and children can be preoccupied with their loss and may be unable or unwilling to recognize or effectively respond to signals of social support, reducing the likelihood of repeated or enduring efforts by well-meaning individuals. This is significant, as the ability to effectively use social support extended by the community and by peers can facilitate both emotional and practical recovery from a loss.

Useful interventions can derive from the communication and emotion regulation exercises described previously. The IGTC model encourages both parent and child to turn their developing skills in communication toward extended family members and friends. The parent can provide a role model and source of instruction to the child in this task. The therapist can ask the child to make a list of friends and identify the kinds of support the child wants or needs, which friends might seem to be providing the support needed or be likely to give it, and how to ask for support from each person. A role play may be useful and should include reminders to thank the person for the help once it is given. Review of social skills beyond those specifically related to requests for social support can be introduced as needed. These can include appropriate assertiveness behavior (e.g., initiating, engaging, and maintaining conversations), management of aggressive behaviors, and emphasizing the importance of the need for different actions and reactions in social behaviors depending on the person and context.

COMPONENT 2: THE TRAUMA NARRATIVE

Some have proposed that PTSD symptoms can undermine the natural process of grieving such that children cannot reminisce about their loved one without experiencing frightening and intrusive thoughts and images about the way the person died (Cohen, Mannarino, & Deblinger, 2006). Bereavement is typically viewed as a process in which individuals think about the deceased in an effort to both accommodate the reality of the loss and maintain memories and a meaningful internal or imagined relationship with the deceased (e.g., Worden, 1996). PTSD symptoms may block access to memories about the loved one and be so disturbing that the bereaved child avoids thinking about the loved one at all.

The presence of the PTSD symptoms and the resulting inability to grieve was first noted in studies of children who were exposed to both violence and loss, including witnessing a parent's murder (Eth et al., 1985) and living in war zones (Saltzman, Steinberg, Layne, Aisenberg, & Pynoos, 2001), and has been described as an independent syndrome called *childhood traumatic grief* (Cohen & Mannarino, 2004). The resolution of PTSD symptoms is viewed as one critical component in paving the way to freeing the individual to think about the person who died and to consider memories other than those related to the fact and nature of the person's death. Toward that end, the treatment of PTSD related to a loss integrates the emotional processing of the death along with further reflection and commemoration of the life of the person. The second component of addressing the needs of bereaved children presenting with PTSD thus involves the development of a trauma narrative, designed to help the child with emotional processing related to the death.

A *trauma narrative* refers to the development of a coherent telling or story of the traumatic experience. It is a core component of most evidence-based trauma interventions, regardless of the type of trauma (Foa et al., 1999), and has been successfully used with adults (e.g., Cloitre et al., 2006) as well as adolescents and children as young as 6 years of age (Cohen, Mannarino, & Deblinger, 2006). The general task involves the telling of the story of the trauma in an organized fashion with a beginning, middle, and end. Children are encouraged to describe their understanding of the traumatic event as well as any thoughts and feelings related to it. The story is repeated several times, such that each telling includes more feelings and thoughts than the one before. The process is associated with a significant reduction in posttraumatic stress symptoms and depression. The loss of a loved one, for example, will likely revise a child's sense of who he or she is or can be. The critical task in narrative work is to help the child and parent find a way not to get stuck in the past or in the pain of the loss and instead integrate it with a frame for continued living and planning for the future.

Various approaches have been taken in the actual construction of the narrative that relate to the age and preferences of the child. Some children will feel comfortable talking about what happened; others will prefer to draw or express themselves in other creative ways. For example, the child can draw and explain what happened while the therapist writes out the story. Later, the text can be transcribed and added to the drawing, creating a book that tells the story of what happened. Some children write as little as a sentence to start (e.g., "My father was very sick and then died"). The therapist can encourage the child to elaborate on feelings and thoughts at repeated tellings or to elaborate on his or her drawings or statements in subsequent sessions (Cohen, Mannarino, & Deblinger, 2006).

Regardless of the manner in which the narrative is constructed, when beginning this type of exposure work, it is important for the therapist and patient to first select a memory together to address. When working with bereaved children who experienced a traumatic loss, this may often involve a memory of the day the parent or other loved one died. This day may be broken up into parts in some cases, depending on the nature of the experience of the individual child. In other cases, the traumatic memory may be more focused on the day the child learned that the parent was sick or was likely to die, seeing him or her in the hospital, and so forth. This is why it is important that the therapist understand the child's individual experience and work collaboratively with the child on identifying the memories that he or she finds most distressing for exposure work. It is also important that the child be given a developmentally appropriate rationale before beginning the construction of the narrative, such as in the dialogue that follows:

> *Therapist:* I know it is really hard for you to think about the day that your [mother–father–caregiver] died. Talking about it might make you feel

really sad and worried or mad. But sometimes when you try not to talk about or think about something that makes you feel upset it affects you in other ways; like you might cry or get angry a lot, or have trouble concentrating in school. (*Use examples from child's presenting problems.*) The good thing about talking about it here with me is that this is a safe place, and I will be right here to help you. And I have a feeling that after we talk about it a few times it will start to get less scary and easier, and you will be able to see that you can get through it and come out feeling OK.

The therapist should instruct the patient to describe the traumatic event, starting from the beginning, speaking in the first person, and preferably in the present tense. This can be explained to the child with an example or by inviting him or her to describe his or her day at school or another specific benign event as an example (e.g., "I am walking into the classroom, and I see my friend Jenny. She invites me to sit with her, and I feel happy"). When beginning the narrative, the therapist should invite the child to close his or her eyes, if he or she is comfortable doing so. Throughout the exposure session, the therapist may encourage the child to adjust him- or herself physically to create a greater sense of grounding and stability (e.g., keep his or her feet on the floor, hold on to the chair). The therapist may also provide some physical reassurance to the child, such as touching the child's arm periodically, if it seems to help the child to feel safe and supported. The following are some questions and prompts to help the child after he or she begins the telling of the trauma narrative:

- Tell me about what happened, starting at the beginning.
- Help me see the way you saw it.
- Help me to see it through your eyes.
- What are you seeing, touching, smelling, hearing?
- Try to focus on your feelings.
- I am right here with you.
- Try to stay in the moment.
- Try to slow down and take it step by step.
- Can you tell me more about that part?
- Let's talk through this part moment by moment.
- How are you feeling right now?

Next is an example of the beginning of a trauma narrative elicited using the aforementioned questions and prompts:

The day my dad died was a Wednesday. I remember that morning really well—my dad left for work before I woke up but my mom and I were arguing about whether I could go to my friend Jackie's house after school. She thought I should come home because I had a history test the next day, and I wanted to go to Jackie's because my other two friends were going. She ended up saying OK. So that's where I was when I found out (at Jackie's house).

My brother called and said he was coming to pick me up. I knew something was wrong right away because he never picks me up unless my mom makes him and he never calls my friends' houses. I guess that's why I didn't ask any questions or complain about not staying longer with my friends. In the car I kept asking what was wrong, and he said mom would tell me. I was really scared by then—I felt sick to my stomach and my leg was shaking.

I came home and my mom was crying and I said "Where's Dad?" She said "Something happened—dad was in an accident." I asked why we weren't at the hospital and she said it was a really bad car accident and he died. I remember I kept asking "What happened?" and I couldn't breathe. My brother hugged me but then I couldn't breathe even more and I had to run outside to get some air. I don't really remember what happened after that . . .

In their presentation of an evidence-based treatment plan specifically designed to work with children experiencing traumatic grief, Judy Cohen and her colleagues spoke to the importance of encouraging the child to share the trauma narrative or book with the parent (Cohen, Mannarino, & Deblinger, 2006). This sharing serves the dual purpose of helping the child to become more comfortable thinking about and talking about the trauma individually as well as discussing these thoughts and feelings with the parent. The parent also benefits by learning what the child is experiencing and by learning in session how to listen to the child without becoming overwhelmed by his or her own distress.

To be ready to focus on the child's needs during the sharing of the trauma narrative, parents require their own preparation for hearing the story from the child's perspective and in the child's voice. Many parents are fearful that their child will not be able to tolerate the process of telling and sharing the narrative. However, in our experience, it is often the parent who has more difficulty than the child. In one case at our clinic, an adolescent boy had created a lengthy narrative of his father's death, including his feelings about his father, his relationship with his father, and his views on how life might be different without him. He initially resisted sharing the narrative with his mother, but with encouragement from the therapist, agreed under two conditions: First, he did not want his mother to interrupt in the telling of the story, and second, he asked that she not cry while they talked about what happened.

His response reflects the importance of effectively responding to the child's own view of what has happened and recognizing the validity of his or her perceptions and feelings. It also reflects another common theme for bereaved children, which is concern about their parents' reactions and reluctance to burden their parents with more pain. Thus, it is critical that the therapist prepare the parent for hearing the narrative. Working in session on the development of emotion regulation and related coping skills should precede sharing of the narrative. In addition, the capacity of the parent to engage with his or her child on this painful topic is more likely to be successful if the parent has completed his or her own narrative work, including his or her beliefs about the impact of the event on his or her children. Last, the therapist should explain the goals of sharing the trauma narrative, including (a) to allow the child to be comfortable in discussing his or her thoughts and feelings with the parent and (b) for the parent to demonstrate his or her ability to effectively listen to and support the child, which may, in turn, lay the foundation for effective communication between parent and child about other emotionally laden matters.

SUMMARY

This chapter outlined interventions to be used when working with bereaved children and adolescents who are presenting with symptoms of PTSD. Specific characteristics and common clinical presentations of children who have experienced a traumatic loss were outlined and described. This chapter highlighted IGTC's dual component approach to treating trauma symptoms, which includes as the first component managing symptoms and improving day-to-day life for the bereaved child and as the second component the creation of a trauma narrative to help decrease the avoidance, re-experiencing, and arousal symptoms that may interfere with a bereaved child's ability to grieve and maintain positive memories of the loved one.

6

TREATING ANXIETY SYMPTOMS IN GRIEVING CHILDREN

Bereaved children have been found to report increased fears and worries in comparison with nonbereaved children (Abdelnoor & Hollins, 2004). Specific anxieties around separation and death are common, with parentally bereaved children indicating concerns about the safety of and separation from family members, particularly the surviving parent (Dowdney, 2000; Sanchez, Fristad, Weller, Weller, & Moye, 1994). The Child Bereavement Study found that bereaved children demonstrated significantly more symptoms of anxiety as compared with nonbereaved children at 2 years after the loss (Worden & Silverman, 1996).

From these findings as well as our own clinical experiences, it is clear that one of the presenting issues that propel bereaved children to seek treatment is symptoms of anxiety—particularly symptoms of generalized anxiety (e.g., worries about everyday things) and separation anxiety (e.g., worries about separating from caregivers). It should be noted that this does not imply that bereaved children are necessarily more likely to meet diagnostic criteria for an anxiety diagnosis (Sanchez et al., 1994), but rather that some bereaved children present with certain types of anxieties of varying severity that impact their daily lives. On the basis of the child bereavement research literature and our clinical

TABLE 6.1
Anxiety Problems Seen Among Bereaved Children

Type of anxiety disorder	Symptoms
Generalized anxiety disorder	Difficulty concentrating (may be evidenced by school problems), irritability (including increased temper tantrums or crankiness), sleep disturbance (trouble falling asleep or staying asleep), and muscle tension (or other somatic problems or physical complaints)
Separation anxiety disorder	Inappropriate and excessive anxiety concerning separation from home or from major attachment figures; persistent and excessive worry about losing, or about possible harm coming to, major attachment figures; reluctance or refusal to go to school or other places because of fear of separation; reluctance or refusal to go to sleep without being near a major attachment figure; repeated nightmares involving separation; and complaints of physical problems during separation or when separation is anticipated

observations, combined with *Diagnostic and Statistical Manual of Mental Disorders* (4th ed.; American Psychiatric Association, 1994) criteria for anxiety disorders, the symptoms listed in Table 6.1 are typical of the kinds of anxiety problems seen among bereaved children.

INTEGRATED GRIEF THERAPY FOR CHILDREN (IGTC) APPROACH TO TREATING ANXIETY IN GRIEVING CHILDREN

A substantial literature supports the efficacy of cognitive–behavioral therapy (CBT) for anxiety disorders among children and adolescents (see Compton et al., 2004; Scott, Mughelli, & Deas, 2005; Silva, Gallagher, & Minami, 2006, for reviews). CBT also has been found to be effective in treating children at risk for anxiety problems, including those with features of anxiety disorders (but not meeting criteria for a diagnosis) and those determined to have mild to moderate anxiety diagnoses (Dadds, Spence, Holland, Barrett, & Laurens,1997; Lowry-Webster, Barrett, & Dadds, 2001).

Given the plethora of evidence on the effectiveness of CBT in treating anxious children, IGTC pulls from these therapies to create a CBT-based approach for use with bereaved children demonstrating significant anxiety symptoms. This chapter presents the IGTC approach for treating anxiety symptoms (including generalized anxiety disorder, separation anxiety disorder, and subthreshold levels of anxiety) following loss. Psychoeducation, cognitive and behavioral coping skills, and the role of the parent in helping children suffering from anxiety are presented. Children are taught to be aware of when they experience anxious arousal and to use anxiety management strategies during these times. A step-by-step plan for coping with anxiety, as well as opportunities for practicing these coping skills, is provided.

Much of the clinical research on anxious children, including studies involving individual and group treatments as wells as preventive interventions, has been based on the work of Kendall and his colleagues (e.g., Kendall, 1990; Kendall, Aschenbrand, & Hudson, 2003). The coping strategies presented in this chapter are based in part on the strategies presented in the *Coping Cat* treatment manual, developed by Kendall (1990) for use with anxious children and adolescents, and other cognitive–behavioral treatments for anxiety. The *Coping Cat* treatment program has been evaluated in several randomized clinical trials (Kendall, 1994; Kendall et al., 1997) and has been deemed empirically supported (Kazdin & Weisz, 1998). Strategies that are thought to have particular relevance to the types of worries and anxieties seen among bereaved children have been selected for the IGTC model. The techniques are illustrated with examples from our clinical experiences with bereaved children and are adapted for use with this population.

INTRODUCTION TO HELPING CHILDREN WITH ANXIETY

It is helpful for anxious children and their parents to understand that worries, fears, and anxieties are normal experiences felt by all people—children as well as adults. Problems sometimes occur when people do not know what to do when they feel anxious, and these problems tend to be exacerbated by stressful life experiences such as loss. Fortunately, coping with anxiety involves skills that can be learned. This concept is an important one to discuss with both the child and caregiver.

> *Therapist:* Lots of children worry about lots of things. For example, some worry about their parents and other family members, some worry about how they are doing in school, and others worry about what other people will think of them. These worries are sometimes called "anxieties." All of these worries or anxieties are normal, but some children know more about what to do when they feel this way than others. Also, some worries seem to get worse or harder to handle when going through difficult times. For example, lots of kids worry about their family after someone they love dies. Part of what we are going to do together is figure out when you feel worried or anxious and what to do when you feel this way.

The therapist can follow up with specific questions:

- Can you tell me about what kinds of worries you have?
- When do you feel the most worried or anxious?
- What kinds of situations seem to cause the most difficulties for you?

If the child has a hard time answering the last question, then the therapist may prompt by asking about specific situations that tend to provoke anxiety among bereaved children, such as the following:

- Situations that draw attention to child's loss (e.g., meet the teacher night, father–daughter dance),
- Meeting new friends or deciding when and how to tell friends about the loss,
- Being away from family members (e.g., sleeping out of the home or being home without a parent), or
- Situations that remind the child of loss or illness (e.g., going to the doctor or hospital).

Therapist: OK, I think I see how some of these worries are getting the better of you. Together, we are going to focus on changing these worries and showing you how to conquer your fears.

IDENTIFYING ANXIETY CUES

Effective treatments for anxious children help them to identify when unwanted anxious feelings arise so that they are able to learn how to cope with and manage anxiety that is causing distress or difficulty (Kendall et al., 2003). Therefore, for a child to learn how to manage anxiety, it is important for him or her to first understand how to identify his or her own unique anxiety triggers and cues.

Therapist: As you know from our previous talks about the Triangle of 3, feelings, thoughts, and behaviors interact to affect us in many ways. Let's take a look at some of the ways that the different parts of the Triangle of 3 work to make you feel anxious or to keep you feeling anxious.

To identify feelings and physical signs of anxiety, the therapist can ask the following:

- What happens when you are anxious or worried? How do you know when you are feeling anxious?

- Which parts of your body give you clues when you are feeling anxious?
- Which parts of your body feel funny or different when you are afraid?
- What does your body feel like when this happens?

If the child needs prompting or additional help understanding this concept, then the therapist may ask specifically about feelings in different parts of the body, including the head, neck, shoulders, muscles, tummy, and so forth.

To identify thoughts and cognitive signs of anxiety, the therapist can ask the following questions:

- What thoughts go through your mind when you're feeling anxious?
- What kinds of things do you say to yourself during these times (e.g., "I can't do this," "People will see that I'm nervous," "I'm afraid something bad will happen")?
- When you feel anxious, what do you expect will happen next (e.g., Will you stay nervous forever? Will you be embarrassed about what other people think? Do you think something bad will happen to you or to your family?)?

To identify activities and behavioral signs of anxiety, the therapist can ask the following:

- What do you do when you feel this way?
- Is there anything you can do to feel better?
- What types of things do you avoid so that you either won't feel anxious or so that your anxiety goes away?

Therapist: All of these cues—including the feelings in your body, thoughts in your head, and things that you do—can be a helpful sign to tell you that you're becoming anxious . . . And knowing this will tell you when to use the skills you will learn as we go along.

COPING SKILLS FOR ANXIOUS CHILDREN

The following strategies may be used by children with anxiety to minimize their worries as well as the impact of those worries on daily life. These strategies have been selected for their ability to help the types of anxieties most common among bereaved children, such as worries about the health and safety of family members. These strategies are also among those included in effective cognitive–behavioral treatments of anxiety for children (see King, Heyne, &

Ollendick, 2005) and are consistent with the IGTC approach of addressing the feelings, thoughts, and behaviors of each problem area.

Relaxation

At this point in the treatment, the child likely understands that feeling states such as anxiety are associated with physiological changes in the body. The body typically reacts to anxiety with tension, such as a tensing of the neck and shoulders. For this reason, relaxation techniques may be a helpful coping strategy for anxious children. The relaxation strategies previously described in Chapter 3, including diaphragmatic breathing and progressive muscle relaxation, should be reviewed with the child and presented as a means of counteracting the tension associated with anxiety.

Depending on the child's age and types of anxieties, the therapist will choose which relaxation strategies to review in session. The therapist should work with the child to determine which strategies are most relevant for the child, how to use the strategies, and under what circumstances the strategies should be used.

The following case example is based on an 11-year-old child named Bobby, who has been sleeping in his father's bed frequently since his mother died about a year ago following a prolonged illness. Most nights, Bobby falls asleep in his father's bed either while they are watching television together or while he is in bed and his father is nearby working on the computer. Bobby occasionally falls asleep in his own bed, but he usually makes his way to his father's bed before morning. Lately, Bobby has been avoiding sleeping at his friends' houses because he feels afraid when trying fall sleep if his father is not there.

This pattern of behavior, in which a child is reluctant to sleep on his or her own for a prolonged period following a significant loss, is something we have seen frequently in the course of our work. For this reason, we encourage therapists working with bereaved children, especially those presenting with anxiety, to ask about the sleeping arrangements in the home. We have found that by sleeping with his or her caregiver, the bereaved child finds comfort for feelings of sadness, fear, and worry that maybe particularly evident at night. In many cases, the caregiver also experiences relief and comfort for his or her own feelings of loss by having the child sleeping near him or her. This is a sensitive issue for many bereaved families and is often best explored with both the child and parent after a relationship with the therapist has been established and coping skills have been developed. During this discussion, it is often helpful to elicit from the parent both the positive and negative aspects of these arrangements. Over time, parents usually begin to recognize the benefits of having their own personal space, as well as teaching their child to tolerate distress and self-soothe.

The following example dialogue illustrates how this issue may be addressed in session.

> *Bobby:* It's not a big deal, but I'm not sure what to say to my friends when they ask me to sleep over.
>
> *Therapist:* What would you like to say?
>
> *Bobby:* Well, I want to sleep over, but the last time I tried that I had to call my dad to pick me up.
>
> *Therapist:* It sounds like you would like to not feel afraid, and that you would like to have a sleepover without feeling anxious.
>
> *Bobby:* Yeah.
>
> *Therapist:* OK, well, let's see what we can do about that. Do you remember that a few weeks ago we talked about relaxation strategies, or things you could do when you're body tells you that you are feeling anxious or stressed?
>
> *Bobby:* I think so.
>
> *Therapist:* Could you tell me one of the strategies that we talked about?
>
> *Bobby:* We talked about breathing deeply—we did that together.
>
> *Therapist:* Right—let's practice that again now. (*Together, inhale slowly through the nose and belly, hold for a moment, and then exhale slowly.*) When do you think would be a good time to use this breathing?
>
> *Bobby:* When I'm trying to fall asleep?
>
> *Therapist:* Yes, it might help to practice deep breathing when you are trying to fall asleep. Are there other times it may be helpful?
>
> *Bobby:* I'm not sure.
>
> *Therapist:* Well, let's think about that last sleepover. When did you start to feel anxious?
>
> *Bobby:* As soon as Thomas asked me to sleep over. It was lunch time on Friday, and I started to get worried that I wouldn't be able to sleep over. Should I do the breathing even when I'm at school?
>
> *Therapist:* Yes! Actually, that's one of the great things about this strategy—you can do it anywhere without anyone noticing.

Decrease Anxious Self-Talk

Given that thoughts and feeling states tend to influence one another, it follows that the child's anxious thoughts (e.g., worries about future loss) may increase his or her anxious feelings (e.g., headaches, nervous stomach). Further, by changing his or her thoughts, the child can also change whether or not he or she feels anxious or at least the extent to which the anxiety impacts him or her.

Because this concept may be somewhat complicated, it is important to present the strategies for changing anxious thoughts in a concrete way. We suggest that the therapist first review the idea of self-talk by presenting the child with cartoons containing empty "thought bubbles" that represent what the character is thinking. The handout *What Are They Thinking?* (Activity 6.1) provides examples of the kinds of cartoons that may be used. The therapist is encouraged to begin by presenting one or two relatively low-stress situations that are not based on the child's loss experience (e.g., it's the child's turn to walk the dog). The therapist then asks the child what he or she might think or say to him- or herself in the given situation. This approach has been used in a variety of effective treatments for children (e.g., Kendall, 1990).

Following a general discussion about anxious self-talk, the therapist may then present cartoons of more ambiguous and potentially stressful situations, asking the child to think of two different thoughts that the character in the cartoon may have. The premise is to illustrate that each of those different thoughts may lead to a different behavior, and that when children expect bad things to happen, they are more likely to feel anxious or worried. The handout *What Are They Thinking?* may again be used to facilitate this discussion, although the therapist is encouraged to develop alternative and creative thought bubbles based on the child's specific age and, later on, the child's specific anxieties.

Although every child is different, certain common themes have emerged in our cognitive work with bereaved children. For example, many bereaved children have a hard time resuming pleasurable activities following the loss, which may be related to feelings of guilt. These children tend to express thoughts such as, "I can't play baseball anymore because I used to play with my dad" or "If I go to the party, my friends will think I don't miss my grandma anymore." Another common theme is the urge that bereaved children may have to protect their grieving parents. Related thoughts such as "If I cry, then my mom will cry too" and "I have to be the man of the house now" are often reported. IGTC encourages clinicians to pay attention to these and other types of thoughts that may be underlying bereaved children's feelings and behaviors.

Those children who are able to grasp the concept that thoughts influence feelings and behaviors may also be able to understand that thoughts may in fact be changed to alter the associated outcomes. First, the child is instructed to pay attention to and recognize his or her self-talk, which will tell him or her when he or she is feeling anxious. Next, the child can ask him- or herself questions

Activity 6.1 What Are They Thinking?

Activity 6.1 What Are They Thinking? (Continued)

ADDRESSING PROBLEMS IN GRIEVING CHILDREN

about how likely it is that the worrisome outcome will happen and whether it has ever happened before. The child may also be taught how to combat the anxious self-talk with positive self-talk. The handout *Thinking Through Your Worries* (Activity 6.2) may be used in session to illustrate these ideas and remind the child how to decrease anxious and negative self-talk.

The strategies that are used in decreasing anxious self-talk are seen in the example of Katie, a 7-year-old whose grandmother died following complications from diabetes. Katie has had a hard time understanding why her grandmother died, but she knows that "Grandma was very sick for a long time." Since this happened, Katie worries about the health of all of her family members and expresses nervousness even when her 4-year-old brother Daniel has a slight cold. When Katie tells her therapist that she is scared because Daniel is not feeling well, the therapist asks her what she is worried about, and Katie replies that she fears her brother getting sicker. The therapist asks Katie to think about all the times she and Daniel have caught colds that she can remember and whether they eventually got better. Katie is able to see that every cold eventually went away and that Daniel will likely feel better soon. The therapist encourages Katie to remind herself that "colds don't last and people get better" whenever she feels anxious. When Katie hears her brother coughing later that night, she tells herself, "Daniel will feel better soon, just like I got better the last time I didn't feel well."

Bereaved children may experience excessive worry about minor illnesses, especially when their loved one died after being sick. This is particularly true in younger children, who often do not know the difference between temporary and fatal illnesses. As illustrated in the previous paragraph, it is important to explain to children that although we all get sick sometimes, people almost always get better.

Facing Fears

The first two coping strategies presented, relaxation and decreasing anxious self-talk, are related to recognizing the feelings and thoughts associated with anxiety. The next step is focused on behaviors associated with anxiety, the most common being avoidance of the feared situation. The key strategy used to address avoidance is exposure to anxiety-provoking situations. The therapist can help the child to practice his or her skills through imaginal exposure (i.e., imagining a scene and role playing responses) as well as through in vivo exposure (i.e., setting up real-life situations in and out of the office, thereby allowing the child to become anxious so that he or she can practice using the coping skills he or she has learned). In vivo exposure is thought to be most useful in helping children face their fears and ultimately reducing their anxiety.

Activity 6.2 Thinking Through Your Worries

- Tune into your self-talk.

- What is worrying you?

- What do you expect will happen?

- How likely is it that something bad will happen?

When preparing for this phase of treatment, it is often helpful for the therapist to work with the child to create a hierarchy of feared situations, including situations that are anticipated as being mildly, moderately, and severely anxiety provoking. The goal is to gradually introduce each situation in the hierarchy, one at a time, with the child remaining "exposed" to the situation until his or her anxiety decreases. After the child successfully learns that he or she can tolerate anxiety in a lower ranked item, the next item on the hierarchy is introduced. For example, a young child who says she is afraid of the dark talks with her therapist about what makes this scary for her. The therapist helps her to see that some situations are scarier for her than others, and they create a hierarchy that includes being in the dark with an adult in the room (a little bit scary), being alone in a dark room with a nightlight on (more scary), and being alone in a dark room with no light (very scary).

By facing the feared situation and remaining until the anxiety eventually decreases or subsides, children are able to see that they can successfully cope and that the feared consequences (e.g., something bad happening to themselves or to loved ones) do not occur. For these points to be made through exposure exercises, the child must be allowed to become anxious. Relaxation and positive self-talk may be used together to help the child cope during exposure work in session and at home.

The use of exposure may be illustrated by the case of Margaret, a 15-year-old girl. Margaret had often been alone in her home before her father died, such as when her parents went out to dinner or when they were still at work when she got home from school. Once in a while, she would become nervous if she heard a strange noise, but she was usually able to forget about it if she called a friend or put on the television. Since her dad died, however, she became increasingly anxious when her mother went out of the home without her, particularly in the evenings. She felt somewhat less afraid when her older brother was around, but even then she had a difficult time. In fact, Margaret described becoming so anxious when she was home alone that she would feel ill with stomach problems and headaches. Margaret began to make plans to get out of the house and be with other people when she knew that her mother and brother had plans. By the time she came to therapy, Margaret had not been alone in her house for months. Each time her mother and brother would be out, she would make plans to sleep at a friend's house. If they had to go out briefly, she would stop what she was doing and go with them, even if it was inconvenient for them all.

In therapy, Margaret learned to identify and reduce her anxious self-talk and to use relaxation strategies to reduce her anxious arousal. She did not spend an evening at home alone, however, until she had discussed this with her therapist as the next step in her progress toward facing her fears. In session, Margaret's therapist encouraged her to imagine herself at home and to talk about what she would be feeling and doing. The therapist even encouraged her to use all her senses and describe what she was seeing and hearing, as if she was actually in the situation. Despite becoming extremely anxious, Margaret was able to continue to imagine the scenario until the anxiety decreased. Following this session, Margaret was able to practice at home, albeit gradually. Together with her therapist and her mother, Margaret decided to be alone first for 15 minutes, then 45 minutes, and then gradually for a couple of hours, using her coping strategies to help her manage her anxious thoughts and feelings. After facing all of the situations on her hierarchy, Margaret continued to experience some anxiety when alone, but she no longer felt the need to avoid being alone completely.

Reward Yourself

A final step among cognitive–behavioral approaches for anxious children is to provide reinforcement for successful coping. Children are encouraged to reward themselves for any progress, including times that they experience anxiety but are able to face or even partially face the anxiety-provoking situation. Rewards may include positive self-statements (e.g., telling themselves they did a good job), sharing the accomplishment with others (e.g., telling a parent or friend), or engaging in an enjoyable activity (e.g., spending time on a special hobby).

PUTTING IT ALL TOGETHER: PRACTICE

Once the coping skills are in place and the child indicates a solid understanding of how to use them, it is important that the skills are practiced in session and in daily life. This is done through exposure exercises as well as through continued monitoring of behaviors, such as avoidance and facing fears. The handout *Facing Your Fears: What to Do When You Are Feeling Anxious* (Activity 6.3) may be used to review the approach presented in this chapter with the child. Some children may find it helpful to post this handout in a place where it can be readily referred to when feeling nervous, anxious, or worried.

This following case example is based on the case of Bobby, described earlier in the chapter.

> *Therapist:* Last time, we talked about how you were ready to put some of your coping skills into action. I'd like to do that today, first by talking through a situation that we imagine and later by coming up with ways for you to continue practicing these skills throughout the week.
>
> *Bobby:* OK.

Activity 6.3 Facing Your Fears:

What to Do When You Are Feeling Anxious

1. Notice when the anxiety is starting to rise. (Pay attention to your body's feelings and cues.)

2. Relax. (Take deep breaths, relax your muscles, and use positive imagery.)

3. Decrease anxious self-talk. (Use positive self-statements.)

4. Face your fears. (Stay in the situation, even if you're anxious—You can do it!)

5. Reward yourself for facing your fears. (Remember that even small steps represent progress.)

Therapist:	Well, I have our list of situations that make you feel nervous that we wrote together early on. Does this list still seem like it fits?
Bobby:	Yeah, I think things are better, but these are still things that bother me—especially the one about feeling nervous to sleep at a friend's house.
Therapist:	OK, so let's use that as an example. I'd like you to imagine that you are in the lunch room, and that your friend has just asked you to sleep over this weekend. Keeping your coping strategies in mind, can you tell me what you would do in this situation?
Bobby:	First, I would notice my feelings. And in this situation, I'd probably start to get a belly ache. So before, I'd probably just make up a reason not to go.
Therapist:	I like how you said what you would have done *before*—does this mean you would do something different *now*?
Bobby:	Yeah, I could do some deep breathing.
Therapist:	That's a great idea—breathing would help reduce your feelings of nervousness. What else do you notice besides the feelings in your body?
Bobby:	I'd notice my thoughts. I'd probably be saying something like, "If I go over to sleep, I'll just get nervous and want to go home."
Therapist:	That's great how you recognized your anxious self-talk. And you also remembered how to help yourself with coping skills based on your feelings and thoughts. Terrific! What happens next?
Bobby:	Maybe decide to go, and plan on calling my dad only if I feel really bad?
Therapist:	OK, so after considering your feelings and thoughts, you are ready to act. Sounds like you have thought of one way to respond—are there any other options to consider?
Bobby:	I can go hang out but not sleep over, and say my dad has to pick me up at 10.
Therapist:	So you have two options—which do you think might be the better choice?
Bobby:	Planning to go would be more like facing my fear, so that's better.
Therapist:	Do you think that would be something you could do?

Bobby: I'll try!

Therapist: Great. Is there anything else you think might be important in this situation?

Bobby: I think I could be proud of myself for making plans to go to the sleepover. I'd tell my dad, and he would be proud, too.

The therapist should encourage the child to continue to practice the skills and to face anxiety-provoking situations, even after the treatment has been completed. Depending on the child and situation, the parent may be extremely helpful in supporting the child to face his or her fears.

PARENT'S ROLE IN HELPING ANXIOUS CHILDREN

Evidence suggests that including the parent in CBT for anxious youth may be important, particularly for younger children. Barrett, Dadds, and Rapee (1996) added what they called *family anxiety management* (FAM) to CBT based on Kendall's (1990) *Coping Cat* program (previously described). FAM trained parents to reward their child's courageous behavior, to better manage their own anxiety, and to help them communicate and problem solve to help their child maintain therapeutic gains. The child and parents met together with the therapist after the child learned each skill, thus helping to reinforce those skills and helping the parents to assist the child. The outcome was that CBT plus FAM was not just effective but significantly more effective than CBT alone for younger children (ages 7 to 10). There was no difference in outcomes between CBT with or without FAM for older children (ages 11 to 14; Barrett et al., 1996).

On the basis of this research as well as our clinical experiences, our IGTC approach suggests that the parent be included in the treatment of anxiety related to bereavement, particularly for children in the preschool and elementary school years. Parents should at minimum be trained in the coping strategies presented to the child and be encouraged to help the child practice those skills between sessions. The degree of parental involvement should likely be based on the age and individual needs of the child. With children aged 10 and under, we have found it helpful to have the parent present at the beginning and end of every session to introduce and review each coping skill. It is also important to have the parent present to facilitate communication between the child and parent and to help the parent know what to do when the child becomes anxious.

As noted earlier, younger bereaved children often experience excessive worry about their surviving parent, and they may have specific concerns that the parent will die and there will be no one left to take care of them. These types of concerns may contribute to worries in other areas (e.g., school, peer relation-ships), so it is important to address them and to discuss these issues in sessions. Such discussions would likely involve the therapist helping the parent to rea-ssure the child of his or her health and safety and of his or her plans to take care of the child until he or she is grown up. It is also often helpful to tell children who would look after them (e.g., grandparent, relative) in the very unlikely sit-uation that something did happen to the remaining parent. The parent is typ-ically the primary source of comfort for the young child, but he or she may need guidance from the therapist about how to address the child's concerns about health and mortality.

Adolescents are less likely than younger children to be interested in their parents' participation in therapy, and the aforementioned research confirms that parental involvement may not be as important for this age group. Even for teens, however, some parental involvement is often helpful. For example, Mar-garet, the 15-year-old previously discussed, agreed with her therapist that it would be helpful to include her mother in at least one session prior to begin-ning the exposure work. Margaret and her therapist talked with her mother about her coping strategies and their plan for Margaret to face her fear of being in the home alone. The therapist encouraged Margaret's mother to praise Margaret for her efforts and to help her by leaving the home for increasing amounts of time as agreed to during the joint session. By including Margaret's mother in the planning for the in vivo practice at home, she was better able to assist her daughter with this challenge.

SUMMARY

This chapter outlined evidence-based interventions to be used when working with bereaved children and adolescents who are presenting with prob-lems related to anxiety. Specific types of anxiety problems most commonly seen among bereaved children were discussed. The IGTC approach involves the instruction of specific coping skills to address feelings, thoughts, and behaviors associated with anxiety, as well as methods of practicing these skills in a way that is designed to ultimately reduce the child's fears.

7

MANAGING BEHAVIOR PROBLEMS IN GRIEVING CHILDREN

Bereaved children have been found to exhibit increased behavior problems in comparison with nonbereaved children (Dowdney et al., 1999; Elizur & Kaffman, 1983; Kranzler, Shaffer, Wasserman, & Davies, 1990). Specifically, common behavior problems in these children include oppositional behavior, school problems, conflict with siblings, and aggressive behavior (Elizur & Kaffman, 1983; Kranzler et al., 1990; Van Eerdewegh, Bieri, Parrilla, & Clayton, 1982). Findings from the Child Bereavement Study indicated that bereaved children demonstrated significantly more emotional and behavior disturbances as compared with nonbereaved children at 2 years after the loss (Worden, 1996; Worden & Silverman, 1996).

On the basis of these findings as well as our own clinical experiences, the integrated grief therapy for children (IGTC) model helps clinicians to conceptualize and troubleshoot behavior problems in the context of the grieving process. As has been emphasized throughout this book, children respond to loss in different ways. Although behavioral problems may not be commonly thought of as grief reactions, some children react with anger and rage after losing a parent. It should be noted that this does not imply that bereaved children are necessarily more likely to meet diagnostic criteria for oppositional defiant disorder or conduct disorder. Rather, when children are troubled by thoughts and feelings related to the death of a loved one, they may express their distress through misbehavior.

This chapter provides guidance on how to manage the types of behavior problems that can develop after a loss. It includes skill-building interventions, such as increasing parental warmth, improving verbal communication, and establishing or reestablishing routines after a loss, and strategies for effective discipline, such as positive reinforcement. The importance of working directly with parents is emphasized to help create positive environments, increase positive parent–child interactions, and use effective limit-setting strategies. The IGTC strategies described in this chapter are based on techniques that have been previously found effective in troubleshooting problem behaviors in young children (e.g., Brinkmeyer & Eyberg, 2003; Kazdin, 2003; Webster-Stratton, 1992). Strategies that are thought to have particular relevance to the types of behavior problems seen among bereaved children have been selected. Depending on the presenting needs of the child, strategies presented in this chapter may be introduced through individual sessions with the parent or by alternating time spent with the child and parent during session.

UNDERSTANDING PROBLEM BEHAVIORS IN THE FACE OF GRIEF

The first step in helping bereaved children and their parents work through problem behaviors is to understand these behaviors in the context of the loss. Some reasons that bereaved children may act out are connected to changes in the structure within the home or disruptions in routines. For example, in families in which the deceased parent was the primary disciplinarian, the child may find a lack of discipline in the home now that the other parent is in charge. This may be off-putting and, in some circumstances, causes children to act out to test where the current limits or rules are. In other families, the two parents may have simply disciplined differently, so the bereaved child may attempt to provoke the surviving parent to respond in the way the deceased parent would have. For example, if the deceased yelled at the child when he or she misbehaved but the surviving parent does not, the child might increase misbehaviors in an effort to get this type of reaction because it is familiar, even if not the optimal means of discipline.

The bereaved child may also act out as a reaction to changes in family dynamics that extend beyond discipline. He or she may miss the types of interactions he or she had with the deceased parent and feel angry toward the surviving parent for not being able to provide the warmth or feedback the other parent did, at least not in the same manner. For example, if the deceased parent tended to be more involved in the child's day-to-day activities at school, the child might sense a lack of (or at least reduction in) involvement or interest and therefore misbehave during or after school.

The therapist might address these types of issues by facilitating a dialogue with the child and parent about what has changed at home and how the two parents differed in how they interacted with the child. Areas where the relationship can be strengthened may be identified, thus helping the parent and child to build on their strengths at the same time that they are both mourning their similar loss. It should be noted, however, that although communication is essential to relationship building and increasing warmth, it is not a substitute for discipline.

Parents of bereaved children and perhaps even clinicians working with these children may be hesitant to enforce rules and provide discipline because of the idea that these children "have been through so much" and that their misbehaviors are in response to grieving and therefore should be empathized with rather than changed. In our work with bereaved families, we have heard countless parents tell us that their feelings of guilt and sadness kept them from setting limits with their children. It is important to emphasize that the interventions described in this chapter work regardless of the reasons the child is acting out. Structure, routines, and discipline are not only effective in curbing misbehavior but also serve to help a bereaved child feel more "normal" in the face of a great deal of stress and change. Reminding parents how much all children yearn for and rely on structure is helpful in easing feelings of guilt and anxiety.

IMPROVING BEHAVIORS THROUGH POSITIVE INTERACTION

This section provides guidance for increasing the frequency of warm, positive interactions between child and parent. This guidance includes specific strategies to help the parent foster a supportive environment, such as focusing on the child's strengths and positive attributes, increasing praise and positive feedback, and engaging in play activities on a daily basis.

Focusing on Strengths

Parents who seek treatment for their child's behavioral problems often feel overwhelmed and inadequate in their attempts to effectively discipline their grieving children. As noted earlier, the daily structure and routine of the household may have been compromised in the aftermath of the loss, resulting in a chaotic environment with few rules. As the child, in turn, becomes more out of control, the parent often begins to focus on the child's problematic behaviors rather than the child's positive attributes. This may inadvertently lead parents to develop a negative view of their children.

To encourage a more positive framework in which to begin addressing the child's difficulties, clinicians should work with the parent to identify the child's strengths and positive characteristics. This emphasis on the positive is in line with the IGTC model as a whole, which is focused on building on and reinforcing strengths to help bereaved children. Discussing strengths is perhaps most important with those parents who are having problems with their children's behaviors, which tend to overshadow positive attributes and relationships. Although parents of such children may feel an urgent need to list all of the problems they are having at home, it is important to contain this type of talk, especially when the child is present in session. Children closely monitor parents' responses and are sensitive to being portrayed negatively. The bereaved child may be especially sensitive to feeling betrayed by the parent and angry that the deceased parent is no longer there to take his or her "side."

Early on in treatment, parents should therefore be encouraged to talk about times the child has done something well or engaged in prosocial behavior. The therapist can begin this dialogue by asking questions such as the following:

- What does your child do well?
- What are you most proud of your child for doing?
- Tell me about a time that your child was kind or helped someone else.
- What do you enjoy most about this child? (What are your child's strengths and positive attributes?)

The process of identifying strengths sets the frame for parents to view their children positively, and it also encourages parents to take a step back and place their concerns about misbehavior in the context of the recent loss and related stressors. The therapist can remind the parent that all children have times when they behave appropriately and other times when they act out or misbehave, especially when they have gone through something as significant as the death of a parent. Again, understanding misbehavior is not a substitute for structure and discipline, nor does it provide an excuse for problematic actions; however, it helps the parent to empathize with the child and work toward getting the child back on track.

Increasing Warmth

Related to helping a parent see his or her child in a positive light is encouraging the communication of this positive viewpoint to the child. Parental warmth and support has consistently been associated with relatively low levels of children's externalizing problems (Caspi et al., 2004; Eisenberg et al., 2005; Rothbaum & Weisz, 1994). Correspondingly, the expression of positive emotions by parents at home in the presence of their children has been related to low levels of externalizing problems, even when the emotions are not necessarily directed toward the child (Eisenberg et al., 2001; see Halberstadt, Crisp, & Eaton, 1999). Therefore, the level of parental warmth and support should be addressed in treatment, particularly in families in which the child is having emotional and behavioral problems. The importance of parental warmth has been documented by Sandler et al. (1992) as particularly significant in bereaved families. In the implementation of their Family Bereavement Program, these authors found that group participation improved bereaved parents' report of warmth in their relationship with their children, as well as increased family discussion of grief-related issues. There was a corresponding decrease in conduct disorder problems, suggesting that parental warmth may be one factor that reduces these types of symptoms in bereaved families.

Parents can be helped to increase warmth through the use of specific strategies. One means of communicating warmth to a child is through the use of active praise. Praise can also be used to reinforce a child's positive behavior, which is described in further detail later. Although the idea of praise sounds simple, some parents will benefit from direction and guidance about how to praise their child. In particular, bereaved children who are often struggling with feelings of guilt, sadness, and low self-esteem will benefit greatly from reassurance and positive feedback from their caregiver. The handout *How to Praise Your Child* (Activity 7.1) helps guide parents on how to give specific and meaningful praise.

When parents are struggling with their own grief or depression, it may be difficult for them to convey feelings of warmth toward their child. During these trying times, parents often need extra resources and support. This may be in the form of supportive relationships in which the parents can express their feelings and obtain help in managing new roles and responsibilities after a loss. In some cases, the therapist may provide a referral for individual counseling to help the parent cope with his or her stress so he or she can function more effectively as a parent. In fact, it has been found that addressing parental stress in treatment for children with externalizing problems enhanced therapeutic change for these families (Kazdin & Whitley, 2003). Later in this chapter, the section Resources for Parents provides strategies to help parents decrease frustrations to better manage their child's misbehavior.

Play

Another important way of communicating warmth and giving positive parental attention to young children is through play. The therapist should encourage the parent to play with his or her child each day to increase positive

Activity 7.1 How to Praise Your Child

1. Be specific when praising instead of providing global praise. Label praise to describe the particular behavior you like and want to see again. *("Great job picking up those blocks when I asked!" instead of "Great job!")*

2. Show enthusiasm—the impact of praise is increased with nonverbal communication. *(Smile at your child, give a pat on the back or a high-five, and use energy in your voice!)*

3. Do not qualify your praise or combine it with criticism. *(Try to avoid statements like, "Great job eating all your dinner. Why don't you do that more often?")*

4. Praise as soon as possible when you see a positive behavior.

5. Praise the behavior every time you see it!

interactions and engage with the child in a nonconflictual way. This helps build and develop the parent–child relationship and decreases the likelihood that children will act out to gain parental attention. It is important to explain to parents that the individual play time with their child can be for a short time period, such as 5 to 15 minutes per day. Emphasizing that even a short period of one-on-one interaction will make a difference in the child's behavior is critical, considering that surviving parents often feel overwhelmed by their grief and stressed by the additional demands placed on them because of the death of their partner. Also, there is no need for expensive toys or elaborate games; the most important function of playtime is the parent interacting with the child. In some cases, it is helpful for the therapist to brainstorm with the parent and child about potential activities to ensure that they choose meaningful, age-appropriate forms of play and to increase compliance by planning daily play activities.

EXPLORING PROBLEM BEHAVIORS

One way to help identify problem behaviors and take a closer look at what is sustaining them is to ask the parent to provide a specific example of a time that his or her child misbehaved. Often, a parent will provide many examples of problematic behaviors without prompting. Parents may describe their child as "out of control" or as "always tantruming." In general, when discussing problems, it is important that the therapist encourage the parent to give concrete examples and not to globalize or overgeneralize problem behavior. After first focusing on the positive, as described earlier, the therapist can then ask the parent to select one example of the child's misbehavior or acting out, and to describe what happened in as much detail as possible. The therapist should encourage the parent to discuss what led up to the behavior, what happened, and what the outcome or consequence was. The therapist can then help the parent to see what parts of the process can be controlled and identify places for intervention and change. Consider the following case example.

Mrs. Smith brought 7-year-old Judy to treatment 1 year after Judy's father died. She began by complaining that Judy was irritable all the time. When the therapist asked Mrs. Smith to identify positive attributes about her child, Mrs. Smith responded by stating that she loved her child but lately she was so frustrated that it was hard to see the positive. The therapist continued to prompt Mrs. Smith by asking what she loved about Judy and what made Judy special. Mrs. Smith commented that Judy helps to take care of her younger brother, especially since her husband died. They then discussed how the loss had impacted the entire family and the series of changes that each of the family members had experienced, which helped Mrs. Smith to put Judy's behaviors into perspective. The therapist later asked for a detailed description of a situation in which Judy exhibited irritable or frustrating behavior, and Mrs. Smith described a time that Judy refused to leave the park to go home for dinner. In talking more about this episode with Mrs. Smith, it became apparent that she was interested in reestablishing routines, such as a nightly family dinner, which had all but disappeared since the death of Judy's father. The reestablishment of routines and positive family time therefore became goals for the ongoing therapy.

REESTABLISHING STRUCTURE AND ROUTINE

As noted earlier and illustrated in the aforementioned case example, bereaved families often have difficulty maintaining structure after the death of a loved one. This may be due to stressors that often arise following a loss, including transitions such as moves, role adjustments, and changes in family structure. Secondary losses are described in further detail in Chapter 8. Often, the stress of the loss itself contributes to the breakdown of structure and routine. In these situations, one important role of the therapist is to help the parent to reestablish rules and consistency in the home. Again, it is important to emphasize to parents that children benefit greatly from structure and clear expectations, especially during times of stress. Clinicians should convey that although this is especially difficult to maintain following a loss, an important part of the work of therapy is to reestablish structure and routine.

> *Therapist:* We know that children respond well to consistency, structure, and clear expectations. Sometimes these things get lost when children and families experience loss or other major transitions. Considering what your family has been through, it makes sense that some of the routines and rules you had before have changed. The behavior problems your child is having are not your fault or your child's fault, and there are plenty of ways to start fixing them. Now is a good time to start rebuilding structure and routine in your home.

To determine which routines to reestablish, the therapist can prompt the parent with the following questions:

- What are some of your responsibilities at home? What are your child's responsibilities?
- What are some things that happen every day in your household (e.g., mealtimes, brushing teeth, activities, bedtimes)?
- What are some things that you would like your family to do every day that do not always get done?

It is important to convey that it is common for parents who have lost a partner to feel overwhelmed by their many responsibilities. The therapist should emphasize that having a routine can help both parents and children know what is expected of them and therefore creates a sense of predictability and security. To help the parent begin establishing a routine, encourage him or her to think about and clarify what tasks are to be done by the child and what tasks are to be done by the parent. Remind parents that by repeating the same tasks every day, children learn what is expected of them more quickly and easily.

The therapist may provide the handout *Daily Routine* (Activity 7.2). The first part of the handout illustrates a sample routine for a school-age child, and the second part provides a blank routine to be completed by the parent and child together, based on their individual or family needs.

PROVIDING CONSISTENT DISCIPLINE

Another important component of reducing problematic behaviors is helping the parent to provide consistent discipline and set limits. In our work with bereaved children, we have found that parents identified having problems managing their children's behavior effectively and consistently as a top concern. As previously mentioned, this difficulty may be due to the parent's feelings of guilt about what the child has been through and/or related to the impact of parent psychological distress on his or her energy level and overall functioning. Role changes following the loss may also interfere with the ability of the surviving parent to maintain consistent rules and discipline. Bereaved parents sometimes describe how they no longer feel in control of their household and instead feel that their child is now in charge. As Worden (1996) pointed out, some parents attempt the opposite and become restrictive and exert excessive control in an effort to manage an environment that feels out of control or to control their children's increasing attention-seeking behavior. He described his findings from the Child Bereavement Study, in which he found that consistent discipline in the pre- and postdeath periods resulted in better outcomes for children. Sandler et al. (2003) also identified these issues as salient for bereaved parents and included effective discipline as a component of their Family Bereavement Program. These authors found that their program improved parenting, particularly for those families who began the program with the poorest scores on positive parenting.

Several strategies that are helpful in providing consistent discipline are discussed in the sections that follow. These include positive reinforcement, ignoring, star charts, clear commands, and time out. The techniques are illustrated with examples from our clinical experiences with bereaved children and are adapted for use with this population.

Activity 7.2 Daily Routine

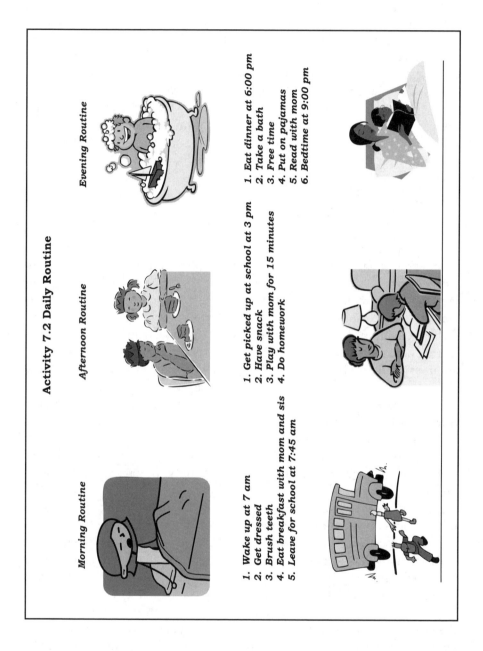

Morning Routine

1. Wake up at 7 am
2. Get dressed
3. Brush teeth
4. Eat breakfast with mom and sis
5. Leave for school at 7:45 am

Afternoon Routine

1. Get picked up at school at 3 pm
2. Have snack
3. Play with mom for 15 minutes
4. Do homework

Evening Routine

1. Eat dinner at 6:00 pm
2. Take a bath
3. Free time
4. Put on pajamas
5. Read with mom
6. Bedtime at 9:00 pm

Activity 7.2 Daily Routine

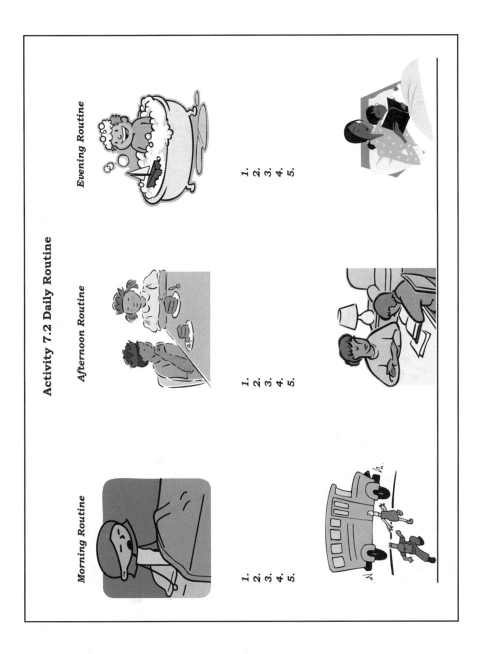

Morning Routine

1.
2.
3.
4.
5.

Afternoon Routine

1.
2.
3.
4.
5.

Evening Routine

1.
2.
3.
4.
5.

Positive Reinforcement

As noted earlier, children who are misbehaving are often seeking attention from their parents. Children typically do not differentiate between positive attention and negative attention and engage in behaviors that elicit either type of response from their parent. This may be particularly true among bereaved children, whose parents may be distracted and/or emotionally unavailable. In addition to gaining attention, misbehaving also serves to activate a parent who is sad, depressed, or otherwise unavailable. This pattern of seeking negative attention can create a cycle in which the child increasingly acts out while the parent becomes increasingly frustrated and less likely to give positive attention to the child.

Positive reinforcement is a means by which a parent tells a child that he or she is pleased with a particular behavior and would like to see that behavior again. Many parents, especially during times of stress, tend to concentrate on negative behavior and forget to reward children for engaging in appropriate or positive behaviors. Earlier in this chapter, the importance of providing specific praise to reward and reinforce a child's positive behavior was highlighted. Rewards can also consist of hugs or physical affection, treats, special privileges, and/or participating in a parent–child activity. The therapist should encourage the parent to "catch the child being good," or, in other words, notice and reinforce each occurrence of positive behavior. This again encourages parents to focus on their children's strengths and recognize when their children are behaving well and also motivates children to increase their positive behavior.

Ignoring

In addition to increasing positive behaviors, parents often also need guidance on how to reduce the frequency of problem behaviors. Ignoring is one discipline technique that is effective in decreasing or stopping minor misbehaviors. As noted previously, children often seek attention from their parents by acting out or misbehaving. If the parent ignores the misbehavior and does not give the attention the child wants, then, in most cases, the child will eventually stop engaging in the behavior. This is especially true when a parent is practicing positive reinforcement, as the child has already begun to notice that the parent is responding with a lot of attention when he or she behaves well. Parents are often reluctant to ignore or have a difficult time ignoring, especially when the child is seen as going through a difficult time him- or herself. It is important to emphasize to parents that behaviors that can be ignored are mild misbehaviors intended to provoke or pester the parent. Behaviors that are destructive or physically harmful to the child, parent, or someone else should never be ignored.

Ignoring is most useful for decreasing a few negative or inappropriate behaviors that the child engages in often. Some examples include whining, kicking the back of the seat when the parent is driving, nagging the parent (e.g., saying "mommy, mommy" or "daddy, daddy" over and over again), tapping a pencil over and over on the table, and even temper tantrums. Ignoring these types of behaviors ultimately serves to reassure the child that there are limits and that it is better to get attention from positive behaviors rather than negative ones.

When a parent begins using the ignoring technique, a child will usually increase his or her negative behaviors in the hopes of provoking a reaction from the parent. It is helpful for the therapist to review strategies with the parent such as relaxation, walking away calmly, and distracting him- or herself with another activity to reduce frustration when trying to ignore his or her child. An important aspect of the ignoring technique is refocusing attention on the child when he or she stops the misbehavior and begins acting appropriately. This reinforces the idea that good behavior earns attention, but misbehavior does not.

Star Charts

Another way of reinforcing positive behavior is by using star charts. Star charts are a simple way of rewarding children for specific behaviors with stars, points, stickers, or other incentives and are most effectively used with preschool- and elementary-school-aged children. Using the handout *Star Chart* (Activity 7.3), the therapist can work with the parent to create a list of behaviors that he or she would like to see the child begin or improve. The first part of the handout illustrates a sample star chart for a school-age child, and the second part is a blank star chart to be used in session and then provided to the parent for use at home.

The star chart also provides another opportunity to help parents to reframe negative behaviors into goals for positive behavior. For example, a parent may indicate that a goal for his or her child is to stop hitting his brother. The therapist can encourage the parent to reframe the goal as "play nicely with his brother after dinner." This creates an observable behavior for the parent to notice and reward with a star or sticker and also encourages the parent to keep his or her eye out for good behaviors. After choosing two or three behaviors that seem most important for the star chart and reframing them in positive terms, the therapist can provide the parent with a sample chart and then enlist the child to help create and personalize his or her own chart. In most cases, it is helpful to create the initial star chart in session, which allows the therapist an opportunity to model clear communication and collaboration for the child and parent.

Activity 7.3

STAR CHART

Name: Andrew

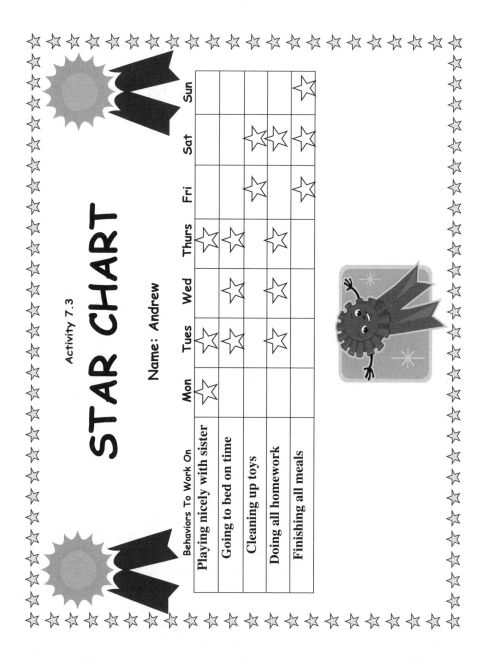

Behaviors To Work On	Mon	Tues	Wed	Thurs	Fri	Sat	Sun
Playing nicely with sister	☆	☆		☆			
Going to bed on time		☆	☆	☆			
Cleaning up toys					☆	☆	
Doing all homework		☆	☆	☆		☆	
Finishing all meals					☆	☆	☆

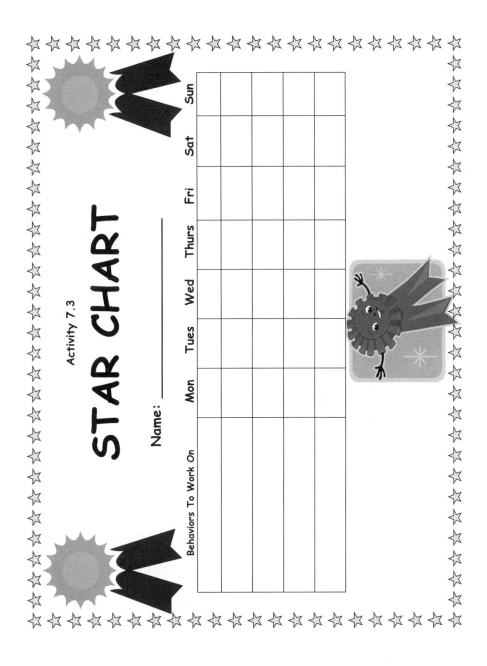

Activity 7.3

STAR CHART

Name: _____

Behaviors To Work On	Mon	Tues	Wed	Thurs	Fri	Sat	Sun

It is important for the therapist to be specific when discussing how to implement a star chart with a family. The use of a chart is most effective when it is done in a thorough and consistent manner. The simple presence of the star chart can be a symbol of routine and structure in a home that has gone through tremendous changes following a loss. The handout *Tips for Using Star Charts* (Activity 7.4) provides tips for parents about how to successfully implement star charts at home.

Clear Commands

A key element in improving a child's behavior is providing clear expectations. One way of doing this is being direct and concise when asking a child to do something and making sure the request is heard by making eye contact and speaking clearly and calmly. It is crucial that a child understand what it is that he or she is being asked to do. This is particularly important in bereaved families, where roles and responsibilities of both the parent and child have likely changed. Many parents inadvertently give vague commands or ask their child to do multiple things at once. For example, rather than telling a young child to "get ready," it is often helpful to say something like, "Get dressed in your room," and then, when that task is complete, "Now brush your teeth." When a child clearly understands what is being requested and still does not comply or misbehaves, then he or she may be given an appropriate consequence. It is helpful if the child knows in advance what the consequence will be for a specific misbehavior. However, the old adage "choose your battles" comes to mind, as not all misbehaviors should be punishable. The therapist should encourage parents to think about which behaviors are best to ignore and which require consequences. Parents must be consistent when setting limits and must follow through with consequences, or a child will quickly learn that he or she can "get away" with misbehaving. Again, consequences for misbehavior should correspond with reinforcement for positive behavior or obedience, with a focus on positive reinforcement. For example, in the case of a child for whom eating at mealtimes is an area of difficulty, on an evening when he is eating his dinner but is also fidgeting or rocking in his chair, the parent may choose to reinforce the positive behavior (e.g., "I like the way you're finishing everything on your plate!") and ignore the negative one. Parents should also be encouraged to give short commands rather than a long rationale or explanation for the behavior they would like to see. When parents are lengthy in their commands, they are more likely to lose the child's attention and are also providing more opportunities for the child to question or dispute what is being asked.

Activity 7.4 Tips for Using Star Charts

1. Clearly label the positive behavior and state in positive terms. (Make clear what you want to see happen!)

2. Discuss with the child exactly how he or she can earn a star (e.g., "Each day that you clean up your toys after playtime, you earn one star at bedtime").

3. Involve the child in deciding what the reward will be (e.g., "You will go out for ice cream with me if you earn 10 stars in one week").

4. Post the star chart in a place where it can easily be viewed. (This helps you remember to fill it in and provides the child with a sense of pride when others see all the stars that he or she has earned.)

5. Be consistent; the star chart should be filled in each day at the same time (e.g., bedtime).

6. If the child does not perform the desired behavior, then he or she does not receive a star for that behavior. The child should not have any additional consequences; not earning a star is enough.

7. Provide weekly rewards.

Time Outs

Another method of effective discipline is the time-out procedure, which is most useful for extreme misbehaviors in young children (ages 3 to 8). This is a form of ignoring and involves a brief period of time during which children are removed from all attention and reinforcement. The child must sit in a chair, preferably in a space that is away from all activity, and stay there for a few minutes without interacting with parents or other family members. This time period is effective because it is a way of disciplining that also gives the child the opportunity to gain control of his or her behaviors and emotions. The handout *Time-Out Procedure* (Activity 7.5) describes the time-out procedure and provides some tips for parents on how to effectively use this strategy.

WORKING WITH ADOLESCENTS

Although many of the strategies described previously are geared toward use with younger children, the conceptual framework also applies to working with preadolescents and adolescents. Adolescence is a time of significant transition and may be especially difficult for teenagers who have recently experienced a loss along with a number of other related changes in and out of the home. Behavior problems in adolescence may involve refusal to comply with parental rules or risk-taking behaviors, such as substance abuse, risky sexual behavior, delinquency, academic failure, truancy, and so forth. For these reasons, it is important for parents to maintain their role as a disciplinarian, a role that may have become more challenging as a grieving and perhaps newly single parent. It is often helpful to review with parents concrete ways of setting age-appropriate limits (e.g., enforcing curfews, setting limits on television and Internet use, providing consequences for disobeying family rules) and to encourage parents to include the teenager in routine family activities (e.g., an established family dinner time, chores, recreational activities). Although it is common for teenagers to prioritize social relationships with peers and to question rules set by parents, evidence indicates that helping parents to provide bereaved youth with consistent discipline in the home promotes favorable outcomes (Lin, Sandler, Ayers, Wolchik, & Luecken, 2004).

As explained previously, teenagers continue to rely on their parents to set limits and provide effective discipline as they seek autonomy and negotiate their independence. Navigating this conflict and achieving a balance can be particularly complex in bereaved families, as the death of a parent can interfere with or create obstacles in an adolescent's path toward independence. The process of mourning and the ensuing shifts in roles and responsibilities may pull these teenagers closer to the family fold, at the precise time

Activity 7.5 Time-Out Procedure

1. Explain how time out works to your child before using it.

2. When your child misbehaves, first calmly ask him or her to stop the undesirable behavior. Tell your child that if he or she does not stop the behavior, he or she will receive a time out. It is OK to provide one additional reminder, and if he or she does not obey, then he or she should be immediately sent to time out.

3. Calmly take your child to the time out chair without further warnings, reprimands, or comments.

Tips:

*   Time out should occur in a quiet place without distractions.

*   Any items that are breakable should be removed.

*   Do not respond to your child's comments or behaviors during time out.

*   The length of time out should correspond to the child's age, with 1 minute for each year of age (e.g., a 5-year-old gets 5 minutes).

*   The timer should start once the child has calmed down and is sitting quietly in his or her seat; should the child begin misbehaving again, the timer should be restarted.

*   Once time out is over and your child is behaving appropriately, reward this good behavior with a lot of positive attention.

*   Use the period when your child is in time out to relax and decrease your own frustration so you can interact positively with your child when the time out is complete.

*   Limit the number of behaviors for which time out is used.

that they were beginning to become more independent. In some cases, teenagers may even fall into the role of becoming a second parent, taking on extra responsibilities such as caregiving for younger siblings and serving as a source of support for other grieving family members. These issues, along with the multitude of feelings associated with grief, may lead to oppositionality and other acting-out behaviors (e.g., Van Eerdewegh et al., 1982). The therapist can work with the parent to set limits and effectively communicate with his or her child and can also help the teenager to express his or her feelings and develop more effective coping skills (see the section that follows and Chapter 9). Like younger children, adolescents are more likely to seek out their parents if they feel that they will be received with warmth and acceptance. In fact, it has been found that increasing parental warmth and consistency in bereaved families has a positive impact on both school-aged children and adolescents (Lin et al., 2004).

IMPROVING COMMUNICATION

Another area to be addressed in joint parent–child sessions is communication between the parent and child. The parent can be trained in techniques such as reflective listening to help foster positive communication, increase understanding, and decrease conflict. The therapist should first model reflective listening by allowing the child to speak his or her mind and giving empathic responses to the child's behavior and statements and then have the parent practice doing the same in session. Continued practice with this strategy can be assigned as homework between sessions. When working with children of school age and older, both the child and the parent can be trained in reflective listening skills, and these can be role played in session and practiced at home. Parents should be encouraged to kneel to the child's eye level and speak clearly and calmly in a soothing voice. The therapist should also review "talking rules" to be followed in session and at home. This includes turn taking, or speaking one at a time; not interrupting; and avoiding threats or insults. In addition, the therapist may encourage the child and parent to use "I" statements rather than focusing on what behavior the other person has done that has upset them. For example, instead of saying, "You always interrupt me when I'm on the phone!" an "I" statement would be, "I feel frustrated when you try to talk to me when I am on the phone because then I have to listen to more than one person." These rules should be framed as a means of helping the parent and child work together to resolve problems and conflict.

With adolescents, it is important to help the family understand that this part of the treatment aims to improve relationships, which should have the effect of decreasing problem behavior as well as increasing the parent's ability to be supportive and helpful. Both the teenager and parent should be provided with the opportunity to discuss issues that may get in the way of their ability to communicate effectively with each other (e.g., anger, lack of trust). In joint sessions, they should be invited to share their concerns with the same talking rules just described, without escalating tone and conflict. Part of improving the communication might involve clarifying and modifying both the parent's and teen's expectations of each other. For example, with a parent who continually becomes angry at a teenager for coming home late, a review of expectations may lead to finding that no curfew has been established or, if it has, that it can be modified relatively easily to a time that is more acceptable for both parent and teen. Improving communication is particularly important when working with bereaved adolescents and their parents, as it is essential that parents be available to talk to their teenagers about their grief and related stressors, as well as about the general challenges that all adolescents face.

Across all age groups, the role of the therapist is to aid the child and parent in working together toward their desired relationship. Examples from daily life are generally helpful and can be used in session. The parent and child can work together on a recent minor problem, such as a difficulty at school or a problematic peer interaction. The therapist can then ask the parent and child to generate potential solutions together, including ones that may have been successful in the past. The child and parent should be encouraged to evaluate the pros and cons for each choice and make a decision about which choice will be most effective. In the next session, the therapist can ask them to report about the effectiveness of the solution and continue to use this strategy around new problems that are presented.

RESOURCES FOR PARENTS

To effectively implement the strategies described in this chapter, parents may benefit from ways to manage their own negative feelings in the face of child misbehavior. Some specific techniques that may help parents reduce their own frustration and focus on managing their children's behavior include increasing emotional awareness, coping skills, self-care, and using social support.

Increasing Emotional Awareness

A common reaction to a child's chronic misbehavior is anger and frustration. However, the parent at times may also feel disappointed, sad, helpless, inadequate, worried, victimized, embarrassed, depressed, or worn out, to name a few. Helping parents to specifically label what they are feeling in a given situation may be useful in reframing their own responses and behaviors in a way that is similar to how they help their children. Parents should be encouraged to notice how their own feelings and behaviors may be impacting or escalating the situation at hand.

Grieving parents may be having their own complex reactions to the loss of their partner or ex-partner, and this may affect how they respond to their child's grief. For example, a parent who is working overtime to fill the role of two parents may perceive a child who persistently acts out as ungrateful, although the child's behavior is likely in response to his or her own grief. Empathizing with parents and helping them tease out their own reactions from the reactions of their children is often helpful.

Coping Strategies

When parents are calm, they can better discipline children in an effective and consistent way. Alternatively, when parents are feeling stressed or agitated, that is often a time when conflict can escalate in the family. Although increased awareness of one's own emotions is important, at times parents may need to actively distract themselves from negative feelings to better focus on the needs of the family. Distraction techniques include shifting their attention elsewhere, using positive self-talk, or leaving the stressful situation until they feel calmer.

It is important to remind parents of other coping strategies, such as deep breathing and relaxation (see Chapter 3 for a review), taking time out for themselves when they are angry or overwhelmed, and seeking emotional support. Although these skills may seem obvious, they are based on emotional and physical resources that are often depleted in grieving families. The bereaved parent is often a single parent, which is arguably one of most the stressful roles in society. Coping skills must be reinforced and practiced, along with encouraging social support and self-care, as described next.

Self-Care

Parents should be encouraged to engage in positive and pleasurable activities on a regular basis and to prioritize taking time for themselves. This is often difficult for parents, especially those dealing with their own grief and operating in a family system affected by loss. Many bereaved parents may feel that they must be continually focused on their children and other responsibilities. It is often helpful to explain to parents that they must take care of themselves to effectively care for their children. It should be emphasized that, like playing with their child, this can be done in a relatively short amount of time (10–15 minutes per day). Providing suggestions of activities that are relatively easy to fit into their schedules, such as taking a bath, phoning a friend, listening to music, gardening, and so forth, can be helpful in increasing their follow through with self-care.

Social Support

Bereaved parents may have to rely on social support in ways they did not before the loss. Those who have lost a spouse are not only grieving for their partner, but also taking on new roles as a single parent. The therapist can help the parent to identify his or her network of extended family and friends and discuss whom he or she can call on for specific needs (such as watching the kids for an hour or talking about feelings of sadness). This dialogue should help the parent to be aware of when he or she needs a break from grieving and household tasks, and should include brainstorming ways to make that happen. It helpful for the therapist to emphasize that many parents are often surprised at how willing others are to help during times of stress when asked for specific requests (such as picking up items at the market and so forth).

SUMMARY

This chapter guided the therapist in working with parents of bereaved children who are exhibiting behavior problems. Specific behavior problems commonly seen in children who experienced a loss were identified and discussed in the context of the grieving process. Strategies for increasing positive behaviors and decreasing negative behaviors were reviewed. The importance of increasing positive family communication and parental warmth was emphasized, as was helping parents of bereaved children to reestablish routines, provide consistent discipline, and communicate effectively following a loss.

III

ADDRESSING CHILDREN'S GRIEF AND BUILDING RESILIENCE

8

INITIATING THE GRIEF-FOCUSED PHASE OF TREATMENT

For those bereaved children who do not exhibit clinically significant symptoms, such as mood disturbance or anxiety problems as addressed in Part II of this volume, the tendency is for grief practitioners to provide non-specific, supportive therapy. Although this may be helpful for some, integrated grief therapy for children (IGTC) presents specific strategies to better address the specific needs of bereaved children. The IGTC model integrates tools from cognitive–behavioral approaches along with narrative therapy and family work to create an intuitive and usable approach to helping the bereaved child. The techniques that are presented in detail throughout Part III include facilitating the child's understanding of death, helping the child and parent to communicate about the deceased, improving problem-solving and coping skills, preserving positive memories, making meaning of the loss, increasing access to and use of social support, and helping children adjust to long-term changes brought about by the loss. Some of these strategies have been used in other bereavement intervention programs (for a review, see Genevro, Marshall, Miller, & Center for the Advancement of Health, 2004), and despite the limited research in this area, our approach uses those interventions proven to be effective whenever possible.

The current chapter provides an introduction to the grief-focused phase of treatment. Important concepts related to bereavement and loss are presented, including ways of discussing these topics with the bereaved child and his or her caregiver. Caregivers will learn normative reactions to loss based on the age of the child, along with information about how to best support the child as they grieve. Changes in family roles and responsibilities along with other secondary losses are also addressed, and goals for this phase of treatment are established. Finally, this chapter emphasizes the importance of fostering resilience and developing problem-solving skills to manage grief-related difficulties and everyday stressors.

ORIENTATION TO THE GRIEF-FOCUSED STAGE OF IGTC

For children who initially present for clinical services with symptoms of depression, anxiety, or behavioral problems, the strategies put forth in this section should generally be postponed until those symptoms have been addressed in treatment (see Part II of this book). For children who do not present with clinically significant symptoms, this chapter may represent the actual start of treatment (following a thorough assessment and determination of the need for therapy).

Getting Started

The first couple of sessions should be spent establishing rapport and generally getting to know the child, the parent, the family system, and how they relate to one another. During these early sessions of the grief-focused phase of treatment, the therapist should assess the family members' grieving process by eliciting the reactions of the individuals as well as the family unit to the loss. This may be done in a family session or individually with child and parent. For children who are preteen and younger, the parent should likely be included in this conversation.

The therapist should use the language of the child and parent when speaking of the loss, especially early on. For example, if the parent says, "When my husband was killed," then the therapist may use similar words when speaking of the death. If the child says, "Since my mom is gone," then the therapist should similarly use this language when talking about the loss. Later on in therapy, particularly if avoidance behaviors are an issue, the therapist may specifically want to help the child or parent to be able to say that their loved one has "died."

The following statements may be used to guide a preliminary conversation about grief with the child.

Therapist: Grief is a painful process that we all go through when someone we care about dies. When we speak about grief, we are talking about the feelings, thoughts, and behaviors that you have following the death of a loved one. It is different for everyone, and there is no one correct way to grieve or set of stages to go through. Grief does tend to be difficult, though. You are coming here for therapy to make the process easier and to help you fit your memories into a life focused on the present and the future.

In Chapter 3, we presented assessment questions about the nature of the death and the mourning process (e.g., rituals, ongoing stressors, coping strategies) for grieving children and their families. If this information has not already been gathered, then the clinician should do so at this point in the treatment. Otherwise, the clinician may choose to review this information and any important changes that have occurred since the treatment began.

In general, the therapist should reinforce any ways in which the family has begun to memorialize the deceased person, particularly strategies that help children remember the way in which the loved one lived as opposed to the way in which he or she died. Families should also be praised for engaging in activities that promote open communication among family members about their grief. If the child and/or parent states that they try to avoid remembering their loved one or that discussion of the deceased does not occur in an open way, then the therapist should let them know that therapy may help them to feel more comfortable facing the thoughts and feelings that typically occur when someone we care for dies.

Establishing Goals of Treatment

After having a preliminary discussion about grief in general, the therapist may discuss how this treatment in particular will help the family to navigate the grief process. Encouraging the parent and child to participate in setting goals for treatment is an important step toward establishing and maintaining a collaborative working relationship with the therapist. The following dialogue may be used to establish goals for the grief-focused phase of treatment.

Therapist: Now that I've had the chance to learn a little bit about you and your family, I'd like to talk to you about some things we will be doing together to help you with the grief process. In general, I will be working with you and your [mom or dad] to provide strategies to feel better and to cope with some of the difficulties you mentioned. (*Refer to specific problems mentioned during the intake and earlier sessions.*) Before we talk about some of these strategies in more detail, what are some things you would like to learn or improve in our work together? (*Make sure to take note of any goals presented by the child or parent and to frame their desires as strategies that may be targeted in treatment.*)

Some of the other things we will discuss during our time together include the way you think and feel about things at home, at school, and with friends, and how certain skills may help you cope with everyday stressors and overwhelming feelings. Later on, we will discuss [the deceased], what [he or she] was like, how you can best remember [him or her], and what life is like now. We will also work on helping you with all of the recent changes in your life.

There will also be times that I meet with your [mom or dad] to talk about strategies that [she or he] can be putting into place at home to help. I will always talk about this with you ahead of time and ask your permission if we are going to discuss anything that you have told me during our one on one time together.

CHILDREN'S REACTIONS TO LOSS ACROSS THE LIFE SPAN

For parents who indicate concern about their children's responses to the loss, the therapist may present the types of reactions that can be expected in the individual on the basis of the child's age and cognitive development. (For details about children's cognitive understanding of death by age, see Chapter 2.)

Although it is important for the therapist to have a working knowledge of children's reactions to death across the life span, the parent should only be presented with the information that is relevant for his or her family on the basis of the age and needs of the children. Because the types of reactions vary widely across families, it is up to the therapist to determine how much information should be conveyed at this point in treatment.

With children preschool age and younger, it is important for parents to provide reassurance that the children will continue to be cared for. Young children also tend to respond best to structure and routine, particularly during stressful situations. Parents of bereaved children should therefore be encouraged by the therapist to maintain a regular routine so that the children have a sense of stability and know what to expect day to day. It is important that adults do their best to maintain as much of a regular schedule as possible. This simple act tends to reassure children that they are being taken care of and that adults will continue to provide for them. Young children may ask a lot of questions, such as, "When is Daddy coming back?" It is helpful for caregivers to try their best to answer all questions that children ask. Responses to questions should be concrete and clear. Caregivers may need guidance from the therapist about how to answer specific questions in ways that are most helpful for the given child.

School-age children may need more help adjusting to some of the life transitions that tend to accompany the death of a significant loved one. For example, if there is a change of school or if the family is moving, children should be told what to expect ahead of time, and they should have an opportunity to express their concerns or worries. Children in this age group may also have more complex feelings about the death, including guilt, self-blame, and anger. The therapist may be able to help such children by providing a safe environment in which to explore these feelings and by helping the parent to support them in effective ways.

Preteens are often increasingly sensitive to feeling different from their peers and may begin to feel isolated after the death of a loved one. The therapist of bereaved children in this age group may help them to seek out and accept support from both family and peers and to figure out when and with whom they choose to share their feelings.

Bereaved adolescents are more likely to respond in ways that are similar to adults, but there are particular reactions to look out for. The therapist working with bereaved teens should assess for increased risk-taking behaviors, such as substance abuse and sexual promiscuity. Adolescents may also take on adult roles and responsibilities or experience tension around how to continue a developmentally appropriate process of separation and individuation. The therapist may help by normalizing this process and by providing the parent with guidance about how to handle changes in family members' responsibilities without placing an undue burden on the adolescent.

GUIDELINES FOR PARENTS IN SUPPORTING GRIEVING CHILDREN

Regardless of the age and comprehension level of their children, caregivers may be encouraged to follow certain basic guidelines to support them. The following section provides a general overview of suggestions to be presented to the parent in preparation for the rest of the grief-related work.

Although describing typical reactions based on children's age groups helps to increase caregivers' understanding of common reactions to loss and grief, it is important to emphasize that the experience of each person is unique and may vary widely among children of the same age range or among siblings in the same family. It is therefore important for caregivers to recognize their children's differences and to interact with them in a way that enables them to feel understood. By being responsive to the needs of each child, the parent conveys that the children are safe to express the many feelings that may accompany grief, including sadness, guilt, anger, ambivalence, and relief.

In general, children tend to react to the responses of those around them, so it is helpful for caregivers to maintain a calm atmosphere and a degree of normalcy during times of grief. For example, regular schedules of eating and sleeping should continue to be applied, as should limits on children's behavior. It should be noted that the suggestion to maintain a sense of normalcy and predictability does not mean that adults should not express their own sadness. On the contrary, it is often helpful for children to learn how to communicate their feelings from trusted and caring adults.

Children tend to benefit most from being around supportive persons who listen to their feelings, answer their questions, and follow their lead in engaging in dialogue about the deceased loved one. Many parents worry about talking too much or too little about death with their bereaved children. A helpful rule of thumb in talking with children is to provide as much information as is being asked and to do so as concretely and honestly as possible.

For example, if a school-age girl wants to play with friends after talking about her deceased mother, it is likely that she has heard enough for the moment and that she will raise the topic again when she is interested in hearing more. In contrast, if she continues to ask when she will see her mother again, an appropriate response may be, "Because Mom died, you will not be able to see her again. I know that you miss her, and that's hard." This answer is preferred over statements referring to abstract notions of death, such as, "You will see her in your dreams" or "She is watching you from heaven." Although such statements are intended to lessen the pain associated with grief, they are often confusing for children and may contribute to feelings of fear and isolation. Guidelines for supporting bereaved children are outlined on the handout *Looking Toward the Future: Guidelines for Helping Grieving Children* (Activity 8.1). This handout may be used in session to guide a conversation about bereavement in children, or it may be given to the parent for future reference.

Just as the therapist has met with the parent to discuss the child's understanding of death during the assessment phase, it is important to discuss the death with the child directly at a later point. This conversation should only occur after the therapist has developed a positive working relationship with the child and should not take place during the first few sessions unless the child raises the topic on his or her own. During the first one to three sessions, the clinician should follow the child's lead regarding whether or not and how much to talk about the deceased loved one.

FOSTERING RESILIENCE

Research regarding outcomes and consequences of early loss has shown that some bereaved children do not have significant clinical problems and instead demonstrate significant resilience (Luecken, 2008). *Resilience* refers to the ability to thrive in the face of adversity and life challenges. A key component of resilience is a focus on the positive (e.g., one's strengths) as opposed

Activity 8.1 Looking Toward the Future:
Guidelines for Helping Grieving Children

- Remember that bereavement is a process that occurs over time and that there are not necessarily right and wrong ways to grieve.
- Listen to your children to find out how they are feeling.
- Follow your children's lead about when and how much to talk about what happened.
- Answer children's questions using language they can understand.
- Keep in mind developmentally appropriate responses.
- Provide reassurance through your own sense of calm.
- Be aware of how your own worries may affect your children.
- Watch for changes in behavior (e.g., changes in sleeping or eating, acting out).
- Expect minor fluctuations in mood.
- Allow children to make choices about attending memorials and dedications.
- Discuss with children how to talk about the deceased loved one with new people or in new situations (such as in school or with friends).
- Talk together as a family about handling special occasions (e.g., anniversaries, birthdays).
- Openly talk about the deceased to preserve memories for your children.
- Use the support of friends, family, and professionals.

to the negative (e.g., one's emotional and behavioral symptoms). In an effort to include work on resilience in treatment, it is important to highlight the strengths of the child and the family both explicitly (e.g., through verbal praise) and implicitly (e.g., by focusing on abilities rather than on presenting problems and symptoms). This may be done throughout the course of treatment, including intake, goal-setting, and therapy sessions.

Talking About Resilience

Although many strategies aimed at fostering resilience are incorporated throughout IGTC, it is suggested that the therapist explicitly introduce resilience as a key target of treatment. By talking about resilience early on in the grief-focused sessions, the therapist conveys that treatment will be focused on providing tools that will help the family to adjust to the loss and on fostering the family's strengths to help the children thrive. The following dialogue illustrates the way in which the therapist may convey this message.

> *Therapist:* Resilience refers to the ability to achieve good developmental outcomes in the face of loss and other stressful life events. It implies that while we are all affected by hurtful experiences, we can continue to grow and thrive in spite of them. This is an important component of the work we will be doing together.
>
> There are many factors related to resilience, including self-esteem, belief in yourself, looking forward to the future, adapting to change, and using humor. So, one lesson is that not only is it ok to think well of ourselves and to have a good time, but it's the healthy thing to do!

Focusing on Strengths

During a discussion about resilience, the therapist should explore with the child and parent individual and family strengths and work to develop factors associated with resilience, such as feelings of self-esteem, self-efficacy, optimism, parental warmth, and a perceived ability to cope with significant change (Lin, Sandler, Ayers, Wolchik, & Luecken, 2004; Luecken, 2008; Sandler et al., 2003).

Bereaved individuals may be hesitant to allow themselves to have or acknowledge positive feelings or experiences during the grieving process. When talking with bereaved individuals, therapists may hear about challenges to adapting to loss, such as feelings of guilt or ambivalence about finding ways to be happy again. It is not unusual for bereaved persons to feel that when they are not actively grieving, they are betraying the person who died. Furthermore, they may worry that if they stop feeling sad, then it is as if they are no longer loving or missing the deceased. Part of the therapist's role is to help the bereaved individual see that it is possible to grieve and to still be involved in some of the pleasures of living at the same time.

The therapist may ask questions to guide a discussion about strengths, to assess challenges to adapting to the loss, and to learn about personal resources that may be fostered throughout the therapy process. The following questions can be asked of children:

- What are some of your favorite things to do? How often do you get to do these things? Does anything stop you from doing things that you enjoy?
- Which of your accomplishments are you most proud of? What do you think your parents are most proud of?
- What are some things you would like to achieve over the next few months? How likely do you think it is that you will meet these goals?
- What, if anything, would you like to change about yourself if possible? What would you like to change about the way things currently are in your family?

The following questions can be asked of parents:

- What are some of your favorite things to do with your child?
- How often do you do things together, spending individual time with your child as well as spending time together as a whole family? What are some things that stop you from engaging in pleasurable activities more often?
- Which of your child's accomplishments are you most proud of? (Notice whether the child was aware of parent's pride, and comment on parent's pride if appropriate.)
- What are some things you would like to achieve for yourself and for your child over the next few months? How likely do you think it is that you will meet these goals?
- What, if anything, would you like to change about yourself if possible? What would you like to change about the way things currently are in your family?

SECONDARY LOSS EXPERIENCES

The loss of a loved one necessarily results in many life changes, some minor (e.g., a child needing to take responsibility for walking the family dog after school) and some quite considerable (e.g., need for family relocation or changes in financial status; Luecken, 2008; Worden, 1996). Felner, Terre, and Rowlison (1988) proposed a framework for understanding the multiple changes that occur in a child's life following a major event such as the loss of a caregiver or other loved one. These additional life changes may be described as secondary losses, in that they stem from a major primary loss and contribute to changes in the daily life of the bereaved. Secondary losses are important to note because they tend to impact the way in which a child, and potentially a whole family, is able to grieve and ultimately resume daily living.

The impact of secondary losses may be particularly relevant when the deceased is a caregiver who previously helped with all of the day-to-day household tasks, such as child care. When families are transformed from dual to single parent households, it usually follows that stress level in the home increases and the ability of family members to properly care for themselves and each other becomes strained. Common changes that may follow the death of a loved one are listed in Table 8.1. The therapist should note that these losses take many forms and that even a single change may impact the child in a number of complex and overlapping ways. For example, the primary loss of a caregiver might result in a series of secondary losses including changes in discipline, reduced

TABLE 8.1
Secondary Loss

Area of loss	Changes
Home life	Changes in daily routine: change in person responsible for waking child–preparing child for school; change in child's mode of transportation to and from school; change in handling of daily scheduling of activities and events; change in meal time or in types of meals provided; change in bedtime routine, such as bath and story time; change in sleeping arrangements; decreased help with homework
	Changes in family member roles: increased participation of children in daily chores and housework, increased responsibilities among children for self-care, change in which parent is providing discipline, change in which parent is the primary wage earner, change in financial stability of family, increased contact and reliance on relatives (aunts, uncles, grandparents), older children and teens feeling like "second parents," widows–widowers feeling overwhelmed about being a single parent
School life	Difficulty concentrating in school, excessive absences from school, decline in academic performance, having to change schools because of relocation
Social relationships	Feeling "disconnected" or "different" from peers, social withdrawal–isolation, decreased time spent with peers because of increased family responsibilities, impact of possible relocation on established relationships

help with homework, and different types of meals being prepared, not to mention the emotional impact of losing a parent. The death of a caregiver may also lead a family to move to a new home, which, in turn, would potentially result in a series of changes, such as decreased contact with close friends, a change in schools, and separation from a familiar home and community.

Although the specific ways in which secondary losses impact a given family must be assessed through ongoing observations and interactions, the following guidelines provide an overview for preliminary education about and assessment of secondary losses with bereaved children and their parents. The clinician's primary goal in this process is to guide the family in identifying areas of life that are most impacted by the loss, to normalize difficulties that the family has as a response to significant changes, and to empower the family to work together in finding more adaptive solutions to problem areas.

TALKING WITH BEREAVED CHILDREN ABOUT SECONDARY LOSS

Depending on the role of the deceased in the child's life, the therapist should assess for secondary losses, including changes in daily routines, family roles, home and school environments, and social relationships.

> *Therapist:* When a loved one dies, we are often left with a lot of changes in our everyday life. So not only do we miss the person, but we are also faced with changes in all of the areas that the person used to be involved in. Sometimes, this leads to a ripple effect of events, so that one change leads to another, and so on.
>
> I'm wondering if you can help me to understand some of the ways in which things are different for you at home, at school, and with your friends. What are some of the noticeable changes for you?

The following questions may be used to elicit information from the child about how things have changed since the death of a caregiver:

- Describe your morning routine before school.
  - (For younger children) How do you wake up in the morning?
  - (For younger children) Who picks out your clothes? Makes you breakfast?
- What about after school and on weekends?
  - Whose responsibility is it to make sure homework is complete?
  - What chores do you do?
  - What do you do for fun?
- How are things at school?
- What are things like with your friends?

- What are things like at home with your mom–dad–siblings?
  - (For preteens and adolescents) After a parent dies, some kids notice that they have started to take on a lot more responsibilities, including doing some things that mom or dad may have done before. Have you noticed any of these kinds of changes in your own life?

For all areas discussed, ask the child how things are different now, compared with how things were before. After evaluating secondary losses across the different domains of the child's life (home life, school, and social support), the therapist should assess for particular areas in which these changes are problematic.

> *Therapist:* It seems that a major area of change has been . . . (*Reflect back on some of the major life changes mentioned by the child.*) What has that been like for you? What are some difficulties resulting from this change? What are some things that are going well with this new change in routine?

PROBLEM-SOLVING SKILLS

Basic problem-solving skills may be introduced at this point as a way of addressing some of the problems identified previously. These skills should be presented in a simple and concrete manner, thus providing the child and parent with strategies that may be readily used to address problem situations.

The therapist should use his or her judgment in deciding which problems to target with the parent and child together and which to address with the parent or child individually. For example, parents and children should work together on problem solving related to trouble adjusting to new routines for young children and for conflicts related to changing roles and responsibilities for teens. For problem solving around instances in which an adolescent feels different from his or her friends, however, it may be more helpful to discuss the situation individually without the parent present.

Problem solving should be presented using a series of discrete steps, with each step following naturally from the previous one (e.g., D'Zurilla & Goldfried, 1971; Shure & Spivack, 1978). The first step in solving a problem is to identify or define it. The therapist should choose a problem already identified by the child to work on in session. Next, the child should brainstorm possible solutions without censoring him- or herself. The child should be encouraged to generate as many alternatives as possible without judging whether these are necessarily the right solutions for the given situation. Because this is a therapeutic exercise, the therapist may want to offer suggestions if the child seems stuck.

After a sufficient number of potential solutions are offered, the next step is to evaluate the pros and cons of each alternative. For each potential solution, the child should be encouraged to question what the likely outcomes are and whether the solution is a practical one to put into action. On the basis of this evaluation, the therapist may help guide the child toward choosing a suitable option. Children should be encouraged to evaluate the outcome of the brainstorming session by using the solution of their choosing. The handout *Problem-Solving Skills* (Activity 8.2) outlines the problem-solving steps described earlier and may be used in session as a tool to help the child work on a specific problem or conflict that has been previously discussed. Children should be encouraged to use these steps during the week and to report on how they were able to solve a problem on their own. Consider the following case example.

Fifteen-year-old Brenda recently moved to a new town with her father and younger brother, following the death of her mother a couple of years ago. She has been struggling with whether to tell her new classmates that her mother has died and with how–when to reveal this part of her life once she makes friends.

Brenda:	In my old school, everyone knew about my mom. I mean, I never even told anyone what happened—they just knew. But now, I feel like I have this big secret.
Therapist:	You feel like it's a secret that your mom died?
Brenda:	Yeah, well, I feel like it's this huge part of my life that people don't know about. But I also like not being known for that, and I really don't want to bring it up. I don't think I would know what to say anyway. There's one girl who is kinda becoming my best friend here, so I'd like to tell her, but I don't know how.
Therapist:	So it sounds like you've been struggling both with when to tell and also how to tell once you've decided that the time is right.
Brenda:	Exactly.
Therapist:	Well, maybe we can brainstorm a bit about this issue using the problem-solving steps we talked about last time. Which part of this would you like to work on first?
Brenda:	The thing with my new friend, Chloe, is really bothering me. I feel like the more time that goes by, the weirder it gets.
Therapist:	OK, so it sounds like you want to talk to Chloe about your mom, but that you don't know where to start. Is that right?
Brenda:	Yes. I mean, what can I say without sounding like I want pity?
Therapist:	Well, before jumping to what it sounds like or how she will respond, let's back up and start with the first step of problem

Activity 8.2 Problem-Solving Skills

1. Define the problem.

2. Brainstorm alternative solutions.

3. Evaluate pros and cons of each potential solution.

   - What is the likely outcome for each?

   - How likely is it that you could put this plan into action?

4. Based on your evaluation, choose the best option and put it into action.

5. Evaluate the outcome.

   - Did you achieve the solution you were hoping for?

   - Why do you think this option did or did not work?

6. Based on your evaluation, do one of the following:

   - Give yourself self-reinforcement, a pat on the back. ("Hey, I handled that really well.")

   - Determine what went wrong and use a coping statement. ("Oh, I made a mistake. Next time I'll take my time thinking more about the outcomes and then I'll do better.")

solving. I have the handout here to remind us of the steps as we go along.

Brenda: OK, so I need to define the problem, which is how to tell Chloe that my mom died.

Therapist: Great, you've defined the problem. What's next?

Brenda: The handout says to come up with solutions, but I don't really know.

Therapist: OK, let's start by coming up with what you would like to say, or some of the things you have thought about saying, without worrying about how they sound. When you think of telling Chloe, have you thought of anything in particular?

Brenda: Yeah, a couple things. I thought of not telling at all, which is what I've been doing. I thought of waiting for her to ask about my mom, and I've also thought about just coming out and saying, "I want to tell you that my mom died."

Therapist: So you've already come up with three alternatives, which is terrific. Sometimes it helps to just get those down on paper, which is why I'm writing these three options down now. Can you think of any other solutions?

Brenda: Not really.

Therapist: OK, so let's go through each one. What do you think of the first option—not telling Chloe about your mom dying?

Brenda: It feels weird, and it's starting to feel like I'm lying.

Therapist: So this choice doesn't seem to feel good for you. Are there any benefits to this option?

Brenda: No, I'm pretty sure I don't want to do that one.

Therapist: Great, so you're already further into making a decision than you may have realized. Let's move on to the second option, waiting until Chloe asks.

Brenda: That's a good one because I can be honest and wait for the right time, and it will give me a reason to tell her.

Therapist: So there are some benefits to waiting to talk to Chloe. Are there any downsides?

Brenda: Yeah, I still kinda feel like I'm lying the more time that goes by. And I don't know when she'll ask me or if she's waiting for me to explain where my mom is.

Therapist: So this option has pros and cons—the good part is you don't have to bring up the topic yourself, but the bad part is the timing. You would be waiting for Chloe to bring it up, and you don't know if or when that will happen.

Brenda: Right, so now I'm thinking that I should just tell her myself.

Therapist: So that's the third option . . . telling her that your mom died sooner, or whenever you're ready. You've already said the benefit of this choice, which is that less time will go by that way. Any downside?

Brenda: Well, it will be hard to say it, but I think that would be true whenever I talk about it anyway.

This example illustrates how problem solving may be conducted in session with a bereaved child. The therapist would then help the child set up a plan for enacting the chosen solution, which, in this case, was telling her friend that her mother died. For example, the therapist might ask the child if she would like to role play the conversation with her friend. The therapist would also follow up with the child during the next session to see how the plan went and to reinforce her use of problem solving in facing a challenging situation.

SUMMARY

This chapter provided an introduction to the grief-focused phase of IGTC. It explained how therapists can assess the child's and family's ability to talk about the deceased, changes that have occurred since the death, and challenges the child may be facing in the process of grieving and resuming daily life.

The chapter also explained how to teach parents about children's normative reactions to death and how children may be best supported in their grief. The child and parent express their own goals and desires for this part of the therapy, and they begin to learn about ways to facilitate their adjustment to the loss. In addition, they learn about some of the factors associated with resilience, and they succeed in problem solving around one or more conflicts related to the loss.

9

COPING SKILLS FOR GRIEVING CHILDREN

Theorists propose that the experience of bereavement tends to bring about changes in thinking about the self, about life, and about the world in general. According to Janoff-Bulman (1992), three basic assumptions may be threatened by loss: (a) the self is worthy; (b) the world is a benevolent place; and (c) the world is meaningful, so that what happens in the world makes sense. The bereaved person is faced with the realization that bad things can happen (to us and to those we love). Janoff-Bulman and Berg (1998) pointed out, however, that coping does not require returning to previously held assumptions or focusing on the loss, but rather maintaining the possibility of loss while living.

This chapter introduces integrated grief therapy for children (IGTC) strategies that may help the bereaved child and parent to cope with potentially overwhelming thoughts and feelings about themselves, others, and the world, so that they can resume the tasks of daily living. It primarily focuses on the cognitive–behavioral therapy (CBT) coping skills previously reviewed for the treatment of specific symptoms and applies them toward distressing grief-related thoughts and feelings. It should be noted that although CBT has not yet been thoroughly examined for use with grieving children in general, it has been recommended for treating children presenting with traumatic grief in particular (Cohen, Mannarino, & Deblinger, 2006) and bereaved adults (Malkinson, 2001), as well as various other problems of child-hood as reviewed in Chapter 3.

THOUGHTS, FEELINGS, AND BEHAVIORS
THAT ACCOMPANY GRIEF

As discussed in Chapter 3, a basic foundation of CBT is the interplay among thoughts, feelings, and behavior. The therapist may ask questions to guide the child in a discussion about thoughts, feelings, and behaviors that tend to accompany the grieving experience.

To assess feelings, the therapist can ask the following:

- What are some things that remind you of the deceased?
  - What kinds of activities did you do together?
  - Are there certain places that remind you of him or her?
  - What time of day were you more likely to be together?
  - Who are the people in your life that make you think of him or her?
- How do you feel when you are thinking about the deceased?
  - What does your body feel like at these times?
  - What do you feel in your chest?
  - Your stomach?
  - Other parts of your body?

To assess thoughts, the therapist can ask the following:

- What are some thoughts that you have when reminded of the deceased?
  - What goes through your mind when you are doing something that you used to do together?
  - What do you say to yourself at these times?
- How do you think you are handling the loss?
- How much hope do you have that things will get better?
- What kinds of changes do you see in yourself since the loss?
- How much control do you think you have in your life now?

To assess behaviors, the therapist can ask the following:

- Are there certain things that you do to help you remember?
  - Is there someplace you go to think about him or her?
  - Do you look at pictures of your mom–dad–other or talk to people about your memories?
- Are there things you avoid so that you will not think about the death?
  - You mentioned that you used to (refer to activity described above) together. How often do you do that now?

- Are there other things that you don't do because they remind you of your mom–dad–other?
- Are there things that you do to help yourself when you feel particularly sad?

During this type of discussion, the therapist should pay particular attention to patterns of negative thinking that may be related to grief. Examples of negative thinking among bereaved children include assumptions about the self (e.g., "I'll never be that happy again") and the world (e.g., "Life is not fair to take away such a good dad"). These types of thoughts may promote negative feelings and increased physiological symptoms. For example, a negative thought such as, "I'll never be that happy again," may be followed by somatic symptoms, such as stomach problems or headaches, which, in turn, may lead to increased negative thoughts, such as, "I feel bad whenever I think about my dad."

Imagined alternatives (e.g., "If only I had done something different, everything would have been OK") are also common among persons struggling with grief (Fleming & Robinson, 2001). This type of thinking, in which the bereaved person imagines how things may have been different if the situation was changed in some way, seems to occur regardless of the actual circumstances surrounding the loss and is often related to self-blame. For example, a bereaved wife may have thoughts such as, "If only I had been using the car that day, my husband wouldn't have been in that accident."

It is not unlikely that bereaved persons will look for a reason for the death and find blame in themselves, perhaps because doing so allows them to lessen their sense of helplessness and randomness in the world (Janoff-Bulman & Berg, 1998). In other words, self-blame may actually be seen as a coping strategy, in that it helps one replace feelings of vulnerability with some sense of control (Fleming & Robinson, 2001). In contrast, self-blame and other cognitive tendencies in the face of loss may hinder the bereaved person's ability to accept the loss and to grieve in a helpful way. Imagined alternatives, self-blame, and the like are therefore important for the therapist to take note of as the child and parent talk about their thoughts and feelings about the death and about themselves. Strategies from the IGTC approach for addressing and changing these types of cognitions are discussed later in this chapter.

GRIEVING IN WAVES

Grieving individuals often describe their feelings of yearning and sadness as "coming in waves," or ebbing and flowing over time. Following the period of active mourning immediately after the death, days or even weeks may go by during which the bereaved person is going about daily life and not thinking much about the deceased. This period may be followed by a seemingly sudden feeling of grief, which is often precipitated by a reminder of the person who died. When these waves occur, family members may experience feelings that further complicate the grieving process, such as guilt over having resumed normal activity, frustration that they are moving backward in their grief, and being overwhelmed by having feelings come when they are not expected. For children, these waves may be particularly stressful, as children may struggle with understanding death and its impact on others and are less likely to have developed effective coping skills to manage their upsetting thoughts and feelings.

It is helpful for the therapist to acknowledge these waves of grief and to normalize these experiences as part of the grieving process. By understanding that certain emotional experiences are to be expected, children and parents may be better prepared to face them. Children and parents can also manage feelings of intense grief with the specific coping skills described in the next section.

COPING STRATEGIES TO MANAGE THOUGHTS, FEELINGS, AND BEHAVIORS

Cognitive, affective, and behavioral coping strategies may be helpful in situations related to grief, including problems that developed following the loss as well as previously existing problems that were exacerbated by the loss. It should be emphasized that some children find certain coping strategies to be more helpful than others. For example, some children are naturally more cognitive in their approach to the world and enjoy thinking things through using logic and evaluation. These children are likely to respond better to cognitive coping strategies than to behavioral coping strategies. Alternatively, other children are more behavioral in nature, meaning that they may respond better to more concrete behavioral interventions. The therapist should therefore not feel that all approaches must be used for all children—this is not a one size fits all type of approach. Instead, we encourage therapists to think of coping strategies to manage thoughts, feelings, and behaviors as different options that may be found in a large toolbox of choices. As with the rest of the IGTC approach, flexibility is key. The therapist may therefore choose to focus on certain strategies that seem to make the most sense for a given child.

It should be similarly noted that some children find certain coping strategies to work best at some times, whereas other strategies are more helpful at other times. For example, a child might find a particular cognitive coping strategy to be helpful in improving his or her mood one day but not the following day. Whether a particular strategy works at a given time may be related to a child's mood, stress level, and other situational factors. For this reason, the therapist is encouraged to present as many "tools from the toolbox" as possible, so that the child has various techniques at his or her disposal.

Cognitive Coping Skills: Managing Negative Thoughts

This section presents three approaches to helping children cope with overwhelming or otherwise distressing negative thoughts: (a) cognitive restructuring, which is focused on changing the thought; (b) managing the thought, which involves strategies to decrease the impact of the thought; and (c) leaving the thought alone, or knowing when the negative thought cannot or should not necessarily be changed.

Before beginning this section, it is important to note that these cognitive coping skills are not meant to minimize the bereaved child's profound loss or sadness, nor are they meant to encourage avoidance of all negative thoughts. The therapist's goal in IGTC is to intervene with those thoughts that are causing persistent distress for the child. At this point in treatment, the child will have had the opportunity to openly express his or her feelings about the deceased in numerous ways and to receive empathy and support. The therapist should encourage continued emotional expression while using the following techniques to modify thoughts that are interfering with the child's ability to resume adaptive functioning. The examples of the different techniques illustrate when cognitive coping skills may be necessary and how they are beneficial in managing grief and fostering resilience.

Cognitive Restructuring

Before introducing specific coping strategies used to change potentially negative thoughts, feelings, or behaviors, it is important for the therapist to review the Triangle of 3 presented in Chapter 3 with the child. This discussion should emphasize the way that thoughts, feelings, and behaviors interact as well as demonstrate how changing one element of the triangle (e.g., thoughts) causes changes in the others (e.g., feelings and behaviors). The following dialogue between therapist and child illustrates this type of review. This dialogue is appropriate for use with school-age children but may be modified for use with older children or adolescents.

Therapist: As you know from our previous talks about the Triangle of 3, thoughts, feelings, and behaviors tend to go together and influence each other. I'm going to tell you a story about a girl your age named Stacy. Stacy had what we called "stinking thinking"—her thinking caused her to feel bad about herself and to do things that kept her feeling bad. One time,

Stacy had a big math test coming up, but she was sure that she was just terrible at math. She thought that there was no way she could do well on the test.

- What is Stacy's stinky thought?
- How do you think Stacy felt when she had these thoughts?
- What do you think she did about the test?

Stacy felt so bad about her math skills that she got a tummy ache whenever she thought about it. The more she thought about math, the more sure she was that she was terrible at this subject. When it came time to study, she felt like it was useless because she was going to fail anyway. So she didn't study at all. The night before the big test, Stacy went to bed early with a tummy ache. She was not surprised when she couldn't understand the questions on the test and she fully expected to get a failing grade, which is in fact exactly what happened. After all, Stacy knew she was terrible at math, and now she had more proof that she was right.

- How do you think Stacy's stinking thinking affected her actions?
- What could she have thought instead? Was there any other way of thinking about the situation?
- What do think might have been different if Stacy had a different thought about herself and her math abilities? How do you think the final outcome would have been different?
- Can you think of any stinking thinking that you have had lately?

After reviewing negative thought patterns and their impact in general, the therapist may move on to specific negative thoughts previously endorsed by the child. If the child reported negative thoughts about him- or herself during the discussion about the cognitive triangle and grief, then these thoughts should labeled as such and further explored for the ways that they affect the child's feelings and behaviors.

Therapist: One of the things you have said is that since your dad died, you feel sad whenever you think about him. Now that we've talked about how thoughts and feelings work together, maybe we can take a look at the thoughts and feelings you have about your dad to see if we can change that connection.

Child: Well, I get sad every time I think about my Dad.

Therapist: And when you say that you're sad when you think about your dad, can you describe some of the feelings that you have in your body when this happens?

Child: Well, I don't feel like doing anything, really.

Therapist: Would you say that you get tired and have less energy when thinking about your dad?

Child: Yes, like it's really hard for me to just to get up and do anything.

Therapist:	So when you remember your dad, you get sad and have less energy. What else?
Child:	I think about how different my life is now that he's gone.
Therapist:	So you think about how different things are now. Could you tell me more about that?
Child:	I think about how things could have been different. I think about how he died and how maybe it didn't have to happen that way.
Therapist:	Different, how?
Child:	Well, he had a heart attack, and I wonder if we could have done something to prevent that. Like if we made sure he ate healthier or if my brother and I fought less.
Therapist:	It kind of sounds like you blame yourself for your dad's heart attack.
Child:	I guess so. I hate feeling this way.
Therapist:	That makes sense—it sounds awful to feel so sad, and also to think that maybe things could have been different.

One of the goals of therapy is to reduce the child's negative thoughts about him- or herself, others, and the world. As described in Chapters 3 and 4, the therapist does this by working with the child to examine the evidence that supports or challenges negative ideas. Questions such as, "What's the evidence to support this view?" and "How would you respond if you had a different expectation?" may be used to guide this exploration. The handout *Be Your Own Detective: Questions to Ask Yourself When Having Negative Thoughts* (see Activity 4.3, Chapter 4) lists typical questions that may be used during this process.

Continuing from the previous example, the therapist can help the child to realize that not only is he or she blaming him- or herself for what happened, but that also these thoughts are detrimental and can be changed.

Therapist:	Remember when we talked a while back about how negative thoughts, feelings, and behaviors go together? We said that when someone has negative thoughts, that negative feelings and behaviors usually follow.
Child:	Uh-huh.
Therapist:	Well, it sounds like that's happening here. You think that you may be to blame for your dad's death, or that you could have somehow prevented it, and you end up feeling bad and then not doing fun things. When bad things happen, lots of people—not only kids, but adults too—blame themselves for what happened. So, it makes sense that you have these

thoughts, but the problem is that it is making you feel bad. I'm going to have us play detective a bit and ask some questions to see if your thoughts are worth hanging on to.

Child: Yeah, I remember when you told me about this.

Therapist: Good. Let's start with the idea that you could have done something to prevent your dad's death. What evidence is there to support this thought?

Child: Well, I know that my dad didn't like when I fought with my brother. He said it made him sad.

Therapist: So we know that when you and your brother fought, your dad got sad. What happened next?

Child: Usually, we stopped fighting when he told us to.

Therapist: So we know that you stopped fighting when your dad asked you to. Do we have any evidence to show that your fighting caused your dad's heart attack? Or that if you fought less, he wouldn't have had the heart attack?

Child: Not really.

Therapist: What about the day that your dad had the heart attack? Were you fighting then?

Child: No, I wasn't even home when it happened.

Therapist: OK, so we don't really have evidence to show that fighting with your brother *caused* the heart attack. Is there any other way that you can think about or explain what happened to your dad?

Child: I'm not sure. I don't really understand why it happened. Everyone says, "He was so young," like it shouldn't have happened. But no one can tell me why it did happen.

Therapist: So, we don't know why it happened, which makes it really hard to understand. But, it seems like you know that it's unlikely that the heart attack was caused by your fights with your brother. How would your feelings be different if you believed that there was nothing you could have done to prevent your dad dying?

Child: I would still miss him just as much, but I wouldn't feel so guilty about what happened.

As mentioned throughout the course of this book, it is important to make abstract concepts such as cognitive processing as concrete as possible when working with children, using age-appropriate language. School-age children tend to be less verbal than adolescents and adults, so a nonverbal, concrete approach to presenting abstract ideas is preferred. One way of doing this is to present the child with cartoons containing empty "thought bubbles" to represent what the characters (which may include animals and people) are thinking, a strategy we first introduced in Chapter 6. Depending on the ideas that the therapist wishes to convey, thought bubbles may be presented with certain content already filled in, or they may be presented empty so that the child can fill in the thoughts that he or she attributes to the characters in the picture. The clinician is referred to the handout *What Are They Thinking?* (Activity 6.1, Chapter 6) for examples of thought bubbles representing various situations. The clinician is encouraged to create different examples or to have the child create his or her own, based on the individual needs of the child. This technique may be valuable in helping children who have difficulty expressing themselves verbally to identify their negative thoughts and feelings.

Managing Thoughts

Whereas the strategies described in the previous section are intended to help children change unhelpful or exaggerated negative thoughts that may be interfering with their daily lives, other thoughts may not be amenable to change for various reasons. For example, an adolescent may think to him- or herself, "I hate that my dad isn't here," when faced with an important life event. This thought reflects a true fact of the adolescent's life that cannot be changed and that must be acknowledged and empathized with. Even these types of thoughts that are based in fact, however, may need to be managed to some extent if they are impacting the bereaved child's daily functioning.

There are also times that the child has a negative or unhelpful thought while in a situation that calls for a response that is quick and immediate. For example, if a child is having negative thoughts when sitting down for an exam, then there may not be time to examine the evidence for and against the thought. For situations during which the child is unable to use cognitive restructuring techniques, alternative strategies for managing the thought (and decreasing its strength and frequency) may be used.

Self-Monitoring. In addition to challenging the child's negative thoughts, there are times when it is helpful to simply monitor the occurrence of these thoughts and their impact on feelings and behaviors. Self-monitoring is useful because it helps the child pay attention to his or her thoughts and slows the thinking process down so that the negative thoughts become more conscious (and less automatic). This process may occur in the form of a thought diary that outlines which parts of the thoughts and situations are important to pay attention to. This format is more preferable than an unstructured diary, which may be more confusing to the child (and in our experience, less likely to be completed). In general, a thought diary should include four components (Stallard,

2002). These components are (a) the child's negative thoughts, (b) evidence supporting these negative thoughts, (c) evidence not supporting (or evidence against) these thoughts, and (d) a more balanced thought.

Self-monitoring may be presented to children as a way to increase awareness of negative or "stinky" thoughts and a way to practice changing those thoughts. For older children, self-monitoring may also be used throughout the course of treatment as a way to monitor the progress they have made. It is interesting to note that we have found children to be more open to thought monitoring than adults, perhaps because they are more accustomed to keeping diaries, doing homework, and engaging in other activities that require monitoring.

The handout *Thought Diary* (Activity 9.1) provides a thought log that may be used by the child between sessions. It should be noted that this handout serves as a template, which the therapist may vary according to the needs and style of the given child. For example, some children may be more interested in being creative and producing their own diary. The therapist should work with the child to create an individualized format, reminding the child to include each of the four elements of self-monitoring listed earlier.

Positive Self-Talk. Positive self-talk is a way to help the child focus on the positive rather than the negative. The basic premise is to have the child identify the negative thoughts or negative self-talk and to recognize that the situation is usually not as dire or catastrophic as it may seem. Again, this strategy is not intended to minimize the child's feelings of loss or to be an oversimplified "think positive" approach, but rather as a way of helping a bereaved child who is having unrealistically negative thoughts to identify this negative pattern and develop a more realistic and adaptive outlook.

For example, 9-year-old Michael often felt sad when thinking about the things he used to do with his dad, and he found that he hardly ever did these things at all anymore. His negative self-talk included thoughts like, "Now I have no one to play catch with." With the help of his therapist, Michael was able to see that this type of thinking made him feel sad and lonely and that he could instead think about who he could do those things (like playing catch) with instead. Again, this does not imply that the therapist should not acknowledge the sadness and empathize with the child, but it does suggest that absolute statements (such as, "I have no one," in this case) be modified whenever possible. In session, Michael developed new positive self-talk statements, such as, "My grandpa can play catch with me," and "I will call my friend Danny to come over and play this afternoon."

Positive self-talk may also be used to reinforce a child's coping skills. For example, 18-year-old Lisa always hated going to the doctor, but she really avoided it after her grandmother died. She thought about all the doctor's visits that her grandmother had and how they had not been able to prevent her from

Activity 9.1 Thought Diary

What were you doing when you had the thought? (Trigger)	List your negative thought	What evidence supports your thought?	What evidence goes against this thought?	What is a more balanced thought?

dying in the end. Eventually, Lisa recognized that her situation was a lot different from her grandmother's, and she decided to make an appointment for her checkup. She was still nervous, however, and she asked a friend to go with her to the doctor's office for support. After the appointment, Lisa told her therapist about it, and she said that she was embarrassed about making such a big deal about a checkup. Lisa's therapist encouraged her to focus on her strengths and to feel good about the fact that she asked for support and that she went to the doctor at all. The therapist not only praised Lisa for facing her fear, but she encouraged her to say, "I did it, good for me!"

Distraction. A third strategy for managing negative thoughts is distraction, which may be useful in situations when the bereaved child is feeling particularly overwhelmed or when other coping strategies are proving unhelpful. There are different ways to distract oneself, including engaging in pleasurable activities, like calling a friend and listening to music, or doing something active, like riding a bicycle.

Another technique that may be useful for those thoughts that are otherwise difficult to manage encourages the child to distract from negative thoughts by focusing instead on narrating what is happening in the present situation (Stallard, 2002). This strategy was used by Alexa, a 9-year-old girl who often worried about her father's health after her mother died. She understood that her father was currently healthy and that there was no evidence that he would get sick, yet she still found the negative and worrisome thoughts running through her mind. When she had such thoughts, she could not seem to focus on anything else. In these situations, she distracted herself from the thoughts by paying close attention to what was going on around her. For example, she would tell herself, "I'm on the school bus on my way home. I am sitting next to the window, and I see all of the trees and houses going by. We are at a red light, next to a big white house. There is a blue car, a station wagon, in the driveway. The house has children's toys, including a red wagon and a baseball, on the front lawn. We are now three blocks from home." Alexa found that when she was narrating her surroundings, she was unable to think about her worries at the same time.

Taken together, the aforementioned cognitive coping strategies provide a toolbox of options the bereaved child can use when he or she becomes overwhelmed by negative thoughts. These strategies are reviewed in the handout *Managing Negative Thoughts: Your Toolbox* (Activity 9.2) to remind the child what to do during times of distress. This handout may also be reviewed with the parent, who can, in turn, help the child practice the strategies at home.

When to Leave a Thought Alone

All bereaved children are expected to experience negative thoughts and feelings related to grief and sadness. These feelings are most likely to be

Activity 9.2 Managing Negative Thoughts:
Your Toolbox

The following strategies are all available to you in your toolbox, to use whenever you need them. . .

• Play detective. What's the evidence for or against the belief?

• Be aware. Pay attention to and monitor your thoughts so that you can see when you're thinking in an unhelpful way.

• Be positive. Use positive self-talk to change negative thoughts.

• Distract. Think about happier times or places.

And remember. . .

• Practice helps! The more you use your tools, the more helpful they will be.

• Any tool might be helpful sometimes and not other times. Don't worry. . . just try to use a different tool!

• You know yourself best. Use whatever tools work most for you.

expressed when the child is talking about the loved one or is otherwise reminded of the deceased. For example, a child telling her therapist about preparing herself to begin high school might comment that she wishes her mother were there to take her shopping for school clothes. Longing for the parent during significant life transitions is a normative response, and there is no reason for the therapist to discourage doing so. Most of these thoughts and feelings are not only normal, but also serve a purpose in allowing children to experience their grief and mourn their loved one.

When the thoughts are so persistent or negative that they are distracting the child from having positive thoughts and feelings, however, they may warrant the types of interventions presented earlier. In other words, negative thoughts that are interfering with daily living and that are prohibiting the child from generally feeling good may be the target of intervention.

Affective Coping Skills: Managing Feelings

Most of the coping strategies presented thus far have been cognitive coping strategies, meaning that they were focused on helping the child to change or at least manage troublesome thoughts. The IGTC model emphasizes that it is equally important to address feelings and behaviors that contribute to the child's overall sense of well-being.

One potentially useful affect management strategy is positive imagery. *Positive imagery*, simply put, refers to using one's imagination to evoke positive feelings. The patient visualizes a situation or place that feels good and imagines all of the sights, sounds, and smells that happen there. The child may choose to imagine a place associated with happy times or a desired outcome that has not yet happened.

The use of positive imagery may be illustrated by continuing the example of 9-year-old Alexa described previously. As mentioned, Alexa often worried about her dad's health, and she continued to experience feelings of sadness and longing for her mother for months after she died. During times when she felt particularly sad or felt like the grief was overwhelming, Alexa found positive imagery to be helpful. Alexa's positive imagery involved the beach, including its sights, sounds, smells, and tastes. For example, Alexa visualized herself standing on the beach in her red bathing suit, feeling the warmth on her face, the sweat on her back, and the sand in between her toes. She also imagined the smell and taste of the salty air and the sounds of the waves crashing. She used all of her senses to evoke an image that helped her to feel calm, safe, and secure.

In this example, Alexa chose to imagine a place that helped her to feel happy but that did not necessarily remind her of her mother. For Alexa, it was important that she be able to generate imagery that could help her distract herself when her feelings of grief became so intense that they were interfering with her school work or sleep. It should be noted that other bereaved children may prefer to generate imagery that includes representations of the deceased loved one. For example, children may feel soothed by imagining that the parent who died is watching over them while they are sleeping or that the parent is whispering words of encouragement in their ears. The important thing to remember with this (and all strategies presented as part of IGTC) is to generate techniques that resonate with the individual child and are helpful for his or her unique circumstances.

Another use of positive imagery is to help a child manage feelings related to potentially difficult situations. In cases like this, the child may envision him- or herself coping with the stressful situation in a successful way, thereby improving self-efficacy. For example, Charlotte had always become anxious before her soccer games. When her mother was alive, she would occasionally complain of stomach aches when it was time to leave the house for a game, and sometimes her mother would let her stay home. Other times, her mother would reassure her that it was just a game and that she would do great. Now that her mother was not available to her, she thought about quitting the team. She told the therapist that she wanted to continue playing but that her stomach aches had gotten more frequent since her mother died. The therapist encouraged her to imagine playing a great game while she was at home getting ready for the soccer game (which is when the stomach aches most often occurred). She was told by her father and the therapist that it was her choice whether or not to continue on the team but that this strategy was available to her if she chose to use it.

In addition to positive imagery, relaxation strategies, such as deep breathing and progressive muscle relaxation, may also be used to help children manage overwhelming feelings. These affective coping strategies have been described previously in Chapter 3.

Behavioral Coping Skills: Managing Reactions and Behaviors

A third area of coping skills, following cognitive and affective strategies, is coping skills for managing behaviors. Although behaviors are typically thought of as reactions to one's thoughts and feelings, there are situations in which behaviors serve to perpetuate negative cognitions and emotions. For example, some studies have found an increased incidence of oppositional behaviors among bereaved children, especially boys (Dowdney et al., 1999; Kranzler, Shaffer, Wasserman, & Davies, 1990). When this occurs, the children and their parents often end up feeling even more overwhelmed and out of control. For bereaved families in which the children demonstrate increased rule breaking and other acting-out behaviors, the therapist should take the time to review with the parent the behavior management skills presented in Chapter 7.

In addition to overtly negative behaviors, such as acting out, more passive behaviors may also perpetuate negative thoughts and feelings. For example, bereaved children and parents may avoid situations and withdraw from people that remind them of their grief and loss. Although the avoidance may bring temporary relief, over time it may become more difficult to reengage in social relationships and pleasurable activities.

Even more so than children, parents often need to be reminded to have fun and add enjoyable activities to their schedules, for themselves (alone or with other adults) and for the family as a whole. For example, Kristen was a young mother of 5-year-old Daniel when she became suddenly widowed. Although she had previously been involved in Daniel's school as a class volunteer, she naturally had less time and energy for these types of activities after her husband died and she became a single parent. She stopped arranging play dates for Daniel, too, mainly because she did not want to face talking about what happened with other parents. A year went by before Kristen realized that Daniel had not interacted with any children outside of school.

The primary behavioral interventions that we have found to be helpful with Kristen and others like her are education about the impact of avoidance and encouragement to resume positive activities. The therapist may also use strategies such as problem solving (introduced in Chapter 8) and cognitive restructuring (introduced in Chapter 3) to address challenges to resuming positive activities, such as hesitation to try new things, difficulty finding a babysitter, and guilt about enjoying oneself in the aftermath of loss.

Children may also have a difficult time reengaging in activities and social situations after a loss. In particular, parentally bereaved children may find it challenging to attend situations where other children will be with their parents, such as school functions and sporting events. The therapist may discuss these events with children to help them anticipate the feelings they might have and problem solve around how they might choose to handle such situations. The therapist may also encourage the surviving parent to facilitate these types of conversations at home.

PARENT AS HELPER WITH COPING STRATEGIES

Most of the coping strategies reviewed in this chapter require practice at home and are more likely to be used by the child who has assistance and encouragement from the parent. For all strategies presented, the parent should be instructed by the therapist on how the technique should be used (by the child as well as by the parent) and how he or she may help the child in using the coping skill effectively.

Praise and other forms of positive reinforcement should also be reviewed with the parents in terms of how they may encourage the use of positive coping techniques. Praising children is most effective when the praise is given immediately after seeing the good behavior, when it is specific (in that it describes the behavior that is being praised), and when it is given in a warm, enthusiastic voice. For example, 9-year-old Alexa (described earlier) told her dad over breakfast that she was worrying a lot about him getting sick. After a few minutes, she remembered that this type of thinking was not helpful and she allowed her dad to talk with her about their plans for the day instead. Immediately following this, Alexa's father told her with a big smile that he was really proud of the way she put her worries aside to focus on the present. This encouraged Alexa to use her distraction techniques and other coping strategies the next time she had worrisome thoughts about her father's health.

SUMMARY

This chapter has described the use of cognitive, affective, and behavioral strategies in the treatment of bereaved children. These children often face overwhelming thoughts and feelings related to their loss and may feel that their basic sense of safety and control has been compromised. It is important to carefully assess what thoughts, feelings, and behaviors are most disturbing for each individual child. The therapist can normalize these grief experiences and help the child to cope more effectively.

Three types of coping skills (cognitive, affective, and behavioral) were presented in this chapter. Cognitive coping skills include cognitive restructuring (including the use of strategies such as the "thought detective"), self-monitoring through the use of awareness and thought diaries, positive self-talk, and distraction. These interventions are designed to help children reduce maladaptive ways of thinking that impact their behaviors, feelings, and general mood. Affective coping skills include the use of imagery to evoke positive feelings, along with relaxation strategies. Affective coping skills are designed to help children reduce overwhelming feelings, including sadness, worry, and anger. Behavioral coping techniques include the encouragement of self-care for both parent and child, psychoeducation about the impact of avoidance, and problem-solving strategies.

Coping skills are important not only for the child but also for the parent. As noted throughout the IGTC approach, it is important for the therapist to aid the surviving parent not only for reducing his or her own distress but also for the impact of parental functioning on bereaved children. Educating the parent about coping skills thus helps parents manage their own thoughts, feelings, and behaviors and reinforce the skills with their child at home.

10

MAKING MEMORIES AND INTEGRATING PAST AND PRESENT

In line with other current grief models (Bonanno & Kaltman, 1999; Klass, Silverman, & Nickman, 1996; Neimeyer & Stewart, 1996; M. Stroebe & Schut, 2005), the integrated grief therapy for children (IGTC) approach proposes that bereaved individuals should preserve and continue a bond with their lost loved one. Our work and the work of others suggest that both bereaved children and adults greatly benefit from maintaining a connection to the deceased and integrating their memories of their loved ones into their current lives (e.g., Rando, 1985; White, 1988). This differs from earlier conceptualizations of grieving as a process that encouraged bereaved persons to work toward saying goodbye or letting go of the deceased, a task that tended to lead to further grief and sadness. In facilitating the grief process, therefore, one important role of the therapist is to help the child put relationships in a new perspective, rather than encouraging separation or detachment from the deceased (Silverman, Nickman, & Worden, 1992).

This chapter provides IGTC strategies and techniques that give bereaved children the space and the opportunity to talk about their loved one and thus to maintain an ongoing connection with the person. The first step in this process is eliciting positive memories of the deceased from the child (e.g.,

Haine, Ayers, Sandler, & Wolchik, 2008) while addressing the complex and potentially conflicted emotions the child has about the person and the loss experience. After allowing the child to reflect and feel connected to his or her lost loved one, the child should then be encouraged and helped to share memories in session with the surviving caregiver. Rituals can be created to help the family to continue this type of remembrance at home, ensuring that the child will have opportunities to reminisce about the person who died with supportive family members and friends. Finally, this process involves addressing changes in identity that often come about after a significant loss. The goal of these strategies is for the child to preserve and organize his or her different memories of the deceased, allowing him or her to maintain an attachment to the parent and also enabling a sense of continuity of self before and after the loss. The framework is consistent with Worden's (1996) tasks of mourning for children, which include (a) accepting the reality of the loss, (b) working through the pain and emotions associated with the loss, (c) adapting to an environment without the deceased, and (d) relocating the deceased into their emotional lives and finding ways to memorialize them.

To begin this type of work with the bereaved child, the therapist must ensure that the child is prepared to manage the multiple and distressing feelings that inevitably emerge when processing memories of the deceased. In light of the challenging nature of this process, the tasks described in this chapter build on everything the child has learned up until this point in treatment. It is particularly important that the child has had the opportunity to build coping skills for managing grief (Chapter 9) and has had the opportunity to work through the potentially traumatic aspects of the parent's death (Chapter 5) before beginning to share and integrate his or her memories of the deceased.

SHARING MEMORIES

Bereaved children in need of treatment are often bothered or distressed by memories of their deceased parent. At times, they even question when it is that they will no longer think about the deceased, as they believe that the only way to feel better is to have fewer memories and thoughts about their loved one. One means by which we have been able to help these children is to find a way to change how they view or experience their memories; in other words, to help them use their memories as a source of comfort and even happiness rather than having their memories cause only distress and sadness.

The distress around memories of a loved one may be associated with a variety of factors. For some, the focus of memories, including one's own and those of the people around them, is on the way that the person died. The child and family think or talk about the circumstances surrounding the death; for example, that the person was too young, that the death was not fair or was too sudden, and so forth. Part of the task for the IGTC therapist, therefore, is to help the child focus not on the way the person died but also on how they lived. This is not to suggest that feelings about the death itself should be avoided, but it does emphasize the benefits of remembering the whole of the loved one's life rather than just the way the life ended. Particularly when the death was violent or traumatic, the images, thoughts, and memories associated with the death may be so frightening or horrific that the child avoids thinking about the person altogether, including thoughts that might otherwise be comforting reminders of the deceased (E. J. Brown & Goodman, 2005). In these cases, the trauma-focused component of treatment (Chapter 5) must be completed before beginning this work.

Another source of distress is often related to the reactions of others when the child shares memories of the deceased. Some children find that they reminisce about their parent on their own but do not feel they can share those memories with family members or friends. This may be because they wish to protect their living parent or other family members from feelings of sadness or worry. They may also have experienced reactions from others such as not knowing what to say, or, at other times, others may have tried to comfort them when they are not seeking comfort. A therapeutic goal, therefore, is for the child to find appropriate ways to talk openly about the deceased with others in a helpful way when so desired.

Yet another aspect of building positive memories is to acknowledge other feelings that conflict with or complicate the sharing of positive feelings about the parent. Children often present with feelings of anger, guilt, and confusion related to their experience of loss (Haine et al., 2008). They may be confused about why the parent died and about the meaning of the death. They may also express angry feelings toward the parent for things he or she did while alive and for, in the child's mind, leaving them alone by dying. Although these complex feelings may have been discussed in previous sessions when working on coping skills for managing grief, they are likely to come up in some form as the child processes memories of the deceased. Ways in which the therapist can help the child to process conflicted feelings are discussed later in this chapter.

Eliciting Positive Memories

The simple act of asking bereaved children to think about positive experiences with their deceased loved one may allow them to reconnect with aspects of the person they have not thought about or considered in a long time. It also provides an opportunity for the child to talk about the loved one in an accepting environment and gives the therapist the chance to both encourage and reward reminiscing. If the child was too young at the time of the loss to recall specific memories about the loved one, then he or she may be prompted to present what he or she has learned from others or from seeing videos and pictures. The child can be engaged in this process using a variety of modes: verbally; through artwork (e.g., creating a book of memories); or by bringing in photographs, videos, and/or other reminders of his or her parent. With younger children, the surviving parent should be encouraged to actively participate in this process by identifying appropriate memorabilia to share. With adolescents, the therapist should encourage the individual to share the memories of the parent that he or she holds most fondly. The dialogue that follows illustrates one way of introducing positive memory making in session.

> *Therapist:* We've talked about a lot of different things in our time together, and I've heard about how your dad died and about how you are doing. I'd love to hear more about your dad and what he was like. Is that something you would like to talk about with me?

The idea is to present sharing memories as an opportunity for the child who feels ready or wants to do this. Children should not be pushed to share memories or talk about the deceased if they are not so inclined. The following example demonstrates how to elicit memories from a child who is ready to share. The therapist is talking with 11-year-old Gina, whose father died 3 months prior to the start of treatment.

> *Therapist:* I'm glad you feel like sharing your memories.
>
> *Gina:* Where should I start?
>
> *Therapist:* Well, what was your dad like? What did you two do together?
>
> *Gina:* He was really tall. We always used to kid around that he wished I was a boy, until he realized that I could play basketball, too.
>
> *Therapist:* (*Smiles*) So did you play with him?
>
> *Gina:* Yeah, we had a hoop in the backyard. When I was little, he used to let me win, but before he died I was really beating him fair and square.
>
> *Therapist:* You're really creating a neat picture in my mind—I can see you beating him!
>
> *Gina:* Can you see that he's bald and sweaty?
>
> *Therapist:* I can now. Actually, if you'd ever like to bring in some pictures that might help me see him even more.

Gina:	Hmm, I haven't really looked at his pictures in a while. I actually don't even know where my mom put the old family albums, and I'm afraid to ask.
Therapist:	Afraid?
Gina:	Yeah, well, I don't want to upset her by asking about pictures of my dad. She's been through enough.
Therapist:	I see. How do you know that asking about pictures would upset your mom?
Gina:	Well, she even cries when we get mail for Dad.
Therapist:	So it sounds like you really want to protect her from feeling sad.
Gina:	Yeah.
Therapist:	So you don't see the pictures because she put them away and you don't want to upset her by asking about them. I'm still wondering, would *you* like to see the pictures again?
Gina:	Actually, yeah, I'd like to show you what my dad really looked like.
Therapist:	How would it feel to ask your mom for the pictures, even if she did get sad or even cry?
Gina:	I'd feel bad. But I also feel bad that I don't know where they are.
Therapist:	So it sounds like there are negatives to saying something and to not saying something to your mom. Which sounds like the better option?
Gina:	Well, if I don't say anything, then I still feel bad. And if I do ask for the pictures, at least there's a chance we can talk about him together or I can look at the pictures on my own.

In this example, Gina readily described her father to the therapist, but she struggled with involving her mom in the process of remembering. As noted in previous chapters, the therapist's understanding of the child's response to the death in the context of his or her family system is essential to IGTC. The surviving parent will have his or her own reaction to the death, and the therapist must delicately address the transactional grieving process between child and parent when facilitating the sharing of memories. In this case, the therapist helped Gina to identify her needs in the context of her family and to problem solve around having those needs met.

Other children may have more difficulty sharing memories that have been avoided or "shut away" for a while. In these cases, it may be helpful to use prompts to ask about concrete aspects of the experience in a way that helps the child remember. The following questions may facilitate the child's reminiscing:

- What did your dad look like?
- What kinds of things did your dad do in his free time?
- What kinds of things did you do together?
- What foods–songs–TV shows did he enjoy?
- How does it feel now to talk about these memories?

If the child has a hard time answering these questions, then the therapist should assess whether this is because they elicit anxious or sad feelings or because the child does not have a clear memory of the event. If the child becomes anxious or upset, then the therapist may use relaxation techniques and other coping skills learned in previous sessions to help the child to feel calmer. At times, it may be helpful to move on to the next step in the IGTC model, which is to enlist the parent to help the child by filling in missing details and to collaborate by creating a shared memory of the loved one that they can return to in the future. It may also be that verbally discussing memories may not be the modality that is most suited for a particular child. We have used everything from art to songs to photos and videos to help children to express themselves.

Specifically, it is often helpful to have the child create a memory book to preserve his or her memories of the deceased. The therapist should encourage the child to be creative, using photographs, artwork, pictures from magazines, and so forth to make the book as lively and meaningful as possible. With teenagers, the book can be presented as a kind of journal, which may include any thoughts, poems, quotes, or other materials that help them express their feelings. The handout *My Memory Book* (Activity 10.1) is a template that may be used to guide the creation of a memory book with a child or adolescent, either after reviewing the child's memories or as a means to help the child to remember. This template should be modified according to the individual needs of the child.

Addressing Conflicted Feelings

As the child discusses memories, it is important to provide space and language for the child to articulate his or her affective response to the loss and to express potential ambivalence about his or her relationship with the deceased. This may be difficult because there is a tendency (among children as well as adults) to sometimes feel pressured to say only positive things about someone who has died. It is important for the therapist to normalize feelings of guilt, shame, anger, and confusion about the deceased, as well as to provide opportunities to resolve conflict and express hurts. Specifically, the therapist can explain to the child that all children have conflicted feelings and thoughts about their parents, whether they are alive or deceased. The therapist can

My Memory Book

(paste photo or picture here)

By

On

Important Things I Know About My Mother

Important Things I Know About My Father

Our Family Traditions and Special Occasions

Activity 10.1 My Memory Book (Continued)

Special Things About Me

My Special Memories

My Favorite Pictures

model acceptance of this conflict by matter-of-factly stating, "That's how people, even parents are—some parts are good, some parts are bad." Integrating both the positive and negative aspects of the parent into memory and accepting the parent for his or her strengths and flaws is an ongoing process and can be considered a lifetime goal for the child to aspire to. Some techniques that are helpful in this process include imaginary dialogue and writing letters to the deceased, which are illustrated in the following two case examples.

Maria, a 14-year-old girl whose mother died in a car accident several months prior to coming to treatment, was continuing to struggle with anger toward her mother and feelings of guilt about the conflict in their relationship prior to the death. With the encouragement of the therapist, she wrote a letter to her mom in which she was able to articulate her feelings of hurt and betrayal. This is an excerpt from that letter.

> You were always so hard on me—you even complained about what I wore when I went out with my friends. Your first question when I came down the stairs was always, Are you sure you want to wear that? It seemed like no decision I made was good in your eyes. I feel like I'm so unsure of myself now.

Maria was invited to read the letter aloud to the therapist, provided that she felt comfortable doing so, and this expression of emotion was of great therapeutic benefit. The therapist talked with Maria about how she felt criticized by her mother at times and helped her to recognize that this was one aspect of their complicated relationship. By allowing her to express these emotions and supporting her ability to describe the range of feelings she had toward her mother, the therapist normalized that conflict is present in many relationships and that it is OK to talk about and remember all parts of who her mother was.

Alison is a 15-year-old girl whose brother committed suicide the year before she began therapy. To deal with her feelings of anger and betrayal, Alison wrote letters to her brother in which she asked him the questions that had been plaguing her about why he chose to end his life. She also expressed how much she missed him and how the family is different without him. The letter writing was followed by imaginary dialogues with her brother in session in which she asked him questions about what he was going through before he died, alternating between playing herself and playing her brother and imagining what he might say. Part of integrating the loss meant knowing that she would never have all the answers, and the therapist helped her to express her feelings about this.

Normalizing Thoughts and Feelings

Another way to explore beliefs, particularly those related to blame or guilt, is to provide the bereaved child with examples of thoughts and feelings that another child expressed following a loss. Learning how other children have felt when faced with similar circumstances may help to normalize complex or unexpected emotions and reduce feelings of isolation. The handout *How I Felt After My Dad Died* (Activity 10.2) illustrates one child's feelings after her father's death. The therapist may read through the list with the child and discuss similarities and differences with his/her own grief experience. The language used in the example provided should help the child to express his/her own difficult or ambivalent thoughts and feelings.

Sharing With the Family

Many bereaved families come to treatment seeking guidance as to how to talk about the deceased parent with their child. Some assume that it is best not to discuss the lost parent in the child's presence for fear of upsetting the child. In the early phase of bereavement, an important task is for the surviving parents to help their children develop a language that allows them to talk about the lost parent (Silverman et al., 1992) and to maintain a place in their minds and hearts for the parent throughout their cognitive, social, and emotional development. To guide this process, the next step in the IGTC treatment approach is to bring the surviving parent to session and have the child share memories with the parent as he or she did previously with the therapist. For example, the child may choose to include the parent in a conversation about the deceased, may share his or her memory book or some artwork, or may ask questions about the deceased that have come up during the memory making exercises. This gives the therapist an opportunity to model for the parent appropriate ways to discuss and remember the deceased with the child and lays the groundwork for continuing these types of discussions at home. The therapist may also encourage parents to provide information about what the deceased parent's values and ideals had been. However, it is strongly urged that using the relationship as a form of indirect discipline be discouraged (e.g., "Your dad would be disappointed!"). The child may be encouraged to instead look to their knowledge of the deceased as a way of seeking comfort during stressful times (e.g., asking, "What would my father tell me now?").

We have found that children and parents benefit from being prepared for the sharing of memories with each other ahead of time. For example, in the case of Gina described previously, she expressed that talking to her mother about her dad was hard for her but that she wanted to be able to do so. It would therefore be therapeutic for Gina if her mother were able to be receptive to the memories and supportive of Gina without being overwhelmed by her own emotions. The therapist could help the mother do this either by preparing her for the types of memories to be shared (with permission from the child) or by discussing

Activity 10.2 How I Felt After My Dad Died

I thought I would never be happy again.

I thought my family was going to fall apart.

I felt bad I did not say goodbye to him.

I felt guilty because I did not spend time in the hospital with him.

I felt deserted.

I thought it was my fault because I stressed him so much.

My friends did not know how to act towards me.

I didn't cry for a long time.

I felt more free. That scared me.

I felt like I loved him more than my mother.

I thought I would never have anyone to give me advice again.

I was afraid my mom would die too and I would be an orphan.

strategies for managing her feelings (see Chapters 3 and 9) so that she could tolerate the material being presented.

When the parent is having difficulty responding in a way that is helpful or comforting to the child, the therapist may use specific exercises to facilitate a meaningful discussion. One example is to have part of a session devoted to the child speaking to the parent while the parent focuses only on giving verbal and nonverbal reassurance (without correcting or otherwise interrupting the child in any way). In cases where the child and parent engage in a dialogue that takes on a negative or unhelpful focus, the therapist may need to meet with the parent alone to provide constructive feedback and more education on reflective listening. In other cases, the child may be encouraged to provide feedback to the parent about what he or she needs to feel supported, but only if the therapist assesses this type of interaction to be tolerable for both child and parent.

In cases where the child indicates a desire to hear more about the deceased from his or her surviving parent, it may be helpful to encourage the parent to share a positive memory of the deceased and the child doing something together. This shifts the focus to the parent temporarily but aids in the child's ongoing recollection of the deceased and sets a template for mutual sharing at home. It also provides an opportunity for a family with a great deal of conflict to remember that there were positive times as well.

In cases where the child–parent relationship is highly conflictual and they are having difficulty engaging in any type of successful dialogue, the therapist may invite the parent to observe a discussion between the therapist and child either in the room or through a one-way mirror with the child's permission. This would allow the therapist to model for the parent how to respond to the child in an appropriate and supportive way. With all of these techniques, it is critical to prepare both the child and parent beforehand and debrief afterward individually when possible.

The use of some of the aforementioned techniques may be illustrated by the case of Diana, a 14-year-old girl whose mother died from AIDS 2 years ago. Her father has been an unstable presence throughout her life, and she was cared for her by her maternal aunt after her mother's death. Diana had few clear memories of her mother, and although some of them were positive, such as playing games and cooking together, they also included memories of her mother using drugs and being sick a lot. Her aunt brought her to treatment because she felt that Diana had begun to engage in some troublesome behaviors, including staying out late, neglecting her schoolwork, and involving herself in unhealthy relationships. Diana reported that she no longer cared about school or pleasing her aunt and that she was feeling depressed and isolated. After working on strategies to reduce her symptoms of depression and oppositional behavior, the next part of therapy consisted of eliciting in detail the memories she had of her mother, both positive and negative.

Diana expressed that she had been reluctant to discuss her mother with her aunt, for she felt her aunt disapproved of her mother and also believed that raising her was a burden to her aunt. The aunt was brought into session, with Diana's permission, to work on their relationship and to help fill in some of the gaps in Diana's memory of her mother. Her aunt explained that she had been trying to protect Diana by not bringing up her mother, as she thought the memories would be too painful for her to bear. The clinician's facilitation of this conversation was helpful in modeling for Diana's aunt the importance of incorporating Diana's mother's memory into their present lives, which, in turn, served to strengthen Diana's relationship with her aunt.

CHANGES IN SELF-IDENTITY

Another key component of treatment is helping the child to understand changes in identity and self-concept related to the loss (White, 1998). In our experience, bereaved children struggle with this in different ways. The loss of a parent may conflict with children's basic sense of trust and safety. It counteracts the perception of parents as a secure base, or, in other words, a place for children to turn to when feeling threatened or alone.

Bereaved children also struggle with the impact of the loss on their identity or sense of self. They may feel that their experience of loss is what defines them, both in how they think about themselves and how they are viewed by others. Many bereaved children describe how family and friends see them as a child who suffered a loss or more simply as "the kid whose dad died." This often comes up when a child meets new people after he or she experiences a loss. In most cases, it is important for the therapist to encourage the child to not see the loss as his or her defining characteristic, but rather to share this experience, just as he or she would share other parts of him- or herself. The therapist must help the child to process the loss but also to recognize that the death of a parent does not wholly define who he or she is. Consider the following case example.

Jenna, a 12-year-old girl whose father was a police officer killed in the terrorist attacks in New York City on 9/11, began junior high school 5 years after her father's death. In elementary school, all the teachers and students had known the circumstances of her father's death, and she felt it defined her in their eyes. When starting in junior high, she decided not to initially disclose about her loss to her new school community. Over time, she shared her experience with close friends and teachers she developed a personal relationship with. Although not directed to tell or not tell, her choice was supported by the therapist, as it allowed her to feel that although her father's death was a piece of her identity, there were other parts of her that were important, too.

Life Story

Particularly for older children and adolescents who are struggling with these types of identity issues, it is therapeutic to expand on the memory book concept described earlier and help the child to create a life story. It is often important to specifically include aspects of what their life was like before and what it is like now. The therapist should encourage the expression of these types of thoughts and feelings verbally or through artwork to help the child build up his or her sense of who he or she was before and who he or she is now without the parent, understanding both what has changed and what has stayed the same. What follows is an example of a life story written by a 14-year-old girl during sessions organized around what life was like before and after the loss of her father, including what is expected for the future.

My Life With My Dad Before:
My dad really liked to do all kinds of things—going to the beach, to the movies, for a walk—he never wanted to stay at home. So he would take us out and my mom would have time to herself. Even if I didn't feel like it, my dad would convince me to go out and I usually ended up having a pretty good time.

Once he took me to a concert and I remember that really well because it was just me and him and I was wearing a really awesome dress that I also wore to a dance at school. Since I was the oldest and had to do more than my little brothers, my dad would once in a while take me to do something just us. I remember my dad said he heard ringing in his ears for days after the concert. Every time I said something to him, he would scream What?? I can't hear you! And we would both laugh.

Every year for winter break in February we would go visit my grandparents in Florida. It was my dad's favorite trip. I think we are going to go this year, but it won't be the same. I think if I can make it through the trip and not be too sad or worried it will be good.

My dad was usually pretty upbeat and happy. Sometimes he would get mad—he would turn red and yell but it was usually over in five minutes. The only time I saw him cry was when his brother died—but pretty quickly he stopped and started trying to comfort us and my mom. He tried really hard not to take sides when I fought with my brothers and to be fair.

What's Different and What's the Same:
Some things haven't changed too much: we all get along pretty much the same, my brothers and I still fight but mom is the one to break it up now. I think I am closer to my mom now, because I'm older and maybe she talks to me more because my dad isn't around. I like that.

I started high school this week. My mom and I talked about what dad would have done had he been there in the morning on my first day: He probably would have made a joke like "You are wearing that?

OK—if you're sure . . . " My mom and I laughed about that, because he always made the same jokes. I think it helped me feel less nervous about starting school.

A lot of my dad's things are still in the house, like his desk is in the den and it has all his papers on it and stuff. It reminds me of him and that he'll never use that desk again. That makes me feel sad because it reminds me that he's not here. I guess we'll just leave his papers and things in the desk.

Other big things will be different now too: my brother's communion in the spring, my graduation in a few years, and when I get married someday. I know he won't be there to make jokes or relax me. But I'll try to remember what he would have said or done. And I've already thought of what music I'll play for him at my wedding: the Beatles. That was his favorite.

For older children and adolescents who are not naturally expressive, it may be helpful to guide the process by asking the individual to talk about him- or herself in the past, present, and future. This helps to establish a cohesive sense of themselves over time (including who they were before and after the loss). Specific questions that may be used in this process include the following:

- How did you see yourself before your parent died?
- What were the attributes your parent may have seen in you in the past?
- How has that changed or how do you see yourself now?
- How do you see the world around you now?
- Who else sees in you the things that your parent appreciated about you?
- What will you be like as a person in the future?
- How has your parent influenced your goals and what you see for yourself down the road?

To encourage the continuation of a psychological relationship with the deceased as well as encouraging relationships with others, the therapist can ask questions such as the following:

- How would it be for you if every day you remembered the things that your parent liked about you?
- How could you show these attributes to other people?
- Who else sees these things in you and reminds you of your parent?

Consider the following case example. Jonathan is a 13-year-old boy whose father died last year. He came to treatment because he has been acting out at school and at home.

Therapist:	So last time we were talking about your memories of your dad. You told me about the times you went fishing and how he used to help you with your homework. I liked hearing those

stories. It helped me to understand how much you must miss your dad and why you love him so much.

Jonathan: Yeah. I do. He was the only one who "got" me.

Therapist: What did he get about you?

Jonathan: I don't know. Like we had the same sense of humor. He got my jokes.

Therapist: So he thought you were funny? What else did he think about you?

Jonathan: That I was smart. Even though I don't always get the best grades, my dad always told me I was smart and he made me feel smart because he listened to everything I said.

Therapist: So he thought you were funny and he made you feel smart. Those are really nice things. Is there anyone else who sees those qualities in you now?

Jonathan: I don't know. Maybe my Uncle Peter. But it's not the same because I only see him once in a while.

Therapist: How could you show those qualities to other people, so more people can see the things your dad saw about you?

Jonathan: I don't know. I guess I could participate more at school when I have an idea or I know the answer. And my mom likes my jokes, too, I just usually don't tell her any.

Therapist: It sounds like there are other people who might appreciate the same qualities about you that your dad appreciated. It won't be the same as sharing those things with your dad, but it can help you to show the things your dad liked about you to other people. In a way, that's keeping a part of him with you.

Jonathan: That sounds good.

Therapist: I'm glad. Are there any qualities that your dad had that you see in yourself?

Jonathan: Well—we're both messy.

Therapist: (Laughs) OK, so that's something you have in common! You mentioned that your dad listened to everything you said. Would you say he was a good listener?

Jonathan: Yeah, he really was. I think I'm a good listener too.

Therapist: OK, so that's another way that you are like your dad and it shows in your personality. By showing that part of you, you are also keeping your dad with you.

Photographs

For younger children, it may be helpful to address the changes in their view of themselves through the use of more creative methods. The following exercise uses photographs to facilitate increased understanding of the changes they have gone through.

Have the child bring in a photo of him- or herself before the loss, along with a recent photo taken after the loss. The therapist should ask the child to describe, in as much detail as possible, who he or she sees in both photos. The therapist can ask the following questions:

- What did you look like before? How about now?
- What is most noticeable about yourself in this picture? What about the one of you now?
- How did you feel this day (happy, sad, scared)? What about now?
- What did you like–not like? How about now?
- Who knows you the best when this picture was taken? How about now?
- What were your hopes and dreams for the future then? How about now?

By asking the same questions about the older and more recent photos, the therapist may help the child see what kinds of things have changed and what has stayed the same. The therapist can also ask the child how the lost loved one, as well as the surviving parent or caregiver, would describe him or her.

KEEPING A CONNECTION

The next goal is to help children maintain their connection to the loved one who died. Bereaved children are faced with the process of continuing to develop their identity and sense of self without the deceased person as a guide. Parents typically serve in the role of a "memory" for their children; they can tell the story of how a child was born, early childhood, how the child's personality developed, milestones, and so on. They also often serve as "mirrors" for their children; parents mirror back qualities, characteristics, and abilities of their children, which helps to shape self-identity. With the loss of a parent, some bereaved children may be able to rely on another parent or caregiver to serve these functions, whereas others may have no one who can truly serve in this role. Although this is a part of loss that is not easily resolved, the therapist can help facilitate healthy development by working to strengthen the relationship of the child to his or her current caregiver and by helping the child to maintain psychological access to the deceased parent, as described next.

Children should be encouraged to continue a psychological relationship or an emotional connection with the deceased that matches their current developmental level (Layne et al., 2001). The idea of continuing a relationship is not to deny that the loss is permanent. Rather, the goal is to help the child recognize that the deceased person continues to affect who he or she is today and that the person may continue to serve as a source of love and comfort. This may be particularly true during times that the child feels the loss to be stronger, such as times of stress or transition. Although it is common for children to try to avoid or forget missing loved ones in these circumstances, it may be more helpful to try to remember. For example, 19-year-old Adam found himself strongly missing his dad on the day he registered for college, knowing that his dad had looked forward to his son attending his alma mater. Adam shared this sadness with his therapist, and they came up with a way to include his dad on this important day by visiting the cemetery with his mother after registration and "telling him" about his classes.

Another important component of working therapeutically with the bereaved is the creation and use of rituals (Rando, 1985). Rituals have been discussed previously but can be used specifically in memory making to help children and families continue to remember their loved one in a structured and meaningful way. At this point in treatment, the parent has already been involved in sharing memories and helping the child to remember the deceased. The therapist can facilitate the continued sharing of memories at home, both now and in the future. For example, when discussing memories of his sister with his therapist, a 7-year-old boy repeatedly mentioned his sister's love of food. With the guidance of the therapist, the boy and his mother decided to eat a meal together with all of his sister's favorite foods as a way of remembering her each year on her birthday. Children may enjoy other activities that help them feel connected to their loved one, such as trying something new that the deceased person would have been proud of, or participating in an activity that they may have avoided doing since the death. It may be enjoyable for children to ask extended family members and friends what they knew of their loved one's favorite things and to engage in a related activity together. Children may also write letters to feel close to the deceased.

CREATING NEW RELATIONSHIPS

It is important for children and adults to feel supported in relaying their experiences of their deceased loved ones. The child's parent may be helpful in identifying additional people who would be open to engaging with the child in conversations about the deceased, such as extended family members and friends. Over time, the memories of the deceased are likely to become less painful and even comforting, and the child will be able to focus his or her energy on other areas of his or her life. Once the child has identified how he or she has incorporated qualities of the deceased into his or her own personality or life, his or her sense of self will strengthen, and new relationships and support systems will form. As the child begins to identify new sources of support and role models, he or she will likely develop closer bonds with these individuals. For example, a bereaved child may develop a stronger relationship with a teacher, coach, aunt, uncle, or grandparent.

SUMMARY

The child has met the goals for this part of the IGTC when he or she demonstrates an ability to reminisce about the deceased loved one and take comfort in the experience. The psychological relationship should be one in which the child feels he or she is able to access memories and feels safe in sharing with significant others. We have observed clinically that when children achieve this type of relationship, they tend to feel less overwhelmed by memories and do not find them intrusive to daily life. If the child continues to demonstrate difficulty in approaching these topics, it may be necessary to review coping skills or cognitive restructuring, in addition to reviewing memories, prior to moving forward.

11

FOSTERING RESILIENCE AND CONCLUDING THE TREATMENT

Resilience is typically defined as continued normative development and the creation of positive outcomes in the face of adversity (Bonanno, 2004; Masten & Obradovic, 2006). Whereas the preceding chapters focused primarily on coping with potential problems commonly associated with grief and with dealing with the loss itself, this final chapter focuses on moving forward by promoting factors thought to be associated with resilience among bereaved children. This emphasis on recognizing strengths and promoting healthy development is a key component of the integrated grief therapy for children (IGTC) approach and has been integrated throughout the presentation of the treatment model, including the more symptom-based phase of treatment (i.e., Part II of this book). Therefore, many of the interventions discussed in this chapter have been previously introduced but are specifically described here for the way they may be used to foster resilience. Reemphasizing those aspects of IGTC that may help the child to thrive well beyond the end of treatment is a natural focus for this last phase of therapy with bereaved children.

Although many processes appear to be involved in children's outcomes following major life stressors, certain factors have consistently been associated with resilience in children. More specifically, the presence of these protective factors seems to be related to positive outcomes in the face of adversity, whereas the absence of or interference with these factors appears to be related to poorer outcomes. These factors include, but are not limited to, the following three general areas: (a) child variables, including temperament, self-efficacy, and cognitive ability (e.g., problem solving, reasoning, comprehension); (b) family variables, including parent functioning and family dynamics; and (c) environmental variables, including cultural factors, peer groups, school systems, and community resources (e.g., Bonanno & Mancini, 2008; Masten & Obradovic, 2006). These three domains, particularly child and family factors, have also been found to be relevant in outcomes for bereaved children (Lin, Sandler, Ayers, Wolchik, & Luecken, 2004; Luecken, 2008).

Bonanno and Mancini (2008) pointed out that there are often remarkable levels of resilience following a loss or other trauma, even without therapist intervention. Bereaved children with significant difficulties or adjustment problems are most likely to present for therapy, and we consider the strengthening of resiliency factors to be particularly essential for these high-risk individuals. Bolstering resilience is particularly important given the role that parental loss in childhood may play in the development of psychiatric disorders and long-term physical health problems in adulthood (Luecken, 2008). Because research has not yet determined the exact pathways that account for resilience, it is important to strengthen the factors that have been linked to positive outcomes in bereaved children, such as parental warmth and discipline, social supports, coping skills, and reducing parental distress (Haine, Ayers, Sandler, & Wolchik, 2008; Luecken, 2008).

Although the literature regarding resilience in children who have experienced loss, trauma, or other adversity continues to expand, it is still a relatively recent concept with limited empirical data. In addition, much of the current research has established which factors are associated with resilience, such as those described previously, with less research focusing on the development of evidence-based interventions to promote resilience. Complicating matters further, many of the factors thought to be related to resilience, particularly child variables such as intelligence and temperament, tend to be stable over time and are therefore less amenable to change. Fortunately, the concept of resilience has broadened to include child, family, and community resources, enabling us to focus on resiliency factors that appear to have the most plasticity for the individual child on a case-by-case basis. The IGTC interventions we propose here are therefore based on the existing literature as well as on our clinical experiences with bereaved children and families, and they aim to target those protective factors that are most likely to be enhanced by therapist-based interventions.

WORKING WITH THE PARENT TO FOSTER RESILIENCE

Research involving bereaved children and adolescents (Lin et al., 2004) and other at-risk children (Jaffee, Caspi, Moffit, Polo-Tomás, & Taylor, 2007) supports the idea that interventions aimed at increasing resilience should target the child as well as the child's family, particularly the parents or caregivers. As often stated throughout the course of this book, the general functioning of the surviving parent is strongly linked to children's outcomes following the death of a loved one. The IGTC model therefore proposes that a key pathway toward fostering resilience among bereaved children occurs through the parent. Strategies for assisting parents with their own functioning as well as strategies for helping parents to create positive environments for their children are presented here.

Provide Psychoeducation About Resilience

In Chapter 8, we provided an introduction to the concept of resilience and described how this concept may be presented to bereaved families. If this was not covered in previous sessions, the clinician may refer back to Chapter 8 at this point to begin a discussion about resilience and about using the strengths of the child and parent to help them through difficult times.

Determine the Parent's Mental Health Needs

Just as the IGTC approach addresses the potential problems of bereaved children (including the clinical domains of PTSD, anxiety, and depression), so must we assess whether the child's parents or caretakers have any significant symptoms of psychological distress. Although this issue was briefly mentioned in Chapter 3, it bears repeating, given the considerable evidence that mental health problems of bereaved parents are significantly related to mental health problems of their children (Cerel, Fristad, Verducci, Weller, & Weller, 2006; Kalter et al., 2002; Kranzler, Shaffer, Wasserman, & Davies, 1990; Lin et al., 2004; Van Eerdewegh, Clayton, & Van Eerdewegh, 1985).

At this point in the treatment, the clinician has likely come to know the bereaved child and his or her family fairly well and therefore should have a good sense of how the parent is functioning. If the clinician has noted that the parent is experiencing significant symptoms of psychological distress, then it is imperative that the parent be referred for further treatment if this has not been done already. Although we understand that people who are experiencing distress do not always respond well to recommendations for individual treatment, we have typically had success in encouraging parents to seek help in these situations, likely because of two factors: (a) Rapport with the parent has already been established and may have even been assisted by the parent's noting significant improvement in the child's functioning, and (b) we convey to the parents the strong link between their own functioning and that of their children, emphasizing how seeking help is beneficial for the whole family.

Aid With Problem Solving to Minimize Family Stress

In Chapter 8, we presented specific ways in which the death of a loved one adds to many additional life changes, and we provided a problem-solving method for coping with some of the potential stressors associated with these transitions. Some parents may simply find it helpful to learn that they are not alone in their experience of the many additional stressors (e.g., social, financial) faced by bereaved families, whereas others may need more structured instruction regarding how to solve specific problems without increasing family conflict. Although the approach introduced in Chapter 8 was initially presented for the clinician's work with bereaved children, a similar approach may be used for work with their parents. The basic premise is that by decreasing the levels of stress within the family and by increasing the parent's ability to cope when stressors do arise, the bereaved parent and child both fare better.

To review, the basic steps in problem solving are as follows:

1. Define the problem.
2. Brainstorm possible solutions without judgment and regardless of how silly or useless they seem. The idea is to generate as many alternatives as possible.
3. Evaluate the pros and cons of each alternative. Consider the likely outcomes and whether the solution is a practical one to put into action.
4. Choose the best option based on the above factors, and use this solution outside of session.
5. Evaluate the outcome and what may be learned from the given situation.

This problem-solving strategy should be introduced to the parent in a step-by-step manner, using a problem from the parent's own daily life as an example. For further work with this technique, the clinician may reintroduce the handout *Problem-Solving Skills* (Activity 8.2), which was initially used with the child in Chapter 8. The clinician may even bring the child and parent together to practice problem solving by working through a recent example from their lives that has been creating conflict for the whole family.

Increase Warmth and Discipline

As previously noted in Chapters 2 and 7, parenting style is another factor that contributes to children's outcomes following the death of a loved one. More specifically, the resilience of parentally bereaved children has been positively predicted by their surviving parents' provision of warmth and discipline (Haine, Wolchik, Sandler, Millsap, & Ayers, 2006; Kwok et al., 2005; Lin et al., 2004). Interventions that aim to increase warmth and discipline among bereaved families, such as those included in Sandler et al.'s (2003) Family Bereavement Program, have been found to improve not only parenting skills but also the outcomes for the bereaved children themselves (Sandler et al., 1992, 2003; Tein, Sandler, Ayers, & Wolchik, 2006). In a similar way, the IGTC interventions presented in the following paragraphs are designed to increase warmth and discipline through building on the family's current strengths to foster resilience among both parents and children.

Increasing Warmth Through Positive Experiences

One aspect of resilience is feeling good about oneself and maintaining a positive perspective about life in general, and this positive outlook stems in part from having opportunities in which life can be enjoyed. Given the link between parental warmth and positive outcomes for bereaved children, it makes sense that one goal for building resilience would be to create an atmosphere of warmth and enjoyment between the parent and child. The following dialogue presents one way of encouraging positive experiences among family members. This particular dialogue is likely most helpful for use with the bereaved child and parent together in a joint session.

> *Therapist:* We have already discussed how part of moving forward includes finding enjoyment in daily life, and that includes enjoying time spent with family. Some families find it helpful to schedule time each week in which they can just have fun. With all of the things you and the rest of your family are up to these days, I thought that scheduled fun time might be important for you, too! You might choose to do something different every week, or pick one activity that you all enjoy and share it together every weekend, for example. Let's start by trying to come up with some activities that the whole family enjoys. What are some things that you all enjoy? (*If the child and parent need prompting, then offer examples like a special meal at home, going to the movies, playing a particular sport, and so forth.*)

Once an activity has been chosen, let the child and parent know that you will be following up with them during the next scheduled session to see how it went. Encourage the family to spend 1 or 2 hours per week simply focused on having fun, without having to face all of the struggles and changes that they have recently experienced in the face of grief.

Encourage Positive Discipline

Chapter 7 reviewed parenting skills at length and included strategies that are likely helpful for all parents. The clinician should refer back to this chapter as needed and review the skills with the parent individually as certain conflicts or problems with the child's behavior arise. The handout *Parenting Skills: A Review* (Activity 11.1) may be used to review these ideas with the parent. This exercise will likely benefit all parents but should be particularly helpful for those who continue to struggle with issues around discipline and/or conflict with their children. The following dialogue between a clinician and the parent of a bereaved 10-year-old boy illustrates how some of the parenting skills may be reviewed in session, and it ties together some of the other concepts discussed in this chapter.

> *Mother:* One thing I would still like help with is reducing the number of arguments that Victor and I get in. Things are definitely better at home, and we are both feeling better than a few months ago, but we still fight a lot. It's like we can't help it since his dad is not around, and it's just the two of us now.
>
> *Therapist:* Can you describe to me what happens when you fight? Let's talk through one specific example, and we'll try to see what can be done differently.
>
> *Mother:* OK, well, just last night we had a typical argument. I asked Victor to take out the garbage and he continued to play his video game. Then he asked me to make chicken salad to bring to school for lunch today, so I told him that I wouldn't do that until he brought out the garbage. He said that he had already helped me that day by going with me to the supermarket. Before you know it, there were doors slamming and we both went to bed angry!
>
> *Therapist:* OK, so it seems that the trigger for the argument was that you wanted him to take out the garbage, but he didn't. Is that right?
>
> *Mother:* Yeah, it's always a struggle and it's not like I ask him to do that much. For all I do around the house, you would think he could do this one thing.
>
> *Therapist:* So it sounds like you're really saying that you are overwhelmed and could use some help around the house.
>
> *Mother:* Definitely.
>
> *Therapist:* OK, that makes sense. You certainly have a lot on your plate. What I'd like to do now is to set that problem—that you have so much to do around the house—aside for a separate problem-solving session. Just like we've handled other

Activity 11.1 Parenting Skills: A Review

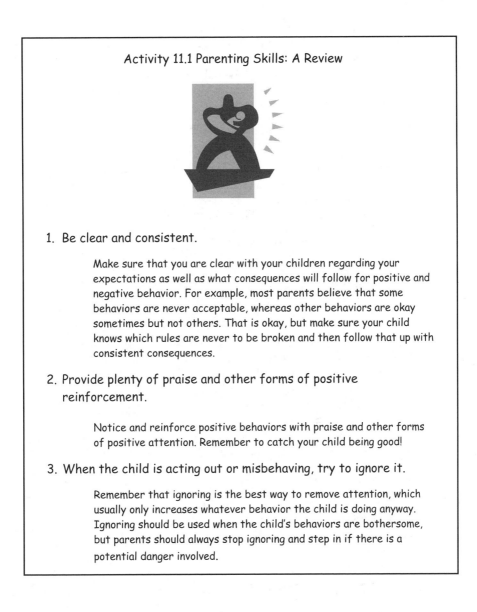

1. Be clear and consistent.

    Make sure that you are clear with your children regarding your expectations as well as what consequences will follow for positive and negative behavior. For example, most parents believe that some behaviors are never acceptable, whereas other behaviors are okay sometimes but not others. That is okay, but make sure your child knows which rules are never to be broken and then follow that up with consistent consequences.

2. Provide plenty of praise and other forms of positive reinforcement.

    Notice and reinforce positive behaviors with praise and other forms of positive attention. Remember to catch your child being good!

3. When the child is acting out or misbehaving, try to ignore it.

    Remember that ignoring is the best way to remove attention, which usually only increases whatever behavior the child is doing anyway. Ignoring should be used when the child's behaviors are bothersome, but parents should always stop ignoring and step in if there is a potential danger involved.

problems, we can brainstorm about how you can get some help and feel less overwhelmed. But first, I'd like to focus on the conflict between you and Victor. Is that OK?

Mother: Sure.

Therapist: Well, it seems like the conflict you described, and a lot of the other arguments we have talked about in session, have a lot to do with your different thoughts about how much he helps and how much he should be helping out. It makes me think about the expectations you have for him, and I wonder if he is clear on what those expectations are.

Mother: Well, he should know that I need help, and do something when I ask. Don't you think?

Therapist: The truth is Victor is a 10-year-old boy. While it might seem obvious to you what he should be doing and when, those things may not be clear to him. Do you remember when we established rules for the house a few weeks back?

Mother: Yes, and there has been a lot less name-calling since then.

Therapist: Great. So once the "house rules" were put into place, it was made clear what words you both should and shouldn't use around each other. And I notice you both have been working hard at getting along in other ways—he's been participating in your one-on-one time on Sundays, and you have been praising him when he asks for things in a calm and pleasant way. I'm wondering if we should add expectations around chores to the house rules. For example, we could pick one chore like taking out the garbage, include what day of the week this should happen, and by what time of day it should be done. This way, it's very clear to everyone what is expected. And part of your job would be to praise Victor every time he helps you out, whether that consists of helping with groceries, the garbage, or other tasks around the house. What do you think?

Mother: Sounds good. I have noticed that we are both happier since I've been paying more attention to all of the good stuff he does and not just the times when there is a problem between us.

WORKING WITH THE CHILD TO FOSTER RESILIENCE

In addition to the interventions targeted for the parent described previously, certain strategies may be targeted for the child to foster resilience and positive outcomes. Most of these strategies have been introduced in earlier sections of this book, but they are briefly reviewed here to emphasize their importance in fostering resilience and to illustrate how skills presented in session may impact various aspects of functioning.

Focus on the Child's Strengths

A key factor in promoting resilience is focusing on the child's strengths and acknowledging ways in which the child has effectively coped with the loss and other significant stressors in his or her life. As highlighted throughout the IGTC approach, one way of focusing on strengths is finding opportunities for both the child and parent to identify positive attributes of the child. The therapist can model how to identifying strengths through questions and statements such as, "How did you handle that?" and "It seems like you managed to get through that even though it was really hard." Focusing on the positive ways that the child copes helps the child to see that despite the distress he or she may have been experiencing, there are areas where he or she has demonstrated great strength. It also shows the parent how hard the child is working and how the parent may make similar attempts to praise the child's efforts at home. At this point in treatment, the therapist can also use his or her knowledge of the child to lead a discussion about how to best use his or her own strengths and resources going forward.

Cognitive Coping Strategies

Research examining resilience among bereaved children has found that mental health problems are less likely when children appraise negative events as less threatening and when children have greater perception regarding their efficacy to cope with life stressors (Lin et al., 2004). In other words, bereaved children with positive coping strategies and strong beliefs in their ability to cope are more likely to do well and function more adaptively in the face of grief. This finding further supports the use of the cognitive coping strategies previously presented in Chapters 3 and 9, such as cognitive restructuring and positive self-talk. Cognitive restructuring is a technique that allows children to challenge negative or unhelpful thoughts about themselves, others, or the world around them. They are able to do this by asking questions about the evidence to support their view and about whether there might be other ways of thinking about the situation. Positive self-talk is a strategy that builds on cognitive restructuring by replacing potentially negative thoughts with ones that are more helpful. This strategy is particularly useful with thoughts that the child acknowledges as unhelpful but that nonetheless continue to persist and to interfere with the child's functioning. The reader is referred to Chapter 9 for a detailed description of how these strategies may be introduced to the child and used to improve coping. Consider the following case example.

Thirteen-year-old Andrea had been in therapy for a few months, and she had learned a lot about grief and about how to go on remembering her mother, who died last year in a sudden accident. She and her therapist had talked about how much she had changed in the past year and about getting ready to end her therapy. However, something happened that caused Andrea to wonder how well she was really doing and whether she had made as much progress as she thought. The school where her mother taught as a second grade teacher made a scholarship fund in her mother's honor, and they decided to publicize the fund on the first anniversary of the death. The local newspaper ran a story about her mother, and people started to talk to Andrea again about what happened. So, just as Andrea was starting to feel "normal" again, she felt like she was brought back to a year ago when her grief was new and defined every aspect of her life. Although she knew that she did not feel quite as bad as before, she thought that this new attention surrounding her and her mother was unfair and unhelpful.

Andrea's therapist reminded her of all the coping skills she had acquired—skills that she did not know about when her mother first died. They reviewed what Andrea could do when she was feeling down, such as who she could talk to about her feelings and how she could use positive self-talk to remind herself of all of the good things in her life (including, but not limited to, memories of her mother). Andrea realized that other people, like the teachers whom her mother had worked with, missed her mom too and that they were simply looking for a way to remember her. Andrea started to tell herself, "Sure they miss her and want to honor her—she was a great person!" rather than focusing on how they were reminding her of what she lost. Of course, there were still times when Andrea needed to tune everyone out by putting on her music and being alone, but she decided that was OK, too.

Increase Access to and Use of Social Supports

In addition to cognitive coping strategies, the child's use of social support is another key factor that may foster resilience. When a child experiences the death of a loved one, changes in family and peer relationships are also likely to occur. Once some time has passed and the child has had the opportunity to find ways of coping with the loss, it is often important to help the child to reconnect with various sources of support, including peers, immediate and extended family members, and other community resources. The clinician may begin by providing psychoeducation regarding the importance of social support, which may come from different types of relationships. For example, friends from the child's peer group may help with emotional support and a sense of identity, whereas positive family relationships may serve to help a child feel safe and secure. Participating in community groups, such as after-school activities, athletics, or volunteering, may promote a sense of belonging and purpose. Therapists can talk to children and adolescents about their use of social supports and community resources.

> *Therapist:* We have been talking recently about how people that we trust and spend time with may be good sources of support and comfort, not only to help us during difficult times but also to help us stay connected during happier times. Let's talk a little bit more about your relationships and ways that you are connected to others.

The following questions can help the therapist explore the child's sense of support and belonging:

- Who do you talk to and confide in about the types of things we have talked about in session?
- How have your relationships with friends changed since the loss?
- How would you like these relationships to be now?
- Have you developed any new relationships since the loss that are now important to you?
- How have your family relationships changed?
- What about with your siblings–parents–grandparents?
- What is your role in your family now?
- How would you like things to be with your family?
- What different groups do you a feel a part of? Can you think of examples of things you feel a part of in your school, town, and city? (The clinician may provide examples here, such as community pool; little league; membership at YMCA; religious affiliation and participation; volunteer organizations; attendance at neighborhood functions, such as sporting events; and school-related activities, such as teams or clubs.)
- What kinds of things do you do, or would you like to do, after school and during weekends?
- Would you like to try any new activities? (If the child needs prompting, then offer the aforementioned examples and/or suggest joining groups of other same-aged peers based on hobby, religion, or even the loss of a loved one.)

The child should be reinforced for all prosocial relationships and activities, and areas in which change is desired or warranted should be further explored through problem solving and additional work.

FINISHING TREATMENT AND CONCLUDING REMARKS

This chapter has reviewed many of the key components of IGTC, with an emphasis on fostering resilience in bereaved children by helping them to use their skills, many of which were learned in therapy, along with their individual and family strengths. At this point in the treatment, the therapist has used those aspects of the IGTC approach that were most relevant for the child, thereby helping him or her to (a) navigate the various difficulties that he or she may have faced following the death of a loved one, (b) develop coping skills to manage distress, (c) maintain memories of and a meaningful, positive connection with the deceased, and (d) bolster protective factors that will help the child do well now and in the future.

We recommend discussing the end of treatment with children and parents in an explicit and well thought out way. Given the significant loss they have recently experienced and the role that therapy has hopefully played in helping them to make progress in the face of that loss, it is important to prepare the family for at least a few weeks prior to the completion of treatment. The child has likely developed an attachment to the therapist, so it is important to guide the child in expressing whatever types of feelings he or she may have about ending treatment by providing a safe environment and at times the language to do so. Feelings related to discontinuing regular sessions may include, but are not limited to, a sense of pride and accomplishment, relief, sadness, anxiety, and fear. The therapist may want to acknowledge his or her own feelings about saying goodbye (e.g., "While I will miss seeing you every week, I am so proud of how hard you have worked and of how well you are doing"), which may increase the comfort of the child and parent in doing the same. Sensitivity to the bereaved child's increased potential for feelings of loss is essential.

Preparation to conclude treatment also involves coming to an agreed on end date as well as deciding whether to end therapy all at once (i.e., with a final "goodbye session") or to taper off gradually (i.e., ending regular weekly sessions but making follow-up appointments on a monthly basis for a limited number of months). The therapist may want to initiate a conversation by acknowledging that the goals set at the start of treatment have been accomplished, asking the child and parent what thoughts and feelings they have about therapy coming to an end, and then discussing specific concerns and questions. This conversation should take place with parents of younger children, with adolescents themselves, or with both the child and parent when appropriate.

> *Therapist:* We have done so much during our time together, and I'd like to talk to you about where we are at now. At this point, it seems to me that we have done a lot of the work that we set out to do. (*Provide*

examples that are specific to the child's initial presentation and progress.) Given how far you've come, I think it makes sense to start planning for how we will finish up treatment. What do you think?

Some of the following points may be useful to guide this conversation:

- Briefly review initial treatment goals, how they were addressed, and how the child is doing now compared with the start of therapy. (A more thorough review of the treatment and the child's progress, as detailed later, may take place during the weeks that lead up to the final session.)
- Ask the child and parent about feelings related to ending therapy.
- Discuss what should be done if the child should start to reexhibit some of the initial presenting problems. This includes using the skills learned in therapy as well as contacting the therapist when necessary. Similarly, discuss some of the warning signs that old patterns or problems are reemerging and that extra steps should be taken to get back on track.
- Offer a checkup by phone or in session 1 month following the last regular session. The purpose of this type of follow-up session is to check in on how the child is doing, to help the child and parent maintain gains made in therapy, and to review skills as needed. This may be particularly helpful for those individuals who express reservation about moving on without the therapist. We have actually found most children and families to be doing quite well 1 month later and that the checkup typically provides reassurance that the child and/or parent are successfully using the skills learned in therapy.
- Decide on an activity for the final session. This final point is particularly relevant for younger children, who are less likely to verbalize feelings about saying goodbye and tend to respond well to concrete farewell activities. For example, many of our own IGTC therapy sessions have ended with an informal "goodbye party" during which the child picked a fun activity to do with the therapist, such as coloring or a light snack. The therapist may choose to provide the child with a colorful certificate indicating "graduation" from therapy. The parent may be included in these activities if the child so desires and if deemed appropriate.

Once the child understands and is comfortable with the idea of therapy coming to an end, the final sessions of IGTC should be spent reviewing the key components of the therapy and the child's gains made during the course of treatment. In our experience, children benefit from a review of what they have learned in treatment and of how far they have come. This type of review serves not only to reinforce their skills but also reinforces a sense of self-efficacy and a feeling of readiness to end therapy and move forward. The therapist might ask the child to indicate which parts of the therapy he or she remembers the most, which skills he or she uses most in day-to-day life, and how he or she feels different from when therapy began. Relevant accomplishments (e.g., specific symptom reduction, coping skills learned, established rituals for remembering the deceased, increased use of social supports) should be reviewed and praised.

The following conversation between a therapist and 18-year-old Ellen illustrates how a therapist may begin to talk about finishing up the IGTC treatment and some of the issues that may arise during this type of discussion.

Therapist: Now that we are getting ready to finish up therapy, I thought it would be helpful to review everything that you have accomplished during our time together.

Ellen: OK.

Therapist: Great. I'd like you to think back to last summer, which was a few months after your mom died and around the time that you and I met. What do you remember most about that time?

Ellen: I was fighting with my dad a lot and I wasn't hanging out with my friends. Looking back, I was really sad.

Therapist: Yeah, you did seem sad. How do you feel now, compared with then?

Ellen: I think I'm doing much better.

Therapist: I'm glad to hear that you're feeling better. What kinds of things do you think helped the most?

Ellen: I think going back to school and seeing my friends again helped. And coming here.

Therapist: So getting back into a regular routine and spending time with friends helped you feel like yourself again. That's a good thing to keep in mind whenever you are feeling sad.

Ellen: I hope I don't ever feel *that* sad again!

Therapist: I'm glad you brought that up. You felt really bad last summer, and you don't want to feel that way again, which makes sense. We can't know for sure that you won't feel so sad again, but we can recognize that you now know what to do if you ever feel that way again. What are some of the things you learned in here about what to do when you're feeling sad?

Ellen:	To watch out for my negative thoughts and to talk to friends. Also, I've been getting along with my dad better, so that helps too.
Therapist:	Terrific! So you learned about how to change your thoughts around, and how to get support from your dad and friends. That makes things a lot different from when you first came here.
Ellen:	That's true.

As noted previously, younger children will likely benefit from more concrete, visual activities, such as listing with the therapist what he or she learned on a large poster board that may be decorated with drawings or stickers. We have found that the child tends to take great pride in these markers of his or her progress and is often eager to share them with the parent. In fact, reviewing the child's gains with the parent in the presence of the child, and having the child actively participate in sharing what he or she accomplished, is another final way of promoting parent–child communication as well as parental warmth and praise as learned in treatment.

Another meaningful way of ending treatment with grieving children and reviewing their progress is to ask the child to provide his or her advice to others that have been through a similar loss experience (Cohen, Mannarino, & Deblinger, 2006). This type of activity helps children to recognize their own wisdom and provides a sense that because of what they have been through, they are able to help others. It also gives children an opportunity to see themselves as a source of strength, rather than as defined by loss. The therapist might ask the child to make a list of things that he or she knows about grief and loss that might be helpful for other bereaved children, including what might have been useful when his or her own loved one died. The following example is a list of tips for other grieving children made by a 12-year-old boy.

Things To Do If Your Parent Dies

1. Be open with your other parent.
2. Be emotional—your parent just died, it's OK. But don't be too emotional.
3. Go on with your life.
4. Do things that make you happy.
5. Comfort your siblings.

The final goal for this phase of treatment is for the child and parent to feel that they are not only equipped to manage but that they will thrive and do well, using their own skills and strengths as well as the skills and strengths of each other as supports. The ending of IGTC is framed as a positive experience that proves how far the child has come.

SUMMARY

This chapter provided guidelines for clinicians to help foster resilience in bereaved children and their families and to complete the therapy process. Focusing on the resilience of children impacted by grief and loss is a key component of IGTC. The ideas presented, which include interventions that promote the development of child, family, and environmental factors that are known to be protective for this population, are weaved throughout the IGTC approach to develop and use existing strengths within the family. The concept of resilience is especially important to discuss in depth as treatment comes to an end to help bereaved children and their families effectively cope and successfully move forward despite their loss. The therapy is considered complete when the child and surviving parent feel that they have achieved their goals and are able to rely on each other for support in times of stress.

REFERENCES

Abdelnoor, A., & Hollins, S. (2004). The effect of childhood bereavement on secondary school performance. *Educational Psychology in Practice, 20*, 43–54.

Achenbach, T. M., & Rescorla, L. A. (2001). *Manual for the ASEBA school-age forms and profiles*. Burlington: University of Vermont, Research Center for Children, Youth, and Families.

Allen, J. P., & Land, D. (1999). Attachment in adolescence. In J. Cassidy & P. R. Shaver (Eds.), *Handbook of attachment theory and research* (pp. 319–335). New York, NY: Guilford Press.

American Psychiatric Association. (1994). *Diagnostic and statistical manual of mental disorders* (4th ed.). Washington, DC: Author.

American Psychological Association Working Group of Psychoactive Medications for Children and Adolescents. (2006). *Report of the Working Group on Psychoactive Medications for Children and Adolescents: Psychopharmacological, psychosocial, and combined interventions for childhood disorders—Evidence base, contextual factors, and future directions*. Washington, DC: American Psychological Association.

Baker, J. E., & Sedney, M. (1996). How bereaved children cope with loss: An overview. In C. A. Corr & D. M. Corr (Eds.), *Handbook of childhood death and bereavement* (pp. 109–130). New York, NY: Springer.

Barrett, P. M., Dadds, M. R., & Rapee, R. M. (1996). Family treatment of childhood anxiety: A controlled trial. *Journal of Consulting and Clinical Psychology, 64*, 333–342.

Beardslee, W. R., Bemporad, J., Keller, M. B., & Klerman, G. L. (1983). Children of parents with major affective disorder: A review. *American Journal of Psychiatry, 140*, 825–832.

Beck, A. T., Rush, A. J., Shaw, B. F., & Emery, G. (1979). *Cognitive therapy of depression*. New York, NY: Guilford Press.

Beck, A. T., Sethi, B. B., & Tuthill, R. W. (1963). Childhood bereavement and adult depression. *Archives of General Psychiatry, 9*, 129–136.

Beck, J. S. (1995). *Cognitive therapy: Basics and beyond*. New York, NY: Guilford Press.

Belsher, G., & Wilkes, T. C. R. (1994). Ten key principles of adolescent cognitive therapy. In T. C. R. Wilkes, G. Belshur, A. J. Rush, & E. Frank (Eds.), *Cognitive therapy for depressed adolescents* (pp. 22–44). New York, NY: Guilford Press.

Bonanno, G. A. (2004). Loss, trauma, and human resilience: Have we underestimated the human capacity to thrive after extremely aversive events? *American Psychologist, 59*, 20–28.

Bonanno, G. A., & Kaltman, S. (1999). Toward an integrative perspective on bereavement. *Psychological Bulletin, 125*, 760–776.

Bonanno, G. A., & Mancini, A. D. (2008). The human capacity to thrive in the face of extreme adversity. *Pediatrics, 121,* 369–375.

Bowlby, J. (1969). *Attachment and loss: Volume 1—Attachment.* New York, NY: Basic Books.

Bowlby, J. (1973). *Attachment and loss: Volume 2—Separation, anxiety and anger.* New York, NY: Basic Books.

Bowlby, J. (1980). *Attachment and loss: Volume 3—Loss, sadness and depression.* New York, NY: Basic Books.

Braswell, L., & Kendall, P. C. (2001). Cognitive–behavioral therapy with youth. In K. S. Dobson (Ed.), *Handbook of cognitive–behavioral therapies* (2nd ed., pp. 246–294). New York, NY: Guilford Press.

Brent, D. A., & Melhem, N. (2008). Familial transmission of suicidal behavior. *Psychiatric Clinics of North America, 31,* 157–177.

Breslau, N., Andreski, P., & Chilcoat, H. (1998). Post-traumatic stress disorder and somatization symptoms: A prospective study. *Psychiatry Research, 79,* 131–138.

Brinkmeyer, M. Y., & Eyberg, S. M. (2003). Parent–child interaction therapy for oppositional children. In A. E. Kazdin & J. R. Weisz (Eds.), *Evidence-based psychotherapies for children and adolescents* (pp. 204–223). New York, NY: Guilford Press.

Bronstein, P., Fitzgerald, M., Briones, M., Pieniadz, J., & D'Ari, A. (1993). Family emotional expressiveness as a predictor of early adolescent social and psychological adjustment. *Journal of Early Adolescence, 13,* 448–471.

Brown, A. C., Sandler, I. N., Tein, J.-Y., Liu, X., & Haine, R. A. (2007). Implications of parental suicide and violent death for promotion of resilience of parentally-bereaved children. *Death Studies, 31,* 301–335.

Brown, E. J., & Goodman, R. F. (2005). Childhood traumatic grief: An exploration of the construct in children bereaved on September 11. *Journal of Clinical Child and Adolescent Psychology, 34,* 248–259.

Burke, L. (2003). The impact of maternal depression on familial relationships. *International Review of Psychiatry, 15,* 243–255.

Campbell, D., Bianco, V., Dowling, E., Goldberg, H., McNab, S., & Pentecost, D. (2003). Family therapy for childhood depression: Researching significant moments. *The Association for Family Therapy, 25,* 417–435.

Carr, A. (2009). The effectiveness of family therapy and systemic interventions for child-focused problems. *Journal of Family Therapy, 31,* 3–45.

Carter, A. S., Garrity-Rokous, E. F., Chazan-Cohen, R., Little, C., & Briggs-Gowan, M. J. (2001). Maternal depression and comorbidity: Predicting early parenting, attachment security, and toddler social–emotional problems and competencies. *Journal of the American Academy of Child and Adolescent Psychiatry, 40,* 18–26.

Caspi, A., Moffitt, T. E., Morgan, J., Taylor, A., Tully, L., Kim-Cohen, J., . . . Rutter, M. (2004). Maternal expressed emotion predicts children's antisocial behavior problems: Using monosygonic-twin differences to identify environmental effects on behavioral development. *Developmental Psychology, 40,* 149–161.

Cerel, J., Fristad, M., Verducci, J., Weller, R. A., & Weller, E. B. (2006). Childhood bereavement: Psychopathology in the 2 years postparental death. *Journal of the American Academy of Child and Adolescent Psychiatry, 45,* 681–690.

Cerel, J., Fristad, M., Weller, E. B., & Weller, R. A. (1999). Suicide-bereaved children and adolescents: A controlled longitudinal examination. *Journal of the American Academy Child and Adolescent Psychiatry, 38,* 672–679.

Charuvastra, A., & Cloitre, M. (2008). Social bonds and posttraumatic stress disorder. *Annual Review of Psychology, 59,* 301–328.

Christophersen, E. R., & Mortweet, S. L. (2001). *Treatments that work with children: Empirically supported strategies for managing childhood problems.* Washington, DC: American Psychological Association.

Clarke, G. N., Hawkins, W., Murphy, M., Sheeber, L. B., Lewinsohn, P. M., & Seeley, J. R. (1995). Targeted prevention of unipolar depressive disorder in an at-risk sample of high school adolescents: A randomized trial of a group cognitive intervention. *Journal of the American Academy Child and Adolescent Psychiatry, 34,* 312–321.

Cloitre, M., Cohen, L. R., & Koenen, K. C. (2006). *Treating survivors of childhood abuse: Psychotherapy for the interrupted life.* New York, NY: Guilford Press.

Cohen, J. A., Berliner, L., & March, J. S. (2000). Guidelines for treatment of PTSD: Treatment of children and adolescents. *Journal of Traumatic Stress, 13,* 566–568.

Cohen, J. A., & Mannarino, A. P. (2004). Treatment of childhood traumatic grief. *Journal of Clinical Child and Adolescent Psychology, 33,* 819–831.

Cohen, J. A., Mannarino, A. P., & Deblinger, E. (2006). *Treating trauma and traumatic grief in children and adolescents.* New York, NY: Guilford Press.

Cohen, J. A., Mannarino, A. P., & Knudsen, K. (2004). Treating childhood traumatic grief: A pilot study. *Journal of the American Academy Child and Adolescent Psychiatry, 43,* 1225–1233.

Cohen, J. A., Mannarino, A. P., Murray, L. K., & Igelman, R. (2006). Psychosocial interventions for maltreated and violence-exposed children. *Journal of Social Issues, 62,* 737–766.

Compton, S. N., March, J. S., Brent, D., Albano, A. M., Weersing, R., & Curry, J. (2004). Cognitive–behavioral psychotherapy for anxiety and depressive disorders in children and adolescents: An evidence-based medicine review. *Journal of the American Academy of Child and Adolescent Psychiatry, 43,* 930–959.

Crenshaw, D. A. (2007). An interpersonal neurobiological-informed treatment model for childhood traumatic grief. *Omega: Journal of Death and Dying, 54,* 315–332.

Currier, J. M., Holland, J. M., & Neimeyer, R. A. (2007). The effectiveness of bereavement interventions with children: A meta-analytic review of controlled outcome research. *Journal of Clinical Child and Adolescent Psychology, 36,* 253–259.

Currier, J. M., Neimeyer, R. A., & Berman, J. S. (2008). The effectiveness of psycho-therapeutic interventions for bereaved persons: A comprehensive quantitative review. *Psychological Bulletin, 134,* 648–661.

Curry, J. F. (2001). Specific psychotherapies for childhood and adolescent depression. *Society of Biological Psychiatry, 49,* 1091–1100.

Dadds, M. R., Spence, S. H., Holland, D. E., Barrett, P. M., & Laurens, K. R. (1997). Prevention and early intervention for anxiety disorders: A controlled trial. *Journal of Consulting and Clinical Psychology, 65,* 627–635.

Davis, M., McKay, M., & Eshelman, E. R. (2000). *The relaxation and stress reduction workbook: Fifth edition.* Oakland, CA: New Harbinger Publications.

Demi, A. S., & Miles, M. S. (1987). Parameters of normal grief: A Delphi study. *Death Studies, 11,* 397–412.

Dowdney, L. (2000). Annotation: Childhood bereavement following parental death. *Journal of Child Psychology and Psychiatry 41,* 819–830.

Dowdney, L., Wilson, R., Maughan, B., Allerton, M., Schofield, P., & Skuse, D. (1999). Psychological disturbance and service provision in parentally bereaved children: Prospective case-control study. *British Medical Journal, 319,* 354–357.

Downey, G., & Coyne, J. C. (1990). Children of depressed parents: An integrative review. *Psychological Bulletin, 108,* 50–76.

Dyregov, A., & Yule, W. (2006). A review of PTSD in children. *Child and Adolescent Mental Health, 11,* 176–184.

D'Zurilla, T. J., & Goldfried, M. R. (1971). Problem solving and behavior modification. *Journal of Abnormal Psychology, 78,* 107–126.

Earls, F., Smith, E., Reich, W., & Jung, K. G. (1988). Investigating psychopathological consequences of a disaster in children: A pilot study incorporating a structured diagnostic interview. *Journal of the American Academy of Child and Adolescent Psychiatry, 27,* 90–95.

Eisenberg, N., Losoya, S., Fabes, R. A., Guthrie, I. K., Reiser, M., Murphy, B., . . . Padgett, S. J. (2001). Parental socialization of children's dysregulated expression of emotion and externalizing problems. *Journal of Family Psychology, 15,* 183–205.

Eisenberg, N., Zhou, Q., Spinrad, T. L., Valinte, C., Fabes, R. A., & Liew, J. (2005). Relations among positive parenting, children's effortful control, and externalizing problems: A three-wave longitudinal study. *Child Development 76,* 1055–1071.

Elizur, E., & Kaffman, M. (1983). Factors influencing the severity of childhood bereavement reactions. *American Journal of Orthopsychiatry, 53,* 668–676.

Eth, S., Silverstein, S., & Pynoos, R. S. (1985). Mental health consultation to a pre-school following the murder of a mother and child. *Hospital & Community Psychiatry, 36,* 73–76.

Felner, R. D., Terre, L., & Rowlison, R. T. (1988). A life transition framework for under-standing martial dissolution and family reorganization. In S. A. Wolchik &

P. Karoly (Eds.), *Children of divorce: Empirical perspectives on adjustment* (pp. 35–65). New York, NY: Gardner Press.

Field, N. P. (2008). Whether to relinquish or maintain a bond with the deceased. In M. S. Stroebe, R. O. Hansson, H. Schut, & W. Stroebe (Eds.), *Handbook of bereavement research and practice: Advances in theory and intervention* (pp. 113–132). Washington, DC: American Psychological Association.

Fleming, S., & Robinson, P. (2001). Grief and cognitive–behavioral therapy: The reconstruction of meaning. In M. S. Stroebe, R. O. Hansson, W. Stroebe, & H. Schut (Eds.), *Handbook of bereavement research: Consequences, coping, and care* (pp. 647–669). Washington, DC: American Psychological Association.

Foa, E. B., Dancu, C. V., Hembree, E. A., Jaycox, L. H., Meadows, E. A., & Street, G. P. (1999). A comparison of exposure therapy, stress inoculation training, and their combination for reducing posttraumatic stress disorder in female assault victims. *Journal of Consulting and Clinical Psychology, 67,* 194–200.

Garmezy, N., & Masten, A. S. (1994). Chronic adversities. In M. Rutter, E. Taylor, & L. Hersov (Eds.), *Child and adolescent psychiatry: Modern approaches* (3rd ed., pp. 191–208). Oxford, England: Blackwell Scientific.

Genevro, J. L., Marshall, T., Miller, T., & Center for the Advancement of Health. (2004). Report on bereavement and grief research. *Death Studies, 28,* 491–575.

Gersten, J. C., Beals, J., & Kallgren, C. A. (1991). Epidemiology and preventive interventions: Parental death in childhood as a case example. *American Journal of Community Psychology, 19,* 481–500.

Glazer, H. R., & Clark, M. D. (1999). A family-centered intervention for grieving preschool children. *Journal of Child and Adolescent Group Therapy, 9,* 161–168.

Goenjian, A. K., Karayan, I., Pynoos, R. S., Minassian, D., Najarian, L. M., Steinberg, A. M., & Fairbanks, L. A. (1997). Outcome of psychotherapy among early adolescents after trauma. *American Journal of Psychiatry, 154,* 536–542.

Greeff, A. P., & Human, B. (2004). Resilience in families in which a parent has died. *American Journal of Family Therapy, 32,* 27–42.

Green, B. L., Korol, M., Grace, M. C., Vary, M. G., Leonard, A. C., Gleser, G. C., & Smitson-Cohen, S. (1991). Children and disaster: Age, gender, and parental effects on PTSD symptoms. *Journal of the American Academy of Child and Adolescent Psychiatry, 30,* 945–951.

Haine, R. A., Ayers, T. S., Sandler, I. N., & Wolchik, S. A. (2008). Evidence-based practices for parentally bereaved children and their families. *Professional Psychology: Research & Practice. 39,* 113–121.

Haine, R. A., Wolchik, S. A., Sandler, I. N., Millsap, R., & Ayers, T. (2006). Positive parenting as a protective resource for parentally bereaved children. *Death Studies, 30,* 1–28.

Halberstadt, A. G., Crisp, V. W., & Eaton, K. L. (1999). Family expressiveness: A retrospective and new directions for research. In P. Philippot, R. S. Feldman, & E. J. Coats (Eds.), *The social context of nonverbal behavior* (pp. 109–155). New York, NY: Cambridge University Press.

Hammen, C., Gordon, D., Burge, D., Adrian, C., Jaenicke, C., & Hiroto, D. (1987). Maternal affective disorders, illness, and stress: Risk for children's psychopathology. *American Journal of Psychiatry, 144,* 736–741.

Harris, T., Brown, G. W., & Bifulco, A. (1987). Loss of parent in childhood and adult psychiatric disorder: The role of social class position and premarital pregnancy. *Psychological Medicine, 17,* 163–183.

Harrison, L., & Harrington, R. (2001). Adolescents' bereavement experiences: Prevalence, association with depressive symptoms, and use of services. *Journal of Adolescence, 24,* 159–169.

Harter, S. (1982). A developmental perspective on some parameters of self-regulation in children. In P. Karoly & F. H. Kanfer (Eds.), *Self-management and behavior change from theory to practice* (pp. 165–202). New York, NY: Pergamon Press.

Hilliard, R. E. (2001). The effects of music therapy-based bereavement groups on mood and behavior of grieving children: A pilot study. *Journal of Music Therapy, 38,* 291–306.

Hilliard, R. E. (2007). The effects of Orff-based music therapy and social work groups on childhood grief symptoms and behaviors. *Journal of Music Therapy, 44,* 123–138.

Horowitz, M. J., Marmar, C., Weiss, D. S., DeWitt, K. N., & Rosenbaum, R. (1984). Brief psychotherapy of bereavement reactions: The relationship of process to outcome. *Archives of General Psychiatry, 41,* 438–448.

Hoven, C. (2003, April). *Lessons learned from 9/11: A public health perspective on children's mental health services.* Paper presented at the Columbia University Mailman School of Public Health Alumni Conference, New York, NY.

Huss, S. N., & Ritchie, M. (1999). Effectiveness of a group for parentally bereaved children. *Journal for Specialists in Group Work, 24,* 186–196.

Jacobson, E. (1938). *Progressive relaxation.* Chicago, IL: University of Chicago Press.

Jaffee, S. R., Caspi, A., Moffitt, T. E., Polo-Tomás, M., & Taylor, A. (2007). Individual, family, and neighborhood factors distinguish resilient from non-resilient maltreated children: A cumulative stressors model. *Child Abuse and Neglect, 31,* 231–253.

Janoff-Bulman, R. (1992). *Shattered assumptions: Towards a new psychology of trauma.* New York, NY: Free Press.

Janoff-Bulman, R., & Berg, M. (1998). Disillusionment and the creation of value: From traumatic losses to existential gains. In J. H. E. Harvey (Ed.), *Perspectives on loss: A sourcebook* (pp. 35–47). Philadelphia, PA: Taylor & Francis.

Johnson, D. R., Feldman, S., & Lubin, H. (1995). Critical interaction therapy: Couples therapy in combat-related posttraumatic stress disorder. *Family Process, 34,* 401–412.

Jordan, J. R., & Neimeyer, R. A. (2003). Does grief counseling work? *Death Studies, 27,* 763–786.

Kalter, N., Lohnes, K. L., Chasin, J., Cain, A. C., Dunning, S., & Rowan, J. (2002). The adjustment of parentally bereaved children: Factors associated with short-term adjustment. *Omega: Journal of Death and Dying, 46,* 15–34.

Kaslow, N. J., Deering, C. G., & Racusin, G. R. (1994). Depressed children and their families. *Clinical Psychology Review, 14,* 39–59.

Kaufman, J., Birmaher, B., Brent, D., Rau, U., & Ryan, N. (1996). *Schedule for Affective Disorders and Schizophrenia for School-Age Children—Present and lifetime version.* Pittsburgh, PA: University of Pittsburgh School of Medicine, Department of Psychiatry.

Kazdin, A. E. (2003). Problem-solving skills training and parent management training for conduct disorder. In A. E. Kazdin & J. R. Weisz (Eds.), *Evidence-based psychotherapies for children and adolescents* (pp. 241–262). New York, NY: Guilford Press.

Kazdin, A. E., & Weisz, J. R. (1998). Identifying and developing empirically supported child and adolescent treatments. *Journal of Consulting and Clinical Psychology, 66,* 19–36.

Kazdin, A. E., & Weisz, J. R. (2003). *Evidence-based psychotherapies for children and adolescents.* New York, NY: Guilford Press.

Kazdin, A. E., & Whitley, M. K. (2003). Treatment of parental stress to enhance therapeutic change among children referred for aggressive and antisocial behavior. *Journal of Consulting and Clinical Psychology, 71,* 504–515.

Kendall, P. C. (1990). *Coping cat workbook.* Ardmore, PA: Workbook Publishing.

Kendall, P. C. (1994). Treating anxiety disorders in children: Results of a randomized clinical trial. *Journal of Consulting and Clinical Psychology, 62,* 100–110.

Kendall, P. C., Aschenbrand, S. G., & Hudson, J. L. (2003). Child-focused treatment of anxiety. In A. E. Kazdin & J. R. Weisz (Eds.), *Evidence-based psychotherapies for children and adolescents* (pp. 81–100). New York, NY: Guilford Press.

Kendall, P. C., Flannery-Schroeder, E., Panichelli-Mindel, S., Southam-Gerow, M., Henin, A., & Warman, M. (1997). Therapy for youth with anxiety disorder: A second randomized clinical trial. *Journal of Consulting and Clinical Psychology, 65,* 366–380.

Kilic, E. Z., Ozguven, H. D., & Sayil, I. (2003). The psychological effects of parental mental health on children experiencing disaster: The experience of Bolu earthquake in Turkey. *Family Process, 42,* 485–495.

Kilpatrick, D. G., Ruggiero, K. J., Acierno, R., Saunders, B. E., Resnick, H. S., & Best C. L. (2003). Violence and risk of PTSD, major depression, substance abuse/dependence, and comorbidity: results from the National Survey of Adolescents. *Journal of Consulting and Clinical Psychology, 71,* 692–700.

King, N. J., Heyne, D., & Ollendick, T. H. (2005). Cognitive–behavioral treatments for anxiety and phobic disorders in children and adolescents: A review. *Behavioral Disorders, 30,* 241–257.

Kissane, D. W., Bloch, S., & McKenzie, D. P. (1997). Family coping and bereavement outcome. *Palliative Medicine, 11,* 191–201.

Klass, D., Silverman, P. R., & Nickman, S. L. (1996). *Continuing bonds: New understandings of grief.* Washington, DC: Taylor & Francis.

Klass, D., & Walter, T. (2001). Processes of grieving: How bonds are continued. In M. S. Stroebe, R. O. Hansson, W. Stroebe, & H. Schut (Eds.), *Handbook of bereavement research: Consequences, coping, and care* (pp. 431–448). Washington, DC: American Psychological Association.

Kranzler, E. M., Shaffer, D., Wasserman, G., & Davies, M. (1990). Early childhood bereavement. *Journal of the American Academy of Child and Adolescent Psychiatry, 29,* 513–520.

Kwok, O.-M., Haine, R. A., Sandler, I. N., Ayers, T. S., Wolchik, S. A., & Tein, J.-Y. (2005). Positive parenting as a mediator of the relationship between parental psychological distress and mental health problems of parentally bereaved children. *Journal of Clinical Child and Adolescent Psychology, 34,* 260–271.

Landolt, M. A., Boehler, U., Schwager, C., Schallberger, U., & Nuessli, R. (1998). Post-traumatic stress disorder in paediatric patients and their parents: An exploratory study. *Journal of Paediatrics and Child Health, 34,* 539–543.

Laor, N., Wolmer, L., Mayes, L. C., & Gershon, A. (1997). Israeli preschool children under Scuds: A 30-month follow-up. *Journal of the American Academy of Child and Adolescent Psychiatry, 36,* 349–356.

Layne, C. M., Pynoos, R. S., Saltzman, W. R., Black, M., Popovic, T., Mušic, M., . . . Arslanagic, B. (2001). Trauma/grief-focused group psychotherapy: School-based postwar intervention with traumatized Bosnian adolescents. *Group Dynamics: Theory, Research, and Practice, 5,* 277–290.

Lewinsohn, P. M., Clarke, G. N., Seeley, J. R., & Rohde, P. (1994). Major depression in community adolescents: Age at onset, episode duration, and time to recurrence. *Journal of the American Academy Child and Adolescent Psychiatry, 33,* 809–818.

Lichtenthal, W. G., Cruess, D. G., & Prigerson, H. G. (2004). A case for establishing complicated grief as a distinct mental disorder in DSM–V. *Clinical Psychology Review, 24,* 637–662.

Lin, K. K., Sandler, I. N., Ayers, T. S., Wolchik, S. A., & Luecken, L. J. (2004). Resilience in parentally bereaved children and adolescents seeking preventive services. *Journal of Clinical Child and Adolescent Psychology, 33,* 673–683.

Lohaus, A., & Klein-Hebling, J. (2000). Coping in childhood: A comparative evaluation of different relaxation techniques. *Anxiety, Stress, and Coping, 13,* 187–211.

Lowry-Webster, H. M., Barrett, P. M., & Dadds, M. R. (2001). A universal prevention trial of anxiety and depressive symptomatology in childhood: Preliminary data from an Australian study. *Behaviour Change, 18,* 36–50.

Luecken, L. J. (2008). Long-term consequences of parental death in childhood: Psychological and physiological manifestations. In M. S. Stroebe, R. O. Hansson,

H. Schut, & W. Stroebe (Eds.), *Handbook of bereavement research and practice: Advances in theory and intervention* (pp. 397–416). Washington, DC: American Psychological Association.

Lutz, W. J., Hock, E., & Kang, M. J. (2007). Children's communication about distressing events: The role of emotional openness and psychological attributes of family members. *American Journal of Orthopsychiatry, 77*, 86–94.

Lutzke, J. R., Ayers, T. S., Sandler, I. N., & Barr, A. (1997). Risks and interventions for the parentally bereaved child. In S. A. Wolchik & I. N. Sandler (Eds.), *Handbook of children's coping linking theory and intervention* (pp. 215–243). New York, NY: Plenum Press.

Mad, sad, glad game [Game]. (1990). Loveland, CO: Peak Potential Inc.

Mahoney, M. J., & Arnkoff, D. B. (1978). Cognitive and self control therapies. In S. Garfield & A. Bergin (Eds.), *Handbook of psychotherapy and behavior change* (2nd ed., pp. 689–722) New York, NY: Wiley.

Malkinson, R. (2001). Cognitive–behavioral therapy of grief: A review and application. *Research on Social Work Practice, 11*, 671–698.

Marmorstein, N. R., & Iacono, W. G. (2004). Major depression and conduct disorder in youth: Associations with parental psychopathology and parent–child conflict. *Journal of Child Psychology and Psychiatry and Allied Disciplines, 45*, 377–386.

Masten, A. S., & Obradovic, J. (2006). Competence and resilience in development. *Annals New York Academy of Sciences, 1094*, 13–27.

McFarlane, M. C. (1987a). Family functioning and overprotection following a natural disaster: The longitudinal effects of posttraumatic morbidity. *Australian and New Zealand Journal of Psychiatry, 21*, 210–218.

McFarlane, M. C. (1987b). Posttraumatic phenomena in a longitudinal study of children following a natural disaster. *Journal of the American Academy of Child and Adolescent Psychiatry, 26*, 764–769.

Melhem, N. M., Walker, M., Moritz, G., & Brent, D. A. (2008). Antecedents and sequelae of sudden parental death in offspring and surviving caregivers. *Archives of Pediatrics and Adolescent Medicine, 162*, 403–410.

Mufson, L., & Dorta, K. P. (2003). Interpersonal psychotherapy for depressed adolescents. In J. R. Wolchik & A. E. Kazdin (Ed.), *Evidence-based psychotherapies for children and adolescents* (pp. 148–164). New York, NY: Guilford Press.

Neimeyer, R. A., & Stewart, A. E. (1996). Trauma, healing, and the narrative emplotment of loss. *Journal of Contemporary Human Services, 77*, 360–375.

New York University Child Study Center. (2006). *Caring for kids after trauma, disaster and death: A guide for parents and professionals* (2nd ed.). Retrieved from http://www.aboutourkids.org/files/articles/crisis_guide02.pdf

Oltjenbruns, K. A. (2001). Developmental context of childhood: Grief and regrief phenomena. In M. S. Stroebe, R. O. Hansson, W. Stroebe, & H. Schut (Eds.), *Handbook of bereavement research: Consequences, coping, and care* (pp. 169–197). Washington, DC: American Psychological Association.

Orvaschel, H., Walsh-Allis, G., & Ye, W. J. (1988). Psychopathology in children of parents with recurrent depression. *Journal of Abnormal Child Psychology, 16,* 17–28.

Parker, G., & Manicavasagar, V. (1986). Childhood bereavement circumstances associated with adult depression. *British Journal of Medical Psychology, 59,* 387–391.

Pfeffer, C. R. (1986). *The suicidal child.* New York, NY: Guilford Press.

Pfeffer, C. R., Altemus, M., Heo, M., & Jiang, H. (2007). Salivary cortisol and psychopathology in children bereaved by the September 11, 2001 terror attacks. *Biological Psychiatry, 61,* 957–965.

Pfeffer, C. R., Jiang, H., Kakuma, T., Hwang, J., & Metsch, M. (2002). Group intervention for children bereaved by the suicide of a relative. *Journal of the American Academy of Child and Adolescent Psychiatry, 41,* 505–513.

Pfeffer, C. R., Karus, D., Siegel, K., & Jiang, H. (2000). Child survivors of parental death from cancer or suicide: Depressive and behavioral outcomes. *Psycho-Oncology 9,* 1–10.

Pfeffer, C. R., Martins, P., Mann, J., Sunkenberg, M., Ice, A., Damore J. P., Jr., . . . Jiang, H. (1997). Child survivors of suicide: Psychosocial characteristics. *Journal of the American Academy of Child and Adolescent Psychiatry, 36,* 65–74.

Pine, D. S., & Cohen, J. A. (2002). Trauma in children and adolescents: Risk and treatment of psychiatric sequelae. *Biological Psychiatry, 51,* 519–531.

Prigerson, H. G., Vanderwerker, L. C., & Maciejewski, P. K. (2008). A case for inclusion of prolonged grief disorder in *DSM–V.* In M. Stroebe, R. O. Hansson, W. Stroebe, & H. Schut (Eds.), *Handbook of bereavement research: Advances in theory and intervention* (pp. 165–186). Washington, DC: American Psychological Association.

Rando, T. A. (1985). Creating therapeutic rituals in the psychotherapy of the bereaved. *Psychotherapy, 22,* 236–240.

Raveis, V. H., Siegel, K., & Karus, D. (1999). Children's psychological distress following the death of a parent. *Journal of Youth and Adolescence, 28,* 165–180.

Reese, M. F. (1982). Growing up: The impact of loss and change. In D. Belle (Ed.), *Lives in stress: Women and depression* (pp. 65–88). Beverly Hills, CA: Sage.

Reinherz, H. Z., Giaconia, R. M., Carmola Hauf, A. M., Wasserman, M. S., & Silverman, A. B. (1999). Major depression in the transition to adulthood: Risks and impairments. *Journal of Abnormal Psychology, 108,* 500–510.

Resick, P. A., & Schnicke, M. K. (1996). *Cognitive processing therapy for rape victims: A treatment manual.* Newbury Park, CA: Sage.

Reynolds, C. R., & Kamphaus, R. W. (2004). *Behavior Assessment System for Children, second edition manual.* Circle Pines, MN: American Guidance Service.

Riggs, D., Byrne, C. A., Weathers, F. W., & Litz, B. T. (1998). The quality of intimate relationships in male Vietnam veterans: The impact of posttraumatic stress disorder. *Journal of Traumatic Stress, 11,* 87–102.

Rothbaum, F., & Weisz, J. R. (1994). Parental caregiving and child externalizing behavior in nonclinical samples: A meta-analysis. *Psychological Bulletin, 116,* 55–74.

Rotheram-Borus, M. J., Stein, J. A., & Lin, Y.-Y. (2001). Impact of parental death and an intervention on the adjustment of adolescents whose parents have HIV/AIDS. *Journal of Consulting and Clinical Psychology, 69,* 763–773.

Rutter, M. (1990). Commentary: Some focus and process considerations regarding the effects of parental depression on children. *Developmental Psychology, 26,* 60–67.

Safran, J. D., & Segal, Z. V. (1990). *Interpersonal process in cognitive therapy.* New York, NY: Basic Books.

Saldinger, A., Cain, A., Kalter, N., & Lohnes, K. (1999). Anticipating parental death in families with young children. *American Journal of Orthopsychiatry, 69,* 39–48.

Saldinger, A., Porterfield, K., & Cain, A. C. (2004). Meeting the needs of parentally bereaved children: A framework for child-centered parenting. *Psychiatry, 67,* 331–352.

Saltzman, W. R., Steinberg, A. M., Layne, C. M., Aisenberg, E., & Pynoos, R. S. (2001). A developmental approach to school-based treatment of adolescents exposed to trauma and traumatic loss. *Journal of Child and Adolescent Group Therapy, 11,* 43–56.

Sanchez, L., Fristad, M., Weller, R. A., Weller, E. B., & Moye, J. (1994). Anxiety in acutely bereaved prepubertal children. *Annals of Clinical Psychiatry, 6,* 39–43.

Sandler, I. N., Ayers, T. S., Wolchik, S. A., Kwok, O.-M., Twohey-Jacobs, J., Lin, K., . . . Tein, J.-Y. (2003). The Family Bereavement Program: Efficacy evaluation of a theory-based prevention program for parentally bereaved children and adolescents. *Journal of Consulting and Clinical Psychology, 71,* 587–600.

Sandler, I. N., West, S. G., Baca, L., Pillow, D. R., Gersten, J. C., Rogosch, F., . . . Ramierez, R. (1992). Linking empirically based theory and evaluation: The Family Bereavement Program. *American Journal of Community Psychology, 20,* 491–521.

Saucier, J.-F., & Ambert, A.-M. (1986). Adolescents' perception of self and of immediate environment by parental marital status: A controlled study. *Canadian Journal of Psychiatry, 31,* 505–512.

Scheeringa, M. S., & Zeanah, C. H. (2001). A relational perspective on PTSD in early childhood. *Journal of Traumatic Stress, 14,* 799–815.

Scheeringa, M. S., Zeanah, C. H., Myers, L., & Putnam, F. W. (2003). New findings on alternative criteria for PTSD in preschool children. *Journal of the American Academy of Child and Adolescent Psychiatry, 42,* 561–570.

Schmiege, S. J., Khoo, S. T., Sandler, I. N., Ayers, T. S., & Wolchik, S. A. (2006). Symptoms of internalizing and externalizing problems: Modeling recovery curves after the death of a parent. *American Journal of Preventive Medicine, 31,* S512–S160.

Schut, H., Stroebe, M. S., van den Bout, J., & Terheggen, M. (2001). The efficacy of bereavement interventions: Determining who benefits. In M. S. Stroebe, R. O. Hansson, W. Stroebe, & H. Schut (Eds.), *Handbook of bereavement research: Consequences, coping, and care* (pp. 705–738). Washington, DC: American Psychological Association.

Scott, R. W., Mughelli, K., & Deas, D. (2005). An overview of controlled studies of anxiety disorders treatment in children and adolescents. *JAMA, 97*, 13–24.

Shalev, A. R., Tuval-Mashiach, R., & Hadar, H. (2004). Posttraumatic stress disorder as a result of mass trauma. *Journal of Clinical Psychiatry, 65*(Suppl. 1), 4–10.

Shaver, P. R., & Tancredy, C. M. (2001). Emotion, attachment, and bereavement: A conceptual commentary. In M. Stroebe, R. O. Hansson, W. Stroebe, & H. Schut (Eds.), *Handbook of bereavement research: Consequences, coping, and care* (pp. 63–88). Washington, DC: American Psychological Association.

Shear, K., Frank, E., Houck, P. R., & Reynolds, C. F., III. (2005). Treatment of complicated grief: A randomized control trial. *JAMA, 293*, 2601–2608.

Sherkat, E., & Reed, M. D. (1992). The effects of religion and social support on self-esteem and depression among the suddenly bereaved. *Social Indicators Research, 26*, 259–275.

Shure, M. B., & Spivack, G. (1978). *Problem-solving techniques in childrearing*. San Francisco, CA: Jossey-Bass.

Siegel, K., Karus, D., & Raveis, V. H. (1996). Adjustment of children facing the death of a parent due to cancer. *Journal of the American Academy of Child and Adolescent Psychiatry, 35*, 442–450.

Silva, R. R., Gallagher, R., & Minami, H. (2006). Cognitive–behavioral treatments for anxiety disorders in children and adolescents. *Primary Psychiatry, 13*(5), 68–76.

Silverman, P. R., Nickman, S., & Worden, J. W. (1992). Detachment revisited: The child's reconstruction of a dead parent. *American Journal of Orthopsychiatry, 62*, 494–503.

Sireling, L., Cohen, D., & Marks, I. (1988). Guided mourning for morbid grief: A controlled replication. *Behavior Therapy, 19*, 121–132.

Social Security Administration. (2000). *Intermediate assumptions of the 2000 trustees report*. Washington, DC: Office of the Chief Actuary of the Social Security Administration.

Sood, B., Weller, E. B., Weller, R. A., Fristad, M. A., & Bowes, J. M. (1992). Somatic complaints in grieving children. *Comprehensive Mental Health Care, 2*, 17–25.

Speece, M. W., & Brent, S. B. (1996). The development of children's understanding of death. In C. A. Corr & D. M. Corr (Eds.), *Handbook of childhood death and bereavement* (pp. 29–50). New York, NY: Springer.

Stallard, P. (2002). *Think good–feel good: A cognitive behaviour therapy workbook for children and young people*. West Sussex, England: John Wiley & Sons.

Stallard, P. (2005). *A clinician's guide to think good–feel good: Using CBT with children and young people*. West Sussex, England: John Wiley & Sons.

Stoppelbein, L., & Greening, L. (2000). Posttraumatic stress symptoms in parentally bereaved children and adolescents. *American Academy of Child and Adolescent Psychiatry, 39,* 1112–1119.

Stroebe, M., Hansson, R. O., Schut, H., & Stroebe, W. (2008). Bereavement research: contemporary perspectives. In M. Stroebe, R. O. Hansson, H. Schut, & W. Stroebe (Eds.), *Handbook of bereavement research and practice: Advances in theory and intervention* (pp. 3–25). Washington, DC: American Psychological Association.

Stroebe, M., & Schut, H. (2005). To continue or relinquish bonds: A review of consequences for the bereaved. *Death Studies, 29,* 477–494.

Stroebe, M., van Son, M., Stroebe, W., Kleber, R., Schut, H., & van den Bout, J. (2000). On the classification and diagnosis of pathological grief. *Clinical Psychology Review, 20,* 57–75.

Stroebe, W., Zech, E., Stroebe, M. S., & Abakoumkin, G. (2005). Does social support help in bereavement? *Journal of Social and Clinical Psychology, 24,* 1030–1050.

Target, M., & Fonagy, P. (2005). The psychological treatment of child and adolescent disorders. In *What works for whom? A critical review of psychotherapy research* (2nd ed., pp. 385–424). New York, NY: Guilford Press.

Tein, J.-Y., Sandler, I. N., Ayers, T. S., & Wolchik, S. A. (2006). Meditation of the effects of the family bereavement program on mental health problems of bereaved children and adolescents. *Prevention Science, 7,* 179–195.

Terr, L. C. (1981). "Forbidden games:" Post-traumatic child's play. *Journal of the American Academy of Child Psychiatry, 20,* 741–760.

Terr, L. C. (1983). Chowchilla revisited: The effects of psychic trauma four years after a school-bus kidnapping. *American Journal of Psychiatry, 140,* 1543–1550.

Thompson, M. P., Kaslow, N. J., Price, A. W., Williams, K., & Kingree, J. B. (1998). Role of secondary stressors in the parental death–child distress relation. *Journal of Abnormal Child Psychology, 26,* 357–366.

Tonkins, S. A. M., & Lambert, M. J. (1996). A treatment outcome study of bereavement groups for children. *Child and Adolescent Social Work Journal, 13,* 3–21.

Treatment for Adolescents with Depression Study Team. (2004). Fluoxetine, cognitive–behavioral therapy, and their combination for adolescents with depression: Treatment for Adolescents With Depression Study (TADS) randomized controlled trial. *Journal of the American Medical Association, 292,* 807–820.

Trowell, J., Joffe, I., Campbell, J., Clemente, C., Almqvist, F., & Soininen, M. (2007) Childhood depression: A place for psychotherapy—An outcome study comparing individual psychodynamic psychotherapy and family therapy. *European Child and Adolescent Psychiatry, 16,* 157–167.

Valiente, C., Eisenberg, N., Fabes, R. A., Shepard, S. A., Cumberland, A., & Losoya, S. H. (2004). Prediction of children's empathy-related responding from their effortful control and parents' expressivity. *Developmental Psychology, 40,* 911–926.

Van Eerdewegh, M. M., Bieri, M. D., Parrilla, R. H., & Clayton, P. J. (1982). The bereaved child. *British Journal of Psychiatry, 140,* 23–29.

Van Eerdewegh, M. M., Clayton, P. J., & Van Eerdewegh, P. (1985). The bereaved child: Variables influencing early psychopathology. *British Journal of Psychiatry, 147,* 188–194.

Webb, N. B. (2002). *Helping bereaved children: A handbook for practitioners* (2nd ed.). New York, NY: Guilford Press.

Webster-Stratton, C. (1992). *The incredible years: A trouble-shooting guide for parents of children aged 3–8.* Toronto, Ontario, Canada: Umbrella Press.

Webster-Stratton, C., & Reid, M. J. (2003). The incredible years parents, teachers, and children training series: A multifaceted treatment approach for young children with conduct problems. In A. E. Kazdin & J. R. Weisz (Eds.), *Evidence-based psychotherapies for children and adolescents* (pp. 224–240). New York, NY: Guilford Press.

Webster-Stratton, C., Reid, M. J., & Hammond, M. (2004). Treating children with early-onset conduct problems: Intervention outcomes for parent, child, and teacher training. *Journal of Clinical Child and Adolescent Psychology, 33,* 105–124.

Weiss, R. (2008). The nature and causes of grief. In M. S. Stroebe, R. O. Hansson, H. Schut, & W. Stroebe (Eds.), *Handbook of bereavement research and practice: Advances in theory and intervention* (pp. 29–44). Washington, DC: American Psychological Association.

Weller, R. A., Weller, E. B., Fristad, M. A., & Bowes, J. M. (1991). Depression in recently bereaved prepubertal children. *American Journal of Psychiatry, 148,* 1536–1540.

White, M. (1998). Saying hullo again: The incorporation of the lost relationship in the resolution of grief. In C. White & D. Denborough (Eds.), *Introducing narrative therapy: A collection of practice-based writings.* Adelaide, Australia: Dulwich Centre Publications.

Wolfelt, A. D. (1983). *Helping children cope with grief.* Muncie, IN: Accelerated Development.

Worden, J. W. (1996). *Children and grief: When a parent dies.* New York, NY: Guilford Press.

Worden, J. W., & Silverman, P. R. (1996). Parental death and the adjustment of school-age children. *Omega: Journal of Death and Dying, 33,* 91–102.

Wortman, C. B., & Silver, R. C. (2001). The myths of coping with loss revisited. In M. S. Stroebe, R. O. Hansson, W. Stroebe, & H. Schut (Eds.), *Handbook of bereavement research: Consequences, coping, and care* (pp. 405–430). Washington, DC: American Psychological Association.

Yamamoto, K., Davis, O. L. D., Dylak, S., Whittaker, J., Marsh, C., & van der West-huizen, P. C. (1996). Across six nations: Stressful events in the lives of children. *Child Psychiatry and Human Development, 26,* 139–149.

Yule, W. (1994). Posttraumatic stress disorders. In E. T. M. Rutter & L. Hersov (Ed.), *Child and adolescent psychiatry: Modern approaches* (pp. 392–407). Oxford, England: Blackwell: Scientific Publications.

Zambelli, G. C., Clark, E. J., Barile, L., & de Jong, A. F. (1988). An interdisciplinary approach to clinical intervention for childhood bereavement. *Death Studies, 12,* 41–50.

Zambelli, G. C., & DeRosa, A. P. (1992). Bereavement support groups for school-age children: Theory, intervention, and case example. *American Journal of Orthopsychiatry, 62,* 484–493.

INDEX

Activities
  Daily Routine, 131–133
  Facing Your Fears: What to Do
    When You Are Feeling
    Anxious, 118–121
  Feelings Monitoring, 86–90
  Helping Children Cope With Death,
    43, 44
  How I Felt After My Dad Died,
    192, 193
  How to Praise Your Child, 127, 128
  Looking Toward the Future: Guide-
    lines for Helping Grieving
    Children, 154, 155
  Managing Negative Thoughts: Your
    Toolbox, 176, 177
  My Daily Schedule, 67–69
  My Goals, 69–73
  My Memory Book, 188–190
  Parenting Skills: A Review, 208–209
  Problem-Solving Skills, 161–164, 206
  Relaxation for Children, 51–53
  Star Charts, 135–138
  Thinking Through Your Worries,
    115, 116
  Thought Diary, 173–175
  Time-Out Procedure, 140, 141
  Tips for Using Star Charts, 138, 139
  What Are My Negative Thoughts,
    78, 79
  What Are They Thinking?, 78,
    112–114, 173
Activity scheduling, 67–73
Adolescents
  activities for, 80
  behavior management for, 140, 142
  communication with, 142–143
  limit-setting for, 140, 142
  and memory book concept, 196–198
  parental involvement in treatment
    of, 122
  and reactions to loss, 17, 153
Affective coping skills, 178–179
Age groups
  and cognitive processes work, 45, 78
  and hyperarousal, 85

and reactions to loss, 15–17, 153–154
relaxation strategies for, 110
risk/protective factors of, 15–17
and therapeutic concepts, 172–173
and Triangle of 3 concept, 49
All-or-nothing thinking, 74–76, 78
Alternatives, imagined, 167
Anger
  coping with, 181
  in depression, 81
  expression of, 31, 44, 153
  normalization of, 188
  in posttraumatic stress disorder, 84, 86
  as reaction to child's misbehavior, 143
  as reaction to loss, 4, 23, 29, 123,
    153, 185
Anticipated death, 23–24
Anxiety, 105–122
  clinical presentation of, 28, 105–106
  coping skills for, 109–121
  cues for managing, 108–109
  and facing fears, 115–118
  parent's role in treatment of, 121–122
  relaxation for, 110–111
  rewards for coping with, 108–109
  and self-talk, 111–115
Approach/avoidance, 57–58
Attachment
  to parent, 22, 64, 184
  theory, 22
  to therapist, 214
Avoidance
  of memories, 187–188
  as protection, 57–58, 96–97
  of traumatic reminders, 84
Ayers, T. S., 20

Barrett, P. M., 121
Beck, A. T., 57
Bedtime, 58, 110–111
Behavioral coping skills, 58–59,
  179–180
Behavior Assessment System for
  Children (BASC), 38
Behavior management, 123–145
  for adolescents, 140–142

Behavior management, *continued*
    approach/avoidance with, 57–58
    with communication, 142–143
    with consistent discipline, 131–140
    coping skills for, 166–167, 179–180
    with depression, 66
    by ignoring, 134–135
    and parental coping, 143–145
    with positive interaction, 125–129
    with structure/routine, 130–131
Behavior problems
    clinical presentation in bereaved
        children, 28–29, 123–124
    consequences for, 138
    as grief reactions, 28–29
    identification of, 129–130
    understanding of, 124–125
Beliefs
    about death, 41, 90–91
    assessment questions about, 40
    following a loss, 90–93, 165
Bereavement, defined, 5
Bereavement support groups, 30–33
Berg, M., 165
Berman, J. S., 30
Betrayal, 191
Be Your Own Detective: Questions to
    Ask Yourself When Having
    Negative Thoughts (Activity),
    74, 75, 171
Bonnano, G. A., 204
Brown, A. C., 24

Cain, A., 19
CBT. *See* Cognitive–behavioral therapy
Cerel, J., 18
Child Behavior Checklist, 38
Child Bereavement Study, 105, 123, 131
Child-centered parenting, 19
Childhood traumatic grief, 27, 100
Children
    cognitive–behavioral therapy for,
        165–166
    cognitive strategies for, 211–212
    coping skills for, 43–45
    excessive worry in, 121–122
    infants, 15–16, 152
    normative grief reactions of, 15–17,
        42–43, 152–153
    previous functioning of, 21

protective factors in, 204
resilience in, 210–213
school-age, 16–17, 152–153
strengths of, 156–157
toddlers/preschoolers, 16, 152
Circumstances of death, 16, 24, 28,
    39–41, 167, 185
Clear commands, 138
Clinical presentations in bereaved
    children, 26–30
    with anxiety, 28, 105–106
    with behavior problems, 28–29,
        123–124
    with complicated grief, 27
    with depression, 26, 63–66
    with posttraumatic stress disorder
        (PTSD), 27–28, 83–85
Cognitive–behavioral therapy (CBT)
    for anxiety disorders, 16–107
    for bereaved children, 165–166
    for childhood traumatic grief, 34
    and coping skills, 43, 45–59,
        165–181
    for depression, 64, 67, 74–78
    with family anxiety management, 121
    and self-talk, 55–57
    trauma-focused, 33–34
Cognitive coping strategies
    and negative thoughts, 169–178
    and self-talk, 54–57
    at treatment completion, 211–212
Cognitive development, 15–17
Cognitive distortions, 73–74, 78–79
Cognitive restructuring
    for negative thoughts, 169–173
    and resilience, 211–212
    as strategy, 54
    techniques for, 54–57
Cognitive triangle, 45–49
Cohen, D., 34
Cohen, J. A., 103
Commands, 138
Completion of treatment, 214–217
Complicated grief, 27
Comprehensive evaluation, 38–39
Conflict
    in families, 82
    in feelings, 188–191
    interpersonal, 80–82
    in parent–child relationship, 194–195

Confusion
    about death, 6, 188
    in posttraumatic stress disorder, 86, 94
    as reaction to loss, 4, 15, 185
Consequences, for misbehavior, 138
Control, 131
Coping Cat (P. C. Kendall), 106, 121
Coping skills/strategies, 45–59, 165–181
    affective, 178–179
    for anxiety, 109–121
    assessment questions about, 40, 42
    behavioral, 58–59, 179–180
    cognitive, 54–57, 169–178, 211–212
    cognitive–behavioral therapy for,
        43–45
    and facing fears, 115–118
    and normative grief reactions,
        42–43
    and parents, 144, 180–181
    physiological exercises, 49–54
    for posttraumatic stress disorder,
        86–90
    practice of, 118–121
    relaxation, 110–111
    rewards for, 118
    and self-talk, 111–115
    and thoughts/feelings/behaviors,
        166–167
    and Triangle of 3 concept, 45–49
Counterexamples, 91
Crenshaw, D. A., 14
Currier, J. M., 30

Dadds, M. R., 121
Daily Routine (Activity), 131–133
Death
    anticipated vs. unanticipated, 23–24
    beliefs about, 90–93
    circumstances of, 39, 41, 185
    nature of, 39–41
    variation in response to, 3–4, 28–29
Depression, 63–82
    activity scheduling with, 67–73
    clinical presentation in bereaved
        children, 26, 63–66
    feelings accompanying, 64–65
    and improving relationships, 80–81
    negative thoughts with, 73–78
    and parents as helpers, 81–82
    rumination with, 65

    and self-esteem, 78–80
    symptoms of, 63, 66
Developmental stage. *See also* Age groups
    cognitive coping strategies in, 45
    depression in, 64–65
    and grief, 13–14
    and reactions to loss, 3–4, 152–153
*Diagnostic and Statistical Manual of
    Mental Disorders,* 65, 83, 106
Diaphragmatic breathing, 50–51
Discipline
    behavior management with, 131,
        134–140
    changes in, 124–125
    and child strengths, 125–126
    consistent, 29, 94
    and mental health of parent, 94
    positive, 208–210
Distorted cognitions, 73–78
Distraction, 176
Dowdney, L., 29

Economic problems, 20–21, 158
Emery, G., 57
Emotional awareness, 143–144
Emotional connections, with deceased,
    22, 200
Emotional expression, 96–99
Emotional modulation, 96–99
Environmental variables, 204
Evidence-based interventions, 6–7
Expectations
    for adolescents, 143
    for child, 130
    for therapy, 9
Exposure treatment, 101–102, 115,
    117–118

Facing Your Fears: What to Do When
    You Are Feeling Anxious
    (Activity), 118–121
FAM (family anxiety management),
    121
Families. *See also* Parents
    changes in dynamics of, 93–96,
        124–125
    conflict in, 82
    context of, 19
    previous functioning of, 21
    protective factors of, 204

Families, *continued*
    responsibilities in, 93–94
    and risk/protective factors, 18–20
    role changes in, 94
    routines in, 94
    strengths of, 156–157
    stress in, 206
Family anxiety management (FAM), 121
Family-based interventions, 64
Family Bereavement Program, 7, 19, 32,
    127, 131, 207
Family therapy, 33–35
Feared situations, 117
Fears, 115–118
Feelings
    conflicted, 188–191
    coping skills for, 166–167
    with depression, 64–65
    management of, 178–179
    and memories, 191–192
    of parents, 143–144
Feelings Monitoring (Activity), 86–90
Feelings Wheel, 97, 98
Felner, R. D., 158
Fight or flight response, 50
Final sessions, 214–215
Financial strain. *See* Economic problems

Gender, 21–22, 29, 179
Generalized anxiety, 105, 106
Goals
    in activity scheduling to reduce
        depressive symptoms, 69–72
    for treatment, 7–8, 151–152,
        214–215
Goenjian, A. K., 32–33
Greeff, A. P., 24
Grief. *See also* Grieving process
    and behavior problems, 28–29
    childhood traumatic, 28, 100
    cognitive–behavioral therapy for, 34
    counseling for, 30
    defined, 5
    and developmental stage, 13–14
    normative reactions with, 15–16,
        42–43
    of parents, 127
    process of, 6
    waves of, 167–168
Grief-focused stage of treatment, 150–152

Grieving process, 6
    and memory work, 183–185
    and posttraumatic stress disorder, 100
    in third phase of treatment, 10–11
Group interventions, 30–33
Guilt
    about enjoying oneself after loss, 180
    in depression, 65, 77
    expression of, 31, 44
    and negative thoughts, 191
    normalization of, 188
    of parents, 29, 95, 125, 131
    in posttraumatic stress disorder, 91
    and praise, 127
    as reaction to loss, 6, 17, 112, 153,
        156, 185
    over resuming normal activity, 168

Haine, R. A., 24
Handouts. *See* Activities
Helping Children Cope With Death
    (Activity), 43, 44
Hierarchy of feared situations, 117
Hilliard, R. E., 31
Home life, 158
Homicide, 20, 23–24, 27, 83, 91
How I Felt After My Dad Died
    (Activity), 192, 193
How to Praise Your Child (Activity),
    127, 128
Human, B., 24
Hwang, J., 31–32
Hyperarousal, 84–85

Ignoring, of behaviors, 134–135
IGTC. *See* Integrated grief therapy for
    children
Illness, 23–24, 39, 41, 83, 115
Imagined alternatives, 167
Individual treatment, 33–35, 205–206
Infants, 15–16, 152. *See also* Children
Initial sessions, 150–151
Integrated grief therapy for children
    (IGTC), 3–12
    and anxiety, 106–108
    and behavior management, 123–124
    as coping skill therapy, 45
    for depression, 64
    as evidence-based model, 4–5
    grief-focused stage of, 150–152

and memories, 183–184
phases of treatment in, 10–11
and resilience, 203
techniques in, 149
terminology for, 5
treatment principles of, 6–10
and variation in responses, 3–4
Interpersonal therapy for adolescents
(IPT-A), 64, 81
Interventions
for anxiety, 106–107
for behavioral problems, 124
for bereavement, 30–35
bereavement support groups, 30–33
customization of, 8–10
for depression, 64
evidence-based, 6–7
family-based, 33–35, 64
for posttraumatic stress disorder,
85–86
IPT-A (interpersonal therapy for
adolescents), 64, 81
Isolation, 25, 80–81

Janoff-Bulman, R., 165
Jiang, H., 31–32

Kakuma, T., 31–32
Kendall, P. C., 107, 121
Kranzler, E. M., 29
Kwok, O.-M., 19

Lambert, M. J., 31
Layne, C. M., 33
Life stories, 196–198
Limit-setting, 95–96
for adolescents, 140, 142
consistency with, 131, 138
Lin, K. K., 20
Listening, 142
Liu, X., 24
Looking Toward the Future: Guidelines
for Helping Grieving Children
(Activity), 154, 155
Luecken, L. J., 20

Mad, Sad, Glad Game, 97
Magical thinking, 65
Managing behaviors
as coping skill, 179–180

Managing behavior problems, 124
Managing Negative Thoughts: Your
Toolbox (Activity), 176, 177
Mancini, A. D., 204
Marks, I., 34
Melhem, N. M., 18, 22, 24
Memories. See also Memory work
avoidance of, 187–188
sharing of, 184–195
Memory book concept, 196–198
Memory work, 183–201
conflicted feelings in, 188–191
connection maintenance as, 199–200
and grieving process, 183–185
and new relationships, 200–201
normalizing thoughts/feelings in,
191–192
positive reminiscing in, 185–188
rituals in, 200
and self-identity, 195–199
sharing memories in, 192–195
trauma narrative for, 101–103
Metsch, M., 31–32
Mind reading, 74–77
Mourning
defined, 5
tasks of, 184
Murder, 23–24, 91. See also Homicide
Music therapy groups, 31
My Daily Schedule (Activity), 67–69
My Goals (Activity), 69–73
My Memory Book (Activity), 188–190

Nature of death. See Circumstances of
death
Needs assessment, 37–42
comprehensive evaluation for,
38–39
factors in, 39, 41–42
questions for, 40
Negative behaviors, 135
Negative self-talk, 54–55, 174
Negative thoughts
alternatives to, 92
cognitive coping strategies for,
169–178
with depression, 73–78
normative, 176, 178
patterns of, 167
Neimeyer, R. A., 30

Normalization, of thoughts/feelings, 191–192
Normative negative thoughts, 176, 178

Oltjenbruns, K. A., 14
Ongoing stressors, 40–42
Oppositional behaviors, 179
Overgeneralization (problem behavior), 129–130

Parent–child relationship
   building on, 8
   and child's recovery, 99
   conflict in, 82, 194–195
   and grief reactions, 85
Parent–child therapy sessions, 121–122, 142–143
Parenting
   child-centered, 19
   and emotional awareness, 97
   and grief reactions of child, 153–154
Parenting Skills: A Review (Activity), 208–209
Parents
   child as support for, 77
   coping strategies for, 144
   deceased, 22–23
   and discipline of child, 29, 94, 208–210
   and emotional awareness, 143–144
   and family routines, 94, 131
   grief of, 127
   and grief reactions of child, 42–43
   individual treatment for, 205–206
   involvement of, in treatment, 81–82, 121–122, 142–143, 180–181
   memory sharing with, 186–187, 193, 194
   mental health of, 17–18, 38–39, 94, 205–206
   as mirrors, 199
   posttraumatic stress disorder in, 85
   problem-solving for, 206
   psychoeducation for, 66–67, 205
   and resilience in child, 205–210
   skills of, 18–20, 208–210
   and social support, 25, 145
   strengths of, 156–157
   surviving, 17–20, 29
   terminology, 5

and trauma narrative, 103–104
   warmth of, 126–127, 207
Passive behavior, 180
Pfeffer, C. R., 31–32, 38
Phases of treatment, 10–11
Photographs, 199
Physiological exercises, 49–54
Play, 127, 129
Play therapy, 33
PMR (progressive muscle relaxation), 51–54
Point system, 72
Porterfield, K., 19
Positive discipline, 208–210
Positive experiences, 207
Positive imagery, 178–179
Positive interaction, 125–129
Positive parenting, 19
Positive reinforcement, 58, 134
Positive self-talk, 174, 176
Posttraumatic stress disorder (PTSD), 83–104
   and beliefs, 90–93
   clinical presentation in bereaved children, 27–28, 83–85
   coping strategies for, 86–90
   and emotional expression, 96–99
   and family changes, 93–96
   interventions for, 85–86
   and social relationships, 99–100
   symptoms of, 84–85
   trauma narrative with, 100–104
Praise, 127, 181
Preschoolers, 16, 152.
   See also Children
Problem-solving, 160–161, 206
Problem-Solving Skills (Activity), 161–164, 206
Progressive muscle relaxation (PMR), 51–54
Prolonged grief disorder, 27
Protective factors. *See* Risk and protective factors
Psychoeducation
   for children, 212–213
   for families, 66–67
   for parents, 205
Psychological relationship, 200
Psychological vulnerability, 21

Psychopharmacological treatment, 64
PTSD. *See* Posttraumatic stress disorder

Rapee, R. M., 121
Reed, M. D., 24
Reexperiencing of symptoms, 84
Reflective listening, 97, 142
Reframing, 135
Re-grief, 14
Reinforcement, 134
Relationships,
    in depressed children, 80–81
    in new sources of support, 200–201
Relaxation, 51–54, 110–111
Relaxation for Children (Activity),
    51–53
Reminiscing, 185–188
Resilience, 203–213
    and children, 210–213
    fostering of, 154–157
    and parents, 205–210
    and treatment conclusion, 214–217
Responsibilities, 93–94
Review of treatment gains, 215–217
Rewards, 118
Risk and protective factors, 15–25
    age/cognitive development, 15–17
    assessment of, 38
    and deceased parent, 22–23
    definitions of, 15
    gender, 21–22
    and parenting, 18–20
    for posttraumatic stress disorder, 85
    and previous functioning, 21
    social support, 24–25
    socioeconomic status, 20–21
    and surviving parent, 17–18
    and unanticipated death, 23–24
Rituals, 40, 41, 200
Role changes, 94, 131
Routine, 94, 130–131
Rowlison, R. T., 158
Rumination, 65
Rush, A. J., 57

Sadness, 64–66
    acknowledgment of, 174
    and cognitive–behavioral therapy, 34
    expression of, 31, 44, 64, 78, 153,
        154

of family members, 125, 185
in grief process, 183
identification of, 97
and memories, 184
and negative thoughts, 74, 176
in posttraumatic stress disorder, 86
and praise, 127
as reaction to loss, 4, 6, 13, 15, 17
and relaxation, 110
sources of, 66
and treatment completion, 214
in waves, 167
Saldinger, A., 19
Sandler, I. N., 19, 20, 24, 32, 127, 131,
    207
Schedule for Affective Disorders and
    Schizophrenia for School-Age
    Children—Present and Lifetime,
    38
School-age children, 16–17, 152–153.
    See also Children
School life, 158
Secondary loss, 157–160
Secondary stressors, 20–21
Self-blame, 90–91, 167
Self-care for parents, 144–145
Self-concept, 195
Self-esteem, 78–80
Self-identity, 195–199
Self-isolation, 25, 80–81
Self-monitoring, 173–174
Self-talk
    anxious, 111–115
    in cognitive restructuring, 54–55
    negative, 54–55, 174
    positive, 174, 176
Separation anxiety, 105, 106
SES (socioeconomic status), 20–21
Setting limits. *See* Limit-setting
Sharing of memories, 192–195
Shaw, B. F., 57
Sherkat, E., 24
"Should" statements, 74, 77
Sireling, L., 34
Social context, 4
Social relationships, 99–100, 158
Social skills, 99–100
Social support
    behaviors of, 99–100
    for children, 212–213

for parents, 145
as risk/protective factor, 24–25
Socioeconomic status (SES), 20–21
Star Charts (Activity), 135–138
Strengths
    building on, 9–10
    of child, 156–157, 211
    and discipline, 125–126
    of family, 156–157
    of parent, 9–10, 156–157
Stressors
    assessment of, 40–42
    influences of, 49–50
Stroebe, W., 25
Structure, 130–131
Sudden death, 39, 41, 83, 99
Suicidal ideation, 26
Suicide
    child's risk of, 38
    of parent, 23–24, 32, 83, 85

"Talking rules," 142
Tasks of mourning, 184
Teenagers. *See* Adolescents
Tein, J.-Y., 24
Terminal illness, 23, 39, 41
Terre, L., 158
Therapist attachment, 214
Thinking Through Your Worries
    (Activity), 115, 116
Thought bubbles, 78, 112–114, 173
Thought Diary (Activity), 173–175
Thought management, 173–176
Thoughts
    coping skills for, 166–167
    and memory work, 191–192
Time-Out Procedure (Activity), 140, 141

Time outs, 138
Tips for Using Star Charts (Activity),
    138, 139
Toddlers, 16, 152. *See also* Children
Tonkins, S. A. M., 31
Trauma narrative, 86, 100–104
Trauma symptoms, 86
Treatment
    completion of, 214–217
    goals of, 7–8, 151–152
    implications for, 35
    individual, 33–35, 205–206
    parental involvement in, 81–82,
        121–122, 142–143, 180–181
    phases of, 10–11
    principles of, 6–10
Triangle of 3 concept, 45–49, 169–170

Variation, in response to death, 3–4,
    28–29

Warmth, parental, 126–127, 207
Waves of grief, 167–168
What Are My Negative Thoughts
    (Activity), 78, 79
What Are They Thinking? (Activity),
    112–114, 173
Wolchik, S. A., 20
Worden, J. W., 131, 184
Worry
    avoidance of, 44
    coping with, 181
    excessive, 115, 121
    of family members, 185
    as reaction to loss, 4, 37
    and relaxation, 110
    in separation anxiety, 28, 106

ABOUT THE AUTHORS

Michelle Y. Pearlman, PhD, is a clinical psychologist in private practice in New York and an adjunct faculty member in the Department of Child and Adolescent Psychiatry at the New York University (NYU) School of Medicine. She was the founding director of the Trauma and Bereavement Service and the clinical director at the Institute for Trauma and Resilience at the NYU Child Study Center. She also was involved with the development and implementation of programming for children and families who lost loved ones during the terrorist attacks of September 11, 2001. Her clinical work and research are specialized in the areas of grief, trauma, anxiety, depression, and positive coping.

Karen D'Angelo Schwalbe, PhD, is a clinical psychologist in private practice in New York. She is an adjunct faculty member of the Department of Child and Adolescent Psychiatry at the New York University (NYU) School of Medicine and an adjunct professor for the clinical psychology doctoral program at Long Island University, Brooklyn Campus. She was previously a staff psychologist at the NYU Counseling and Behavioral Health Service and completed a postdoctoral fellowship in the Institute for Trauma and Resilience at the NYU Child

Study Center. Her clinical work and research areas include attachment, childhood trauma and resilience, grief, and eating disorders.

Marylène Cloitre, PhD, is the founding director of the Trauma and Resilience Research Program at the New York University (NYU) Child Study Center. She is also the Cathy and Stephen Graham Professor of Child and Adolescent Psychiatry at the NYU Langone Medical Center and a research scientist at the New York State Nathan Kline Institute for Psychiatric Research. Her clinical work and research for the past 20 years has focused on the assessment and treatment of the effects of childhood maltreatment, trauma, and loss across the life span.